THE FEDERAL ROAD
through Georgia,
the Creek Nation,
and Alabama,
1806–1836

THE FEDERAL ROAD
through Georgia, the Creek Nation, and Alabama, 1806–1836

HENRY DELEON SOUTHERLAND JR.,
AND JERRY ELIJAH BROWN

MAPS BY CHARLES JEFFERSON HIERS

Sponsored by the Historic Chattahoochee Commission

The University of Alabama Press
Tuscaloosa

∞

The paper on which this book is printed meets the minimum
requirements of American National Standard for Information
Sciences-Permanence of Paper for Printed Library Materials,
ANSI Z39.48-1984.

Library of Congress Cataloging-in-Publication Data

Southerland, Henry deLeon, 1911–
Federal Road through Georgia, the Creek Nation, and Alabama
Henry deLeon Southerland, Jr., and Jerry Elijah Brown: maps by
Charles Jefferson Hiers.
p. cm.
"Sponsored by the Historic Chattahoochee Commission."
Bibliography: p.
Includes index.
ISBN 0-8173-0518-1   ISBN 978-0-8173-0443-0 (pbk. : alk. paper)
1. Federal Road (Ala. and Ga.)—History.   2. Alabama—
History—1819-1950.   3. Georgia—History—1175-1865.   4. Creek
Indians—History.   5. Indians of North America—Alabama—
History.   6. Indians of North America—Georgia—History.
I. Brown, Jerry Elijah, 1945- II. Title.
F326.S73 1989
975.8—dc19   88-35698
CIP

To Louise Harris Southerland
and to the Memory
of John M. Fletcher of Hallewokee Farm

CONTENTS

ILLUSTRATIONS

FIGURES

MAPS

ACKNOWLEDGMENTS

HISTORIES OF ALABAMA are replete with references to the Federal Road, but except for an unpublished thesis written in 1936 by Mary Ida Chase at Birmingham-Southern College (dealing with only the Alabama portion of the road), a documented history drawn from original sources does not exist. This book began as a master's thesis at Samford University in 1983 and has been extended with joint authorship to a larger exploration of the topic.

The authors are indebted to many who have gone before, particularly to Peter A. Brannon, who wrote widely and well of Alabama's formative period, and to Fletcher Hale, a topographical draftsman who traced the exact route of the Federal Road by studying aerial photographs. Special gratitude is due to the late Dr. James Lewis Treadway, who collected and shared much data on the Federal Road.

Acknowledgment to scholars, in the notes and bibliography, seems too small a way to express appreciation. Special acknowledgment is made to Joseph Hobson Harrison, Jr., Bert Hitchcock, and Frank Lawrence Owsley, Jr., professors at Auburn University, for their thorough scholarship and their helpful comments.

The gratitude of those who have been delivered from ignorance, error, and sometimes desperation by kindly stewards of knowledge is extended to Miriam C. Jones, of the Alabama Department of Archives and History; Mary Bess Paluzzi and Yvonne Crumpler, of the Birmingham Public Library; Elizabeth Wells and Shirley Hutchens, of the Samford University Library; Joyce H. Lamont, of the University of Alabama Library; Mary Ann Neeley, of Old Alabama Town, formerly the Old North Hull Street Historic District in Montgomery; Glenn Anderson, Gene Geiger, Barbara Bishop, and Marilyn Thomas, of the Ralph Brown Draughon Library at Auburn University; and Francis Bouilliant-Linet and William M. Russell, Jr., of Macon County, Alabama.

Leah Atkins, formerly of Samford University and now the director of the Auburn University Center for the Arts and Humanities, and Douglas Clare Purcell, executive director of the Historic Chattahoochee Commission, have been faithful shepherds of this work. Special thanks also are expressed to two whose hands brought words to the page—to Elsie Reynolds, of the Auburn University Journalism Department, for creating a first draft from near-indecipherable writing, and to Bettye Campbell, for expeditious word processing that produced the finished work. Charles Jefferson Hiers studied our sources, explored the terrain of the Federal Road himself, and read our manuscript before drawing and lettering the maps; he was ably assisted in final preparations by Heather Timmons, graphic artist. Thanks are due to Craig Noll, our able copyeditor, for setting the manuscript on its true course, to Wendy Haught for proofreading, and to Jay Lamar for preparing the index. Serlester Williams's help with other projects indirectly expedited the completion of this book.

Finally, the authors express sincere appreciation to their respective families: to Louise Southerland and the Southerlands' daughter Carolyn Long for their help, encouragement, and understanding; and to Libby Brown and the Browns' daughters, Brooks and Lindsay, for patiently abiding scattered papers, strange mumblings, and a typewriter welcoming the dawn.

Henry deLeon Southerland, Jr.
Birmingham, Alabama

Jerry Elijah Brown
Auburn University, Alabama

THE FEDERAL ROAD
through Georgia,
the Creek Nation,
and Alabama,
1806–1836

INTRODUCTION

"But for the Federal Road . . ."

IN 1806, A PATH FOR THE HORSES OF POST RIDERS was opened from middle Georgia to lower Alabama, through Indian country in the section of the United States once called the Old Southwest. Five years later the mail path was widened and rerouted over much of its length to create a military lane for the movement of troops, supply wagons, and ordnance. Instantly, use transcended intention: the road built for soldiers, who would confront the Creeks before engaging the British, became a major pioneer highway, an artery for all travel. Now, after more than 175 years, during which time the road has virtually vanished into the landscape, we can understand how it has meandered into history; we can recognize it as a source and a solution of conflicts, a factor in the location and growth of cities, a consideration in decisions civil and military, and a contributor to local, state, and national identities. Now we can see that one road as more important than it ever appeared in its own time, when it was merely a track, muddy or sandy, through forests and swamps; when, as the official highway, it afforded pioneers the strength of numbers and the refuge of forts and inns.

Although the insight now possible into that Federal Road approaches epiphany, it is not unique with respect to rivers and roads. When T. S. Eliot saw the full influence of the Mississippi on Huckleberry Finn—on the book, the boy, and the writer, as well as on the country—he called the river "a strong brown god"; similarly, twentieth-century Americans who made their escape to the West knew that, when U.S. Route 66 was replaced by the interstate highway system, more had disappeared than cracked pavement, Burma Shave signs, and lonely diners.

Though the sense that a road may be more than a route for travel or a conduit for commerce comes readily, it is difficult to specify par-

1

ticular contributions. Because a road is not a human character and because it may appear simply as part of the scenery, wandering through the events that occur on or around it, we hold back from arguing that even a prominent road is the sine qua non of a major historical change; none but the naive are likely to be convinced. One may suggest, however, without forcing the thesis, that such a thoroughfare was the Federal Road, sometimes called the Old Federal Road. It was built in 1811 from west-to-east, from Fort Stoddert, near Mount Vernon, on the Mobile River, to Fort Wilkinson, near Milledgeville, on the Oconee, then the capital of Georgia. From Fort Stoddert to the Chattahoochee, across present-day Alabama, the Federal Road coincided with the post riders' horse path that had come down from Athens, Georgia, to make the New Orleans connection in 1806. Where the horse path had turned north, at the falls where Columbus would be located, the Federal Road continued east, to areas where soldiers could be recruited and supplies procured. There, too, in Georgia and the Carolinas were waiting the Americans eager to settle in the fertile new lands to the west.

Started as a post route during the first administration of Thomas Jefferson and fulfilling its usefulness as a military road near the end of the presidency of Andrew Jackson (who made and maintained his reputation by suppressing Indians in its proximity), the Federal Road has been so central that no complete history of the southeastern United States can be written without a mention of it. In 1927, Peter A. Brannon, a historian to whose spadework this study owes a considerable debt, agreed with a nineteenth-century counterpart who compared it to the Appian Way.[1] "But for the Federal Road with its forts," Peter Joseph Hamilton had declaimed in 1898, "there had been no Alabama as we know it."[2] Over this route passed post riders for remote New Orleans, militiamen to reinforce forts, stagecoaches bearing European travelers and touring theatrical companies, Aaron Burr under arrest, freight wagons, the maverick evangelist Lorenzo Dow and Peggy (his sensible wife), the horses of highwaymen, the Marquis de Lafayette in a grand entourage, Creeks taking a last look at what had been their lands, and, of course, thousands of pioneers seeking a fresh start. The chances are good that all who trace their ancestry to anywhere in Alabama south of the Tennessee Valley have a forebear who came over the Federal Road. During its period of maximum use, when "Alabama fever" was epidemic in the Carolinas and Georgia, the population of the territory (later, the state) increased by over half a million.

If the road has been so important, why is this book, published about 150 years after its demise, the first full study of it? One simple reason is that the story of the road has not been assembled; details of the conception and construction, which might seem interesting mainly to historians of civil engineering, have been strewn piece-meal in hundreds of government documents, articles and books, and private letters. Even now, we know too little of the day-to-day work involved in cutting the road, building the causeways, or establishing the ferries. The single most important reason for the absence of a book devoted solely to the road is the overwhelming presence of other subjects of such magnitude that they have obscured the story of why this road came to be, where it was located, and how it has fig-ured in sectional development. To be sure, other stories have been more spectacular: the movements of the white traders, the War of 1812, Andrew Jackson's career, the Creek and Seminole wars, and the social and political issues pointing to the Civil War. Although a history of the Federal Road cannot be written without retelling some familiar stories (occasionally with new information), this work as-sumes that they are but bright beads concealing the string that joins them.

Naturally a study that proposes to isolate one element from the complex of national, regional, and state histories must steer between Scylla and Charybdis—avoiding, on the one side, the tendency to fo-cus too narrowly and, on the other, the temptation to veer into digressions. Once upon a time historians could navigate past these perils simply by adding the phrase *incidentally of* after their main ti-tles. (The best-known example is probably Albert James Pickett's *His-tory of Alabama, and Incidentally of Georgia and Mississippi from the Earliest Period*.) This history of the Federal Road is "incidentally of" the territory and the states it influenced, with more attention paid to Alabama and to the courageous but doomed natives whose last days in the southern United States were synchronous with the appearance and disappearance of the Federal Road.

To write about these people, the places they inhabited, and the streams they lived by is to discover how little we know and are likely to know. If it was not easy for the white pioneers to understand how the world looked to the Indians, it is only slightly less difficult now that the races are no longer at war. In the latter part of the twentieth century, we can at least empathize with the Indians' concept of stewardship of the land; the savaging of wildlife, streams, and forests, only recently an issue with us, was recognized immediately by the Indians as alien and destructive. Not directly threatened by death at the hands of the Indians, we, the de facto heirs of their land, are in a position to give a fairer assessment than our ancestors could have, a privilege that is forfeited only when sympathy for the underdog lapses into sentimentality.

What we can see now, maybe more clearly than ever, is how protracted and invasive the process of transition was. Intermarriages of whites and Indians, acceptance of the whites' mode of dress and conduct, and efforts to make Indians into farmers and craftsmen all point to the changing of ways. Though it may seem less significant, the switching over of names was a more critical signal, an indication that conceptions of man and the role of nature were changing. Unfortunately, this important point is easily lost on students struggling with the welter of alternative spellings and pronunciations that have resulted from Americans' efforts to record Creek speech. (This book uses modern spellings for names and places and standardizes punctuation and capitalization, except in those instances when the original provides a glimmer of the writer's individuality or some sharp insight into the times.) Dual Indian and English names reveal how close and how distant the red and white worlds were. As every schoolchild used to know, William Weatherford, the Creek leader who put his horse off a bluff into the Alabama River to escape death and who was so honorable that Andrew Jackson granted him a pardon, was also called Red Eagle. Few have occasion to know that Creek names, in and out of translation, were also used. In some official correspondence, Big Warrior signed his Creek name Tustenugge Thlucco, followed by the initials of the English name in parentheses. Alexander Cornells, a member of an extended family of mixed bloods, was also Chief Oche Haujo; but William McIntosh, both a Creek chief and an American general, usually went by the name of his Scots ancestors. Many whites also had Indian names; the raconteur-historian Thomas S. Woodward said he was called Chulatarle Emathla. Streams everywhere bear euphonious Indian names (Chattahoochee, Cubahatchee) or names given to honor settlers or describe uses (Milly's, Line). In these small particulars is revealed the true course of transition.

Looking larger to understand how the Federal Road became a character in national development, one may discover an array of motives for its existence. Although the horse path from Georgia to Alabama was opened as one link in the mail route between Washington City and New Orleans, it penetrated the territory of the Muscogees—actually a confederation of tribes and clans called Creeks by the white men, who saw their villages along the watercourses—and stimulated hostilities. As a military road, the passage encouraged exploitation and made expulsion inevitable. Although the stated intent of the horse path or the road was not to remove the Creeks, the passage forced a social, military, and diplomatic confrontation with these fierce, proud people. Their final thirty years in the South were, to say the least, anguishing. As their land was being crossed by the Federal Road, they were crossed and double-crossed by the government and by unscrupulous white men and betrayed, some felt, by their own kind.

It is tempting to speculate on the motives of United States officials. Did they realize that a war with the Creeks would be a likely consequence of the road building? Obviously the more far-sighted were aware of what the intrusion would bring to the wilderness that was wedged between white-dominated sections of the lower South. In his third annual message to Congress, delivered in 1803, Jefferson defined, perhaps unintentionally, the irreconcilable forces. He referred to the "ulterior measures which may be necessary for the immediate occupation and temporary government" of the newly purchased Louisiana Territory, and the strategy he outlined was the same his administration was following in the Mississippi Territory, created in 1798. The "ulterior measures" were necessary "for confirming to the Indian inhabitants their occupancy and self-government, establishing friendly and commercial relations with them, and for ascertaining the geography of the country acquired."[3] Even as Jefferson was speaking, Georgia and South Carolina were making claims to western lands. With such a manifestly contradictory mission—believing that Indian autonomy could be confirmed while their lands were being examined for later use—the country was set on a course that would subdue one people to make room for another.

It is also tempting to see parallels between that earlier time and our own. In extending the authority of the presidency beyond the limits set in the Constitution, Jefferson not only purchased a vast tract of land, he also left a precedent for later chief executives. Andrew Jackson effectively dealt with guerrillas and terrorists, even if his Draconian tactics now offend some sensibilities. Since the construction and implementation of the Federal Road were exercises in the use of raw power, our sense of justice is engaged as we review the consequences. Only students wearing star-spangled blindfolds can ignore the brutality that made the section safe for white travel and settlement—or pretend that the ultimate price was not paid by the Creeks. The heightened consciousness of the nation, to no one's surprise, was late in rising. In fact, the status of the black race has occupied the nation far more than have the injustices committed against the Indians.

Along with the negative moral judgments, circumspection requires that the positive results also be considered. The action started by Jefferson in response to the commonweal and completed by Jackson yielded a unified section of the country, a South that by the late 1830s was emerging from an Old Southwest and becoming an important part of the country's economy and politics. To study the changes wrought by the Federal Road is to understand the formation and the transformation of a section of the United States.

And yet the Federal Road is more than a symbol for the metamorphosis of a single geographic region. Begun in an age when travel and overland communication were synonymous, when no messages, no news, and no military dispatches moved except by horse or foot, the road lasted until rails were being laid across the swamps and ridges, steamboats were plying the Chattahoochee and the Alabama, and telegraph poles were being set in the rights-of-way. A modern world of communications options, one of them electronic even then, was in the cradle. What was happening along and to the Federal Road provides a dramatic illustration of the country's direction.

As alternate routes and alternative communications became available, the Federal Road became less central. No longer needed as the single passage through the Creek Nation, it did not become the spine of a twentieth-century infrastructure—a network of roads, communications, and governmental functions—and gradually it faded. Today only a few remnants remain, familiar for the most part only to local historians. Over most of its length the road is obliterated, and the ruts cut by the wagon wheels of the pioneers are returned to a landscape no longer virginal and haunting, with streams decidedly less clear. To get some inkling of the world implied in the few ruins still visible involves a delving into the facts of how the road was built and maintained and how it affected and was affected by the people who passed over it. Also needed, as always in a pleasurable study of history, is the exercising of an informed imagination. If this study succeeds, the Federal Road will be regarded as a living part of our past, and an illumination of its brief life will help present-day inhabitants appreciate how we came to where we are.

1

THE NATIONAL PERSPECTIVE

 By 1803, THOMAS JEFFERSON'S OPINION on the subject of federal post roads had taken a dramatic turn. Seven years earlier, while serving as George Washington's secretary of state, he had seen such projects as a source of patronage that would "open a bottomless abyss for public money."[1] Although Jefferson had a point, the fiscal conservatism of the moment apparently blinded him to a lesson in his own experience. During the Revolutionary War, when a weak defense marked by inadequate military communications allowed the British to move across Virginia, Jefferson himself was forced to flee Richmond and Monticello.[2] Nevertheless, at his inauguration in March 1801, he was committed to a policy of peace and austerity; ships were sold, and the army was reduced to its status of four years earlier, when John Adams had taken office.[3] Contributing to the mind change evident as Jefferson began his third year in office was what his predecessor later called "an assumption of implied power greater in itself and more comprehensive than all of the assumptions of applied powers in the years of the Washington and Adams Administrations taken together."[4] Adams referred, of course, to the complicated process by which Jefferson stretched the constitutional authority of the presidency to institute the Louisiana Purchase, a doubling of the country's land area.

The bold assertion approved by Congress in April 1803 and sealed in the ratification of a treaty with France the following October was politically perilous from start to finish. It was not immediately apparent that the purchase of 828,000 square miles for about $15 million was a bargain. Jefferson was on shaky constitutional ground in initiating the action; during the long negotiations with Talleyrand and the Bonaparte government in Paris, when he had to fret over the terms being considered by his envoys, Robert R. Livingston and

James Monroe, he also learned anew what frustration the absence of clear, fast communication can bring. With the acquisition of the new territory, that concern was heightened to anxiety. Jefferson had created for the country an underbelly with a vulnerable vital organ, New Orleans, a ready target for the British by sea and the Florida-based Spaniards by land.

Occupying the newly created southwest corner of the country, New Orleans had gone through a change of ownership only three years before the purchase. Settled by the French, it was ceded with all lands west of the Mississippi to Spain in 1762, during a time when France was losing its other North American possessions to Great Britain. In 1800, a more powerful France under Napoleon Bonaparte asked for the territory back and got it in a swap with Charles IV of Spain for an obscure duchy in northern Italy. Included in the transaction was the fragile promise that Louisiana would not be given over to another country.

When it became known that a retrocession agreement, called the Treaty of San Ildefonso, had been signed in secret, the American government became disturbed. Settlers in the Ohio, Cumberland, and Tennessee river valleys already were shipping on the Mississippi and using New Orleans as a port, taking advantage of an agreement with Spain in 1795. By 1802, according to one account, sugar exports from the city totaled $3 million and cotton $1 million. Upland settlers undoubtedly contributed to the ten thousand barrels of flour and the large volume of cordage, cider, apples, and pork which passed through the port that year. Of the 267 ships sailing in 1802 from New Orleans, 104 were Spanish and 158 were from the United States.[5] In light of this commercial activity it is no surprise that, instead of laying to rest an old specter, the transfer of ownership to France raised a new one. The port was too tempting a prize and too critical to U.S. commerce to be in the hands of any other country, even an established ally. "There is on the globe one single spot, the possessor of which is our natural and habitual enemy," said Jefferson. "It is New Orleans, through which the produce of three-eighths of our territory must pass."[6] The purchase removed the likelihood that the United States would be forced into an alliance with the British—hardly a friend—to rout the French. An American flag flying over New Orleans did not make the port more secure, and it was apparent in the capital that action would be necessary to draw the possession into the country.

The passing of enabling legislation on October 31, 1803, gave the president full authority to protect the new territory. The funding from Congress was a signal for Jefferson to act, and quickly, to establish lines of communication between the capital and New Orleans. Homework had already been done by the postmaster general, Gideon Granger; in September he had ordered a trial run to New Orleans over the Natchez Trace. If horses were changed every thirty miles and riders every hundred, Natchez could be reached in fifteen days. Still, the exchange of dispatches between Washington and what a Jefferson biographer called "the periphery of the republic" would take more than a month at the least. Jefferson lost no time in starting the process. Immediately after the enabling act was signed, a post rider left Washington, carrying important documents for officials in the new region.[7]

The 450-mile Natchez Trace, which started in Nashville, was actually the last leg of the post riders' long route from Washington City to New Orleans. A likely journey would have been from Washington west across the Blue Ridge Mountains, or south to Fredericksburg or Richmond, and then west across the Blue Ridge for an intersection with the "Great Valley Road," also known later as the "Great Philadelphia Wagon Road." The route through the Shenandoah Valley was clear as far as Salem, Virginia; there the back-country settlers would continue on the Wagon Road south through the upper Carolinas to Columbia or Camden, and a few on to Augusta and Milledgeville. The post riders to New Orleans would continue southwest from Salem to Abingdon, then on to Knoxville, where the Holston and French Broad flow together to form the Tennessee River. Southwest of Knoxville a turn west directed the rider over the Cumberland Mountains into middle Tennessee and Nashville. By the time the Natchez Trace was reached, almost a third of the journey remained.

Realizing that the Constitution empowered the Federal Congress to "establish Post offices and Post roads," James Madison in 1796 had called for surveying "a general route most proper for the transportation of the mail from Maine to Georgia."[8] A shorter route from Washington City to Georgia, and on through to Louisiana, could be created nearer the Atlantic seaboard. Among the first to call attention

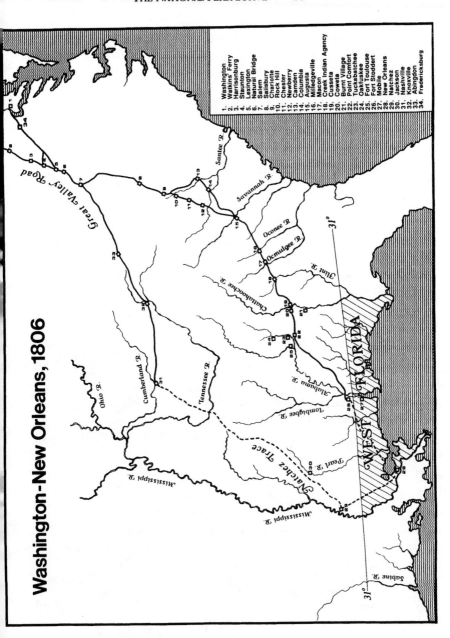

Washington–New Orleans, 1806

1. Washington
2. Watkins' Ferry
3. Harrisonburg
4. Staunton
5. Lexington
6. Natural Bridge
7. Salem
8. Salisbury
9. Charlotte
10. Rock Hill
11. Chester
12. Newberry
13. Camden
14. Columbia
15. Augusta
16. Milledgeville
17. Macon
18. Creek Indian Agency
19. Cusseta
20. Coweta
21. Burnt Village
22. Point Comfort
23. Tuckabatchee
24. Oaktuskee
25. Fort Toulouse
26. Fort Stoddert
27. Mobile
28. New Orleans
29. Natchez
30. Jackson
31. Nashville
32. Knoxville
33. Abingdon
34. Fredericksburg

to that possibility was Samuel Latham Mitchill, a New York Republican congressman and an admirer of Jefferson, whom he described as "more deeply versed in human nature and human learning than almost the whole tribe of his opponents and revilers."[9] In the first session of the Eighth Congress, Mitchill took a major step in pushing construction of a postal horse path through the Mississippi Territory. According to the *Annals of Congress*, Mitchill "called the attention of the House to a subject of considerable importance growing out of our possessions on the Mississippi." He argued that the Natchez route was difficult and circuitous; he contended that the country was infested with robbers and in some sections was so spare of necessities that a rider had to carry subsistence and water for himself and his horse. Mitchill said four hundred miles could be saved and twenty days removed with an improved land route, and he requested that the Committee on Post Offices and Post Roads investigate the means by which mail could be conveyed from Washington to Natchez and New Orleans.[10]

Jefferson gave the project his blessing, and in November 1803, Henry Dearborn, the secretary of war, asked that the Indian agent in Georgia, Col. Benjamin Hawkins, suggest a location for the road. Dearborn also asked Gen. James Wilkinson in New Orleans to report on the feasibility of a road from Hawkins's place on the Flint River, in western Georgia, to New Orleans by way of the Alabama and Tombigbee rivers.[11] Hawkins's reply is not on record, but the general reported that two routes used by the Indians from Coweta, a central Indian village on the west bank of the Chattahoochee, to Mobile "traverse in general a smooth surface and open pine woods perfectly convenient to the passage of loaded pack horses; the lower route passes no settlement Christian or Savage but the upper one near the Indian settlements on the Tallapoosa."[12]

Wilkinson's circumspection reflects the standing, general knowledge of Indian trails in the region and the history of the white man among the Creeks—in particular, the varying alliances of the Indians. The trail Hernando DeSoto and his fortune hunters traveled as they moved from northwest Georgia across Alabama down the Coosa and Tallapoosa toward the bloody battle of Maubila apparently was well established in 1540 and was part of the route that was later called the Lower Creek Trading Path.[13] By the late seventeenth and early eighteenth centuries, explorers, traders, agents, and a few missionaries, all from European colonies in America, converged on the Creek Nation from three directions. The British came west from Charles Town to Oakfuskee and Tuckabatchee, the Spaniards northwest and north from St. Augustine and Pensacola to Apalachicola Fort, near Coweta, and the Frenchmen northeast from Mobile to Fort Toulouse. Each of these European nations wanted to dominate the land that later became the state of Alabama.[14]

Among the early British representatives was Capt. Tobias Fitch, who was sent from Charles Town into Creek Indian territory in 1725 to counteract French influence after the construction of Fort Toulouse and to obtain proper treatment for English traders. He kept a journal of his visit and of his efforts to gain friendship between the Indians and the English. Between Augusta and Tuckabatchee, Fitch generally followed the Indian packhorse path, which later became the Federal Road.[15]

Soon after Gen. James Edward Oglethorpe landed in Georgia, he assembled some chiefs of the Lower Creeks and formed a treaty in which the Indians released land between the Altamaha and Savannah rivers and permitted English traders to enter the Creek Nation.[16] In 1739, Oglethorpe traveled to the headquarters of the Creek Nation to take the leaders presents and to court their friendship.[17] Then, and later, the Indians did not woo easily. In 1771, Capt. John Stuart, the British colonial superintendent of Indian affairs for the southern district from 1762 until the end of the colonial period, failed in his attempts at Pensacola to negotiate for a thirty-five mile strip of land on each side of the Escambia River.[18] Stuart passed the chore on to David Taitt, whose trip to the Creeks in 1772 to negotiate for this land also proved unsuccessful. He traveled from Pensacola, with Joseph Cornells as an interpreter and guide, to Tuckabatchee, Fort Toulouse, Wetumpka, Tuskegee, Chehaw, and Coweta; he crossed the Chattahoochee, Flint, Ocmulgee, and Oconee rivers; and he proceeded to Augusta, Silver Bluff, and Charles Town, making frequent reports and keeping a detailed journal of his travels.[19] He saw the behavior of the Indian traders, which was as bad as that of any of the young Indians, and wondered how they could get along so well together.

During the Revolutionary War, the famous naturalist William Bartram traversed a greater portion of the Old Federal Road area. He crossed the Oconee River on July 1, 1775, and, except for going north to Tallassee about July 15 to 19, followed the old Indian trading paths which became the Federal Road, all the way from Milledgeville to Mobile.[20]

A number of British colonists had settled along the lower Mississippi River after the Treaty of Paris of 1763, and many British traders were in the Upper Creek country. Settlements containing the British colonists were isolated by the Spaniards—also at war with England—at the beginning of the American Revolutionary War. From New Orleans, Gálvez took over Baton Rouge in 1779, Mobile in 1780, and Pensacola in 1781. British Loyalists at Natchez revolted against the Spaniards and were forced to flee, in a well-documented hegira. By a circuitous route, the Loyalists—men, women and children, with minimum personal effects—traveled eastward over the path that later became the Federal Road, to Augusta and on to refuge in Savannah, Georgia.[21]

The negotiations for the rights to a post road through the Creek territory must be seen against this backdrop of exploitation, conflict, and attempts at settlement. The divisiveness among the Creek clans, the absence of a single spokesman for the entire diverse confederation, and the collective cultural anxiety about their eventual displacement by the whites are all reflected in the various loyalties and in the complex of treaties. The role of the United States at this critical juncture is best represented by Hawkins, a North Carolinian and a former senator, who was appointed by his friend George Washington in 1795 to serve as "Principal Agent for Indian Affairs South of the Ohio River." Apparently Hawkins, unlike his predecessors, took the term *agent* literally. His own writings and the several studies of his life reveal the actions of an even-handed advocate who supported the claims of the Indians against land pirates and the government itself from 1796, when he assumed the duty, to his death, twenty years later. He was able to ascertain where Indian political power lay so that stronger treaties could be negotiated with real leaders. Described as a "born dirt farmer," he was, in fact, Princeton-educated, a translator of French, and an accomplished husbandman who tried to teach the Indians to live by European agricultural practices.[22] The Treaty of Washington, signed in 1805, after Hawkins had nearly a decade of experience in dealing with the Creeks, attempted to give the Indians advantages in controlling and trading with these latest official intruders.

Before the clutch of chiefs arrived in the capital in November 1805 to negotiate the treaty, the will of the United States and the physical difficulty in carrying it out already were becoming clear. Dearborn, who, as secretary of war, was a principal signatory of the treaty, had asked Hawkins in February of 1804 to seek permission from the Creeks for the open road.[23] In July of that year Isaac Briggs, an assistant surveyor general of the United States, offered to return to his station in Natchez through Georgia and the Creek Nation and to take observations of latitude and longitude at important points along the route. This offer was accepted by President Jefferson, and Briggs proceeded, but not without difficulties.[24] He was furnished with an accurate sextant to permit proper delineation of these points on a map. By September 2, 1804, Briggs reported from Gen. David Meriwether's place in Georgia that he had found this "both to body and mind, the most fatiguing journey" that he had ever undertaken.[25] At General Meriwether's home, near the eastern boundary of Indian Territory and more than five hundred miles from Washington, Isaac Briggs obtained a packhorse and provisions for the journey as far as the Flint River.[26]

Briggs and his companion, Thomas Robertson, departed on September 6 and in two days progressed only about thirty-one miles to the store of an Indian trader. After fruitless efforts to secure a guide, they proceeded and wandered without one until they arrived at Colonel Hawkins's place on the Flint River. For four days they had not seen another person. Colonel Hawkins gave them additional provisions and a guide. They proceeded to "Point Comfort," a second home that Hawkins had established, two miles south of the Tallapoosa River. Here they arrived on September 27, after a laborious journey of seven days, covering 120 miles. The horses swam the Chattahoochee River and six creeks along the way. One of the principal Indian chiefs, Oche Haujo, with whom Briggs talked at Point Comfort, thought that a road through the Nation "would be highly beneficial to the red people as well as to the white."[27] (It is not coincidental that Oche Haujo was one of the chiefs who signed the Treaty of Washington.)

BENJAMIN HAWKINS, INDIAN AGENT

The single most important white man in the Creek Nation in the Federal Road period was Benjamin Hawkins, who from 1796 until his death in 1816 was the Indian agent. Hawkins instituted programs to teach the Creeks farming and crafts, but even his limited success excited the nativist Creeks who resented new ways. Hawkins also negotiated for the postal horse path cut in 1806 and told a council of Creek chiefs in 1811 that, despite their objections, the Federal Road would be opened. (Photograph by Mark E. Fretwell, St. Augustine, Florida)

On October 3, 1804, Briggs left the Tallapoosa and arrived on the ninth at the home of Nathaniel Christmas on the west side of the Tombigbee River, about two miles above its confluence with the Alabama. Here, while down with a fever, Briggs learned that the yellow fever raged in New Orleans. After about three weeks of recuperation, he left the Tombigbee, traveling through Mobile. He crossed the Pascagoula River, passed around Biloxi and Bay St. Louis, crossed the Pearl River about ten miles above its mouth, and went on through the rigolets, or canals, to New Orleans. He had traveled a little more than 1,000 miles since he left Washington four months before. His letter from New Orleans on December 22 to President Jefferson presented the latitude and longitude of the principal places along the proposed route and the distances between each. Using the instruments of celestial navigation, he determined that the sum of the airline distances between principal places from Washington to New Orleans was 979.5 miles, only 14.5 miles farther than the 965-mile straight-line distance calculated between the two cities. Briggs suggested a route by Athens, Georgia, where a university had recently been located, to Point Comfort, and thence to Mobile and New Orleans.[28] On February 1, 1805, Jefferson transmitted the three letters from Briggs to the House of Representatives, stating that Briggs was in New Orleans and not well but that his special report with accompanying maps would be forwarded when received. This was done on February 23. The last letter from Briggs had been dated December 22, 1804.[29]

Briggs's illness in New Orleans was attributed to his journey through the Creek Nation. Three years later Jefferson reminded Congress of Briggs's service and the excellent map which he had prepared, suggesting that he receive compensation for this work. Although additional requests were made from time to time, it was 1818 before Congress authorized the Treasury Department to pay Briggs "a reasonable charge for exploring the route of the road from Washington to New Orleans."[30]

Congress passed an act on March 3, 1805, to establish a post road, partly in Orleans Territory, "from Washington City by Athens, Georgia, to New Orleans."[31] Thomas Jefferson, in his second inaugural address, March 4, 1805, mentioned that surplus revenue "may, by a just repartition of it among the States and corresponding amendment of the Constitution, be applied in time of peace to rivers, canals, roads, arts, manufacturers, education, and other objects within each state."[32] It may seem incongruous, in light of the presence of federal funds and the pressure to establish the faster communication with New Orleans, that an act of Congress and a formal treaty would be required to open a post road through the Creek territory. A network of paths allowed riders to carry messages before the formalities were enacted. Moreover, accounts of the new country almost always embrace a tacit paradox: the land was isolated, hostile, and threatening; at the same time, it was populated with people of all races and loyalties, and exchanges among these inhabitants were common. There was, however, no public postal service in the new territory. Indian traders and other travelers carried letters only on a personal basis; furthermore, the presence of a regular system of communication was a threat to the traders, half-breeds, and escaped slaves who were living outside the law and who preferred that their records and whereabouts remain unknown.

A more formal system, supported by diplomatic accords, was also needed because early optimism about the cooperation of the Spaniards through West Florida did not hold. On May 4, 1805, William C. C. Claiborne, the territorial governor, wrote Jefferson that there would be no difficulties with the Spaniards, a claim he repeated to Postmaster General Granger on June 7 and again on June 17.[33] He informed Secretary of State James Madison on July 5 that Governor Vicente Folch y Juan of Spanish West Florida "had no objection to the Post Route and that his protection would be afforded the Post Riders." Again, on July 14, Claiborne wrote Jefferson that, not only would the Spanish permit the new road, they also promised protection.[34] Francis Abrahams, later identified as a post rider, had been from New Orleans to Fort Stoddert and back twice, though the road was often flooded and difficult. Although the regularity of the route had not been established, Claiborne, for his part, had arranged for a ferry across Lake Pontchartrain and had contracted for conveyance of the mail.

By fall, Claiborne's sanguine attitude and his estimate of Spanish good will had changed. On October 17, he informed the postmaster general of the frequent delays in the passage of the mail to Fort Stoddert, of jealousy on the part of the Spaniards, of the murder of one rider, and of shots being fired at another. By October 30, Claiborne found that the Spaniards were of "a hostile disposition."[35]

Neither Claiborne nor Granger had realized the difficulties with the Spaniards, the Indians, the terrain, or the weather. In July, Granger had reported to Claiborne that the route to Coweta was in perfect order, that nine mails had been sent through Georgia toward New Orleans, that steady persons had been employed, and that the Indians had consented. Nothing, however, had been received from New Orleans, and the postal agent there had not been heard from since May.[36] Granger, on August 2, 1805, questioned Benjamin Hawkins as to whether the mails were moving properly between Coweta and New Orleans.[37]

Just how perilous the movement of mails was during this time was revealed in an act of Congress in April 1806, appropriating a sum not to exceed $250 to enable the postmaster general to defray the expenses of Joseph H. Webb, who, in August 1805, "was wounded by persons unknown while carrying the U.S. Mail and who is now under the care of the commandant at Fort Stoddert."[38] Webb lived, but he must have been wounded seriously, for on December 28, 1831, Congressman Dutee Jerauld Pearce, from the Committee on the Post Offices and Post Roads, reported on the petition of Jonah H. Webb (apparently the same Webb identified as Joseph) for an increase in his pension. The committee was satisfied that Webb was "aged and poor; that the wounds he received while employed to carry the mail of the United States from Athens, in Georgia, to New Orleans, rendered him unable to labor, and made him a cripple for life; that he is now in a suffering condition, the present allowance of fifty dollars per annum being insufficient to procure him the necessaries of life."[39] The committee requested a bill to give Webb eight dollars per month, the same compensation given a soldier who had been totally disabled by wounds suffered while in the service of his country. On August 19, 1805, Granger wrote to President Thomas Jefferson that the service had failed, that Francis Abrahams, who had tried to establish a mail route from Coweta to New Orleans, was sick at Fort Stoddert, that the mails had vanished, and that the post horses had died or had been stolen by Indians. Granger said that, after six months, not a single mail had been furnished by Abrahams.[40]

The most recent events gave special urgency to a conference between the United States and the Creek Indian Nation in the capital, completed on November 14, 1805, with the signing of the Treaty of Washington. The Indians ceded to the United States certain lands between the Oconee and Ocmulgee rivers, which brought the boundary of Indian territory to what later became Macon, Georgia. But more important, the treaty stipulated:

> that the government of the United States shall forever hereafter have a right to a horse path, through the Creek country, from the Ocmulgee to Mobile, in such direction as shall, by the President of the United States, be considered most convenient, and to clear out the same, and lay logs over the creeks; and the citizens of said State shall at all times have a right to pass peaceably on said path, under such regulations and restrictions as the government of the United States shall from time to time direct; and the Creek chiefs will have boats kept at the several rivers for the conveyance of men and horses, and houses of entertainment established at suitable places on said path for the accommodation of travellers; and the respective ferriages and prices of entertainment for men and horses shall be regulated by the present agent, Col. Hawkins, or by his successor in office, or as usual among white people.

The Treaty of Washington provided for the United States to pay the Creek Nation twelve thousand dollars annually for eight years and eleven thousand dollars thereafter for the next ten years. A line was to be run by the United States from the high shoals of the Apalachee to the mouth of the Ulcofauhatche to form the northwesterly boundary of the ceded lands. The treaty was signed on behalf of the United States by Dearborn, and on behalf of the Creek Nation by Oche Haujo, William McIntosh, Tuskenehau Chapco, Enehau Thlucco, and Chekopeheke Emantlua. Among those representing the United States were Benjamin Hawkins and James Madison.[41]

The Creek cession was urged on by the Pensacola-based trading company of John Forbes, the successor to Panton, Leslie & Company and a powerful influence among the Indians of the Southeast. From the monies to be paid to the Creeks, the company wanted assurances that the Creek debt, amounting to about forty thousand dollars, would be paid. In another treaty, also involving the trading company and later influencing traffic on the Federal Road, the Choctaws ceded certain of their lands between the Mobile and Mississippi rivers. Mindful of the international conflicts reflected in the region, Jefferson pressed for stronger defenses along the West Florida boundary.[42] The stipulation allowing for a horse path through the Creek lands would establish communications with troops that could face the Spaniards and the British in that critical corner of the United States.

On March 21, 1806, Granger sent to the House of Representatives a cost estimate for construction of the post route from Athens, Georgia, to New Orleans, detailed in three sections.[43] Congress came through with the exact appropriation of $6,400 on April 21, 1806; the formal declaration authorized the president to open a road from the Indian frontier near Athens—not far from the Ocmulgee River, then the western boundary of Georgia—to New Orleans, as far as the thirty-first degree of north latitude, north of Mobile and just below the junction of the Tombigbee and Alabama rivers.[44] Brush was to be cleared to a width of four feet; trees which had fallen across the paths were to be cut away; causeways across the swampy bogs were to be made of logs five feet long; and logs were to be laid across the creeks. According to these projections, the distance from Washington to New Orleans would be 1,152 miles, or 320 miles less than the route over the Natchez Trace.[45] In the push for faster communication, Jefferson would gain ten days with the new route—if the riders moved at the same rate of speed. More than speed, however, and more than a mere post route were to be the results of the project. A feat of frontier engineering, complicated by politics, confusion, and incompetency, and urged on by new necessities, was about to begin.

2

STAYED COURIERS

ATTEMPTS BY THE UNITED STATES POSTAL Department to build the mail route through the Creek Nation provide a study in frustration—in particular, the failure of the young central government to comprehend the mission. Initially, authorities in the Postal Department, aware of the national impetus for the shorter, faster route to New Orleans, did not regard the construction of a post road as a hazardous or slow undertaking. The first comments from Gideon Granger indicate that the postmaster general approached the project with the confidence of an absentee administrator. In 1803, he had written to the chairman of the House Committee on Post Offices and Post Roads, "As New Orleans will unquestionably be the place of deposit for the products of the Western World, its connection with the Atlantic Capitals must be incalculably great and important. The road to and from thence will become the great thoroughfare of the United States."[1]

Granger and other officials believed that, in the Treaty of Washington of 1805, they at last had a binding agreement with the Creeks—not knowing that not even Alexander McGillivray, the powerful chief who died in 1793, had had the power to speak for the entire confederation. National attention was directed to larger threats—to the British, with their eye on New Orleans, and to the Spaniards, still strong enough to cause trouble from their base in West Florida.

Col. Benjamin Hawkins, the seasoned Indian agent who lived among the Creeks and who had established a reputation for being fair but firm, appeared to be the man to direct the project. Accordingly, on April 14, 1806, Granger informed him of the congressional act appropriating $6,400 for the post road and instructed him to begin the construction at Athens.[2] Although the point of origin of the postal horse path is sometimes given as Athens, actually the "High

22

Shoals" of the Apalachee, in the headwaters of the Oconee in upper central Georgia, was the point at which it entered lands that had belonged to the Creek Indians prior to the recent Treaty of Washington in 1805. The ax work on the critical part of the path building in the Creek Nation began in 1806 on the west bank of the Ocmulgee.

Granger instructed Hawkins to begin the construction and to continue toward Fort Stoddert by way of Burnt Village, just south of the Creek village of Coweta on the west bank of the Chattahoochee, below present-day Columbus.[3] If followed, this route would have passed through Tuckabatchee, northeast of the junction of the Coosa and Tallapoosa rivers, not far from the site of Montgomery, in the heart of the territory of the Upper Creeks. General Wilkinson had earlier pointed out to Granger that a route could be established that skirted these settlements to the south.[4] For whatever reason, Granger changed his instructions to Hawkins to say that the route could run more directly south below Coweta to strike the ridge on the east of the Alabama watershed. Hawkins was told that it was his responsibility to superintend the conveyance of mail from Coweta to Fort Stoddert; in addition, he was to keep the route passable and to move the mail at 120 miles in twenty-four hours. The order was a tall one, even for a man of Hawkins's stature and experience, and doubtless he could have done the job well; but on August 4, Granger had to inform Jefferson that Hawkins was sick and unable to attend to the construction.[5] As events transpired, this misfortune set the tone for the entire post-route project.

In Washington, and "at a loss and unable to determine what is best," Granger had a choice of two successors to Hawkins.[6] One Samuel F. Bloomfield, a post rider who was living at Tuckahatchee, offered a description and an estimate for a road to be constructed from "Coweta to Tombeckby," although his description, as it came to Granger, stopped at a point on the east side of the Tensaw River, twelve miles from Fort Stoddert. Bloomfield's knowledge of the land and the climate is reflected in his careful, precise estimate. Numerous bridges and causeways would have to be constructed along the 208-mile route from Coweta. Timbers would be placed across the road and dirt packed between these logs to complete the causeways and keep horses from bogging to their bellies in the swamps.[7] Bridges would keep the oiled, deerskin mailbags, or portmanteaux, above the water and preserve contents, which even the postmasters were forbidden to tamper with; "filing the chain of the mail portmanteau" was an expressly stated offense.[8] In building these bridges, the planners would have to take account of the seasonal floods. Bloomfield noted that one stream, to be crossed where it was not flanked by the usual swamps, would require "a very high bridge otherwise the rise of water being too rapid it will be carried away." According to Bloomfield's projection the construction could proceed at less than 23 miles a day, or not more than 180 miles in eight days.[9] This conservative estimate did not please Thomas Jefferson; on August 9, he wrote Granger that "Col. Hawkins's illness and the feeble idea of Bloomfield for making only 23 miles a day are sufficient grounds for our looking to other resources."[10]

The other bid Granger had in hand was from Col. Joseph Wheaton, who offered to cut the road from Athens to Coweta—and presumably beyond—and to carry the mail from Washington to New Orleans in fourteen days. The Postal Department quickly contracted with Wheaton for both jobs. Trimming to a bureaucratic fine point, the contract signed on August 15 specified that, instead of fourteen days, the mail was to be moved from Washington to New Orleans in thirteen days and seven hours. Wheaton was also put in charge of constructing the entire road from Georgia to Fort Stoddert.[11] Two days later he got his cash advance of $2,700, representing $2,000 for carrying the mail and $700 for cutting the road, a ratio which reflected the priorities of the postal officials but not a comprehension of the terrain or the principal chore. Furthermore, Wheaton accepted a short deadline; he was given three months, to November 15, 1806, to come from Washington, put his crew together, and complete the horse path, with some assistance from Bloomfield and one other party.[12]

A report prepared by Wheaton as a special pleading and presented to Granger two weeks after the deadline had been missed traces his efforts in the wilderness. On August 20, he left Washington, stopping by Monticello for consultation with the president on some points important to the safety and dispatch of the mail. At the "high shoals of the Appalachy river on the frontier of Georgia," between the ninth and thirteenth of September, he collected horses, provisions, and men. A march of twenty miles the next day brought him to Little

River, one of several southern streams by that name, where he hired two more men, making a total party of thirteen. They crossed the Ocmulgee River at Lloyd's Ferry the next day and camped on Indian lands. Since there was no ford, he found a place for a permanent ferry with a good and sufficient flat and there "Marked a Large Oak with the initials of the Orleans Post Road."[13]

Wheaton's party began cutting, clearing, and blazing the path for the mail on a course west-southwest to connect the Indian trail from Coweta with the four fords of the Ocmulgee where the mail had previously passed. On September 16, they made about twenty miles to the crossing which led to the Upper Creeks and to McAllister's store. On September 17, Wheaton sent Robert Stirry ahead to arrange for carrying the mail between Fort Stoddert and New Orleans. He also sent Swan Hardin to the Marshalls' house at Coweta for an Indian runner and provisions. They camped on the Flint River and caught plenty of fish. The next day they cleared the road and stopped at Crow Creek. On the morning of September 19, Wheaton wrote a letter "on my knee to Col. Hawkins," telling the Indian agent he had a message for him from the president. By late afternoon the party arrived at Coweta and was invited into the town-house square by Chief William McIntosh, the Long Lieutenant, and others.

September 20, 1806, was spent in preparing provisions, conferring with McIntosh, and attending Indian ceremonies at the council square. Colonel Wheaton informed McIntosh that the mail had to be exchanged on the east side of the river. McIntosh drew a map on the ground with his pipe hatchet, indicating a shorter route than the old path, and Wheaton agreed to be guided accordingly. Speeches were exchanged. On the twenty-first the party crossed the Chattahoochee and cleared the path to McIntosh's plantation, where Wheaton dined with him in his two-story log house, where one of his wives lived. Wheaton then went on to "one Miller's house," where another McIntosh wife lived, and was caught in a heavy rain. The next day they cleared a path into low, swampy ground, and finally McIntosh had to acknowledge that a path in that location could not be built. Abandoning their work of the past two days, they reverted to the old path leading to Tuckabatchee. After clearing beyond the Pensacola path, they found a little-used trail, not one of the proven, high-ground Indian trails, leading in what Wheaton thought to be the right direction.

They took it, without a guide, trying to avoid the swamp—a costly mistake for Wheaton, as it turned out.

On September 23, he received a message from Hawkins, stating that Bloomfield and six axmen, acting under separate orders from Hawkins, were to have cut a path all the way from Alexander Cornells's between Coweta and Tuckabatchee, to Fort Stoddert, but had cleared only about twenty miles. In addition, a party under Rhode Early was to make a path from Early's mill to Burnt Village. The guide, John Field, reported that they had met so many streams of the Ocmulgee and so many swamps and mountains that, after preparing about forty miles, this route had been abandoned.

To make matters worse, Wheaton, who was already off track, became ill with a "high billious fever" and fell from his horse after having cleared about fifty miles from Coweta to Alexander Cornells's. He took Cornells with him as an interpreter and proceeded in search of Bloomfield, first to Zachariah McGirth's house and then to Colonel Hawkins's former residence. After a march of twenty-five miles, they came to a large stream of the Alabama River and were drenched by a heavy rain. Wheaton's fever reached its highest, and on September 25, he was having "fainting fitts" and was unable to sit on his horse. Three of his men were in similar condition. He abandoned his objective and ordered travois, or horse litters, made of the tents. After two nights at Bloomfield's, one at Cornells's and one on the path, he reached Coweta on the twenty-ninth and received aid from Capt. Thomas Marshall. The men were paid and all reached the frontier safely.[14]

On October 1, Wheaton went to Colonel Hawkins's house to arrange for expediting the mail and to recover from his illness. There he made a contract with McGirth, who owned some property in the vicinity. When McGirth realized the difficulties in carrying the mail from Coweta to Fort Stoddert in three days, he became alarmed and abandoned the contract before getting started. At the special recommendation of Hawkins, temporary arrangements were made with Bloomfield to carry the mail from Coweta to Fort Stoddert in only three days instead of the usual eight. On October 16, Wheaton left Colonel Hawkins's residence and returned to Washington by way of Fort Wilkinson, taking thirty-four days for the trip.

Neither cutting the horse path nor carrying the mail ran smoothly for Wheaton. On December 22, 1806, a circular was sent by Gideon Granger to all postmasters on Wheaton's route, requesting them to report immediately any neglect or inattention of any contractors or riders in conveying the mails. Granger also asked some postmasters, by postscript, why Wheaton frequently failed to deliver the mails on schedule and to report, for the next three months, the condition of the mail services along the line serviced by Wheaton.[15] On January 20, 1807, Granger advised Wheaton that he would be responsible for the delivery of mail to the postmaster in Athens in accordance with the schedule. Wheaton was to dispatch an express on the road and also to send a circular by each rider, "authorizing and commanding him and them" that, whenever the rider or horse should give out, a new rider and horse be furnished, so that, whatever the peril, the mail would be delivered on time.[16]

On February 12, Capt. Edmund Pendleton Gaines at Fort Stoddert received letters of instruction from Granger dated December 18 and 20, 1806. Gaines's reply mentioned repeated failures of the mail service between Fort Stoddert and Athens, but previously he had not been convinced of any wrongdoing by Bloomfield. Gaines had sent dispatches to the War Department by John Holcroft, who found "at Coweta three portmanteaux" which should have been carried to Fort Stoddert by Bloomfield's post rider the next day. The rider arrived at Fort Stoddert with only one portmanteau and could not account for any others.

The most graphic evidence of bungling came in a report from Lt. H. R. Graham, who had been requested by Gaines to investigate abuses of the mail between Fort Stoddert and Athens and to convey his findings to Granger.[17] He found the route "by no means calculated to ensure a safe or speedy conveyance of the mails." He had met a post rider named Allen and another named Len McGee and had learned that post riders sent to Fort Stoddert had not passed each other, because they had traveled old and new roads, alternate routes cut in places to avoid hazards. On February 19, at Bloomfield's, where Graham had been assured that every attempt had been made to expedite the mail to Fort Stoddert, he found that a mail bag that left Washington January 24 was at Coweta on February 5, but not until February 10 was it recognized as an express mail. "This discovery however did not add to it acceleration," Graham reported to the postmaster general. Whatever smugness that might be inferred from Graham's account is offset by his own apologies. "You will perceive, Sir, I traveled very slowly—my horses were extremely jaded—some of them with sore backs—the waters very high—all swimming, and roads very bad." He recommended that Gaines hire two carriers at Fort Stoddert, that Alden Lewis, the postmaster at Athens, employ two others, and that each rider make the entire trip in seven or eight days by changing fresh horses at appropriate points within the Creek Nation.[18]

While the U.S. government was concerned with Wheaton and the particulars of mail delivery, two other incidents heightened the need for a military communication route. The Spaniards, evicted from New Orleans and still unfriendly to the United States, moved into the old French garrison at Natchitoches, which had been established sometime between 1714 and 1716.[19] It was located on the east bank of the Sabine River, formerly the French boundary and, after the Louisiana Purchase, considered the western boundary of the United States. When the Spaniards posted cavalry east of the Sabine in 1806, the United States sent troops to occupy Natchitoches; by September, the Spaniards returned to the west side of the Sabine, and by December the U.S. militia had returned home.[20]

Tensions among settlers of the Old Southwest and the settlers in West Florida were further increased by the Aaron Burr episode. Burr, who had served as vice president during Jefferson's first administration, had been discredited following the death of Alexander Hamilton from their duel in July 1804 and was thought to have developed grand plans with the controversial Gen. James Wilkinson to establish an empire west of the Mississippi River. Influenced by the proclamation of President Thomas Jefferson, Col. Ferdinand L. Claiborne arrested Burr in January 1807. In court held at Washington, near Natchez, Burr's demands that he be released were denied. By the next day, when the court convened, Burr had forfeited his bail bond of $10,000 and fled.[21] Burr spent the nights of February 18–19, 1807, at the home of Col. and Mrs. John Hinson in Wakefield, Washington County, in the Alabama area of the Mississippi Territory. The following morning, he was again arrested by Capt. Edmund P. Gaines and taken to Fort Stoddert. After March 6, Col. Nicholas Perkins headed an expedition to accompany and guard the prisoner on his trip to Virginia for trial.

Accounts of Burr's removal show how travel had to proceed through the Creek Nation. Burr and his captors rowed up the Mobile and Tensaw rivers to the boat yard near Fort Mims and began their journey through Indian Territory, essentially along the post route that became the Federal Road. The route went about eight miles south of Econchate (now the site of Montgomery), by the residence of "Old Milly," and crossed Okfuskee (Line), Cubahatchee, and Calabee creeks, which the travelers swam. At the Chattahoochee, Flint, and Ocmulgee rivers, they crossed in canoes, with the horses swimming alongside. At Fort Wilkinson (near Milledgeville) they crossed the Oconee River by ferry, and a few miles to the east they stopped for breakfast at a house of entertainment, the first seen on their trip.[22]

Failure to complete the horse path on time and to establish dependable mail service along this route, together with publicity from the Burr conspiracy, invited congressional inquiry. A more subdued Postmaster General Granger stated, on February 5, 1807, that he was not against the mail route, but that he was opposed to "large expenditures in unsuccessful attempts to force rapid mail service through an immense wilderness filled with streams and marshes where no sustenance or aid can be given to either man or beast."[23] On February 11, Granger informed Josiah Meigs, at Athens, that express mail service had been instituted between Washington and New Orleans. Horses and riders were provided by the government, and certain persons were authorized to remove "any one, though faithful, where there was reasonable ground to believe that the Officer or Agent was directly or indirectly implicated by, or attached to the existing conspiracy."[24]

On February 16, 1807, Granger appointed Denison Darling as agent for running regular express mail between Athens and Fort Stoddert and for improving the route, and as postmaster of the Lower Creek Nation, with headquarters at Coweta. Granger suggested that Darling purchase the horses that Bloomfield and others were using. Col. Benjamin Hawkins was considered ill and aged, though he was only fifty-two, and Granger, on February 25, authorized Gen. David Meriwether of Georgia to complete the road be-

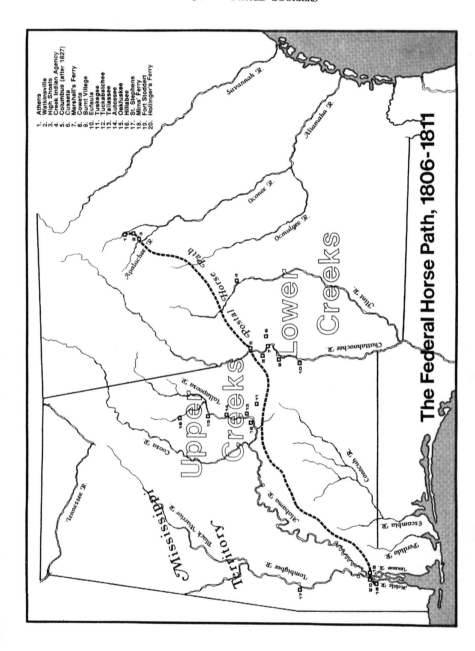

1. Athens
2. Watkinsville
3. High Shoals
4. Creek Indian Agency
5. Columbus (after 1827)
6. Cusseta
7. Marshall's Ferry
8. Coweta
9. Burnt Village
10. Eufaula
11. Tuskegee
12. Tuckabatchee
13. Tallassee
14. Autossee
15. Oakfuskee
16. Hillabee
17. St. Stephens
18. Mims' Ferry
19. Fort Stoddert
20. Hollinger's Ferry

The Federal Horse Path, 1806-1811

Upper Creeks

Lower Creeks

Mississippi Territory

Savannah R.

Altamaha R.

Oconee R.

Ocmulgee R.

Federal Horse Path

Apalachee R.

Flint R.

Chattahoochee R.

Tallapoosa R.

Coosa R.

Tennessee R.

Black Warrior R.

Alabama R.

Tombigbee R.

Conecuh R.

Escambia R.

Perdido R.

Mobile R.

Tensaw R.

tween the high shoals of Apalachee and Fort Stoddert and to establish stages where horses could be kept and riders housed at thirty-mile intervals.[25]

Granger and Wheaton had yet to come to terms over the broken contract. The account of the General Post Office for Wheaton showed the cash advance on August 17, 1806, of $700 (part of the check for $2,700) and a notation claiming that the road had been opened as far as Tensaw. Trees had been felled over all streams whose width could admit such bridges between Coweta and Fort Stoddert, but none of the marshy places were causewayed. Twenty miles of the road had been opened by Colonel Hawkins, and the distance from Tensaw to Fort Stoddert was nineteen miles, making a total of thirty-nine miles. A deduction of $65 was made for the road not cut and $57.62 for the causeways and bridges not made, for a balance due from Wheaton to the General Post Office of $122.62.[26]

Granger and Wheaton signed a statement dated July 6, 1808, before C. Swan and John P. VanNess, referees, that all depositions, affidavits, letters, and certificates should be allowed in evidence. On July 9, Granger outlined to these referees the incidents of breach of contract by Wheaton.[27] Alden Lewis, the postmaster at Athens, informed Granger on January 17, 1807, that Wheaton's wages were not sufficient to retain faithful mail riders and, as if to sink a barb, stated that Wheaton was a great admirer of Aaron Burr and thought that Burr would be the next president of the United States.[28]

Other evidence of confusion was the status of Samuel F. Bloomfield, who was at a loss to know whether he had been acting under the authority of the General Post Office or on behalf of Wheaton. On May 31, he was carrying the mail for Wheaton and also at the same rate for Darling. This past due account for carrying the mail and expense of opening the horse path amounted to $1,671.37. After crediting the government for horses he had acquired from the government, $256.50 was due him, which he requested, apparently without reservation, by the next mail.[29] Bloomfield claimed that he had not made an accurate survey of the path but had cut the path as near a direct line as practicable; he had cut the path six to ten feet wide nearly to the "Bigbee" settlement, placing logs over all streams not too wide for the length of the tree; he had been instructed only to ascertain the length of causeways needed, not to build them; and he found that, on Wheaton's portion of the path, not a bush had been cut, even in the thickets.

Although some letters did move through Georgia and the Creek Indian territory, most of the heavy mail for New Orleans continued to travel by Knoxville, Nashville, and the Natchez Trace.[30] The horse path through the Creek Nation had not relieved the pressure for the fast route needed to communicate with New Orleans. If anything, the post road had increased pressure; more traffic by the white man through the Nation over the next five years contributed to warmongering among one faction of the Creeks, who were receiving arms and ammunition from the British through the Spanish at Pensacola. These natives would see to it that a new hazard was added to the route by 1813.

3

THE WAR ROAD

T HE LIKELIHOOD OF A WAR WITH THE BRITISH and the certainty that an attack would occur somewhere on the central Gulf coast had by 1809 redirected attention to the need for a land route across the Mississippi Territory. In the waning months of Thomas Jefferson's presidency, two thousand men were sent by sea to Gen. James Wilkinson at New Orleans.[1] Before James Madison had been in office a year, half of that number were dead, killed by sickness, and Wilkinson was relieved of his command for refusing to obey a direct order from the secretary of war to move most of his fever-plagued troops to higher ground. Wilkinson, who had survived his association with Aaron Burr, was later court-martialed for insubordination and acquitted, a verdict President Madison signed "with regret."[2] Under the new commander, Brig. Gen. Wade Hampton, steps were taken to bolster defense and prepare for the coming confrontation. If the men and supplies were to be moved overland to reinforce the Gulf coast between the Apalachicola and the Sabine rivers, of immediate necessity was a military road.

On June 23, 1810, Secretary of War William Eustis directed Col. Richard Sparks, the commanding officer at Fort Stoddert, to order Capt. Edmund P. Gaines, the same officer who had sent a subordinate to inspect Wheaton's horse path, to take noncommissioned officers and privates on an exploration of the country along the ridge between the Tuscaloosa, later called the Black Warrior River, and the Coosa River, to the "Highwassee," then up, across, and down the Connasauga, Coosa, and Alabama rivers.[3] (Earlier maps had shown that the Highwassee, also spelled Hiwassee and Hawassee, was much farther west and south of its actual location, in southeast Tennessee near Chattanooga. The Connasauga is a small stream, a tributary of the Coosa near its headwaters in northwest Georgia.)[4]

Sparks was also ordered to send out a second party, east by Indian trails eventually to join Gaines's party at the Highwassee. Both parties were to return to Fort Stoddert by way of the Coosa and Tallapoosa rivers, completing a circuit generally across and down present-day Alabama. Each party was to keep a journal of daily progress, distances, soil, timber, water, and other remarks on the character of the country.

The action of the second party was to prove of great significance. Its commander, 1st Lt. John Roger Nelson Luckett of the Second U.S. Infantry, undertook what is probably the first simple, one-line or center-line survey for road construction in Alabama.[5] Beginning on September 12, 1810, at a red oak on the east bank of the Tensaw River, about fifteen miles from the fort, Luckett made a careful survey, marking each mile by carving Roman numerals on a tree. (Since his use of these numbers did not include the usual contractions, even the V for five, the ninety-ninth mile-post tree was inscribed "LXXXXIIIIIIIII." He must have been glad to approach the next tree, markable with a single C.) In particular, Luckett was charged with laying out the road from the Tensaw, northeast to the junction of the Coosa and the Tallapoosa. In addition to charting a line northeast from Fort Stoddert, Luckett prepared a "brief delineation," an account which offers more insight into how the Creek country appeared to a Maryland native who had already seen the territorial lands as far as Natchitoches, where he had gone in 1806 with other U.S. troops to confront the Spaniards at the Sabine River.

Although Luckett acknowledged that he was traveling during a dry season—a providential blessing, considering other accounts—he noted the presence of many springs of pure, good, and transparent water. The hardwoods he mentioned—Spanish oak, white oak, black oak, post oak, beech, sycamore, and chestnut—were standing in their virgin state. At the 114th mile-post tree, he took note of an "extensive cane brake," which would serve as important forage for horses. But his overall view was of a land of "Sterile Sandy Soil" in "Pine Woods Land," where the only fertile or better quality soil lay along the small watercourses, precisely where the white people would want to settle. He found grass in abundance, "a circumstance favorable to the raising of large Herds of Cattle."[6]

Gaines's party never met Luckett's; after proceeding 125 miles from St. Stephens over country that would "admit of a good road," Gaines was surrounded by a large body of Creeks and was forced to return to Fort Stoddert.[7] At Pintlala Creek (also called in various accounts Palawla, Palaula, Pintlas, and Manack's Creek), at "7 Chains 126 Miles," Luckett also stopped. His account does not mention an encounter with the Indians, but that is probably why he returned. In a letter to the secretary of war dated July 2, 1811, Luckett said, "You are apprized of the circumstance which opposed the fulfilling of the objects comprehended on this Order,"[8] which probably means that the officials knew the operation was covert and did not want mention made of contact with the Indians. The party of soldier-surveyors was, in fact, on the edge of the territory of the Upper Creeks, near the Hickory Ground, at a time when hostilities were increasing. Whatever the reason, Luckett returned to Fort Stoddert. He had two assignments to Baton Rouge and spent the remaining thirty months of his life attached to the fort on the Mobile River. According to military records, Capt. J. R. N. Luckett died there on May 5, 1813, less than three months before the first formal battle with the Creeks.[9]

Although Luckett's effort might be the single most important contribution by one man to the Federal Road, he and the soldiers under his command did not build it, as some earlier histories claim.[10] On July 11, 1811, General Hampton was directed by his superiors in Washington to begin without delay the construction of three wagon roads. The first of these roads Captain Gaines had been ordered to survey earlier, from the Tennessee River to Fort Stoddert; the second, which became the Federal Road, was described as running "from Fort Stoddert to Colonel Hawkins' place on the Flint River"; and the third, from Fort Stoddert to Baton Rouge.[11] Preliminary work on this third road, from the Mobile River to New Orleans, had already been done under the authority of Judge Harry Toulmin. He had been requested by the postmaster general on April 25, 1806, to take charge of cutting a horse path west from Fort Stoddert to intersect with a road from Pinckneyville on the Mississippi to the Pearl River.[12] Five years later, a more direct route to New Orleans still was not possible because of the Spanish presence in West Florida, who regarded the thirty-first parallel, running about six miles below Fort

Stoddert—a projection into lower Mississippi of the line that became the straight, southern boundary of the state of Alabama and of the state of Mississippi—as inviolable by the Americans.

The orders issued from Fort Stoddert in July 1811 included one historically significant proviso: "Give to the Creeks the necessary information and explanations—the United States must have roads for the purpose of transporting their Ordnance and military stores from one military post to another, as occasion may require."[13] This notice was to be given to the Indians, and the soldiers were to treat them kindly. There is little evidence that this attitude of the Americans—if it was expressed—was a palliative to the more hostile Creeks; in fact, the presence of Luckett and other soldiers, as opposed to post riders, traders, or Indian agents, must have had the opposite effect. Hawkins himself was blunt after attempting diplomacy. At a special meeting in September 1811, the Creek council, including deputations from the Choctaws, Cherokees, and Shawnees, gathered at Tuckabatchee to discuss the road. At the end of the three days of debate, permission was denied. According to a Savannah newspaper report, "Hawkins, at length, told them he did not come there to ask their permission to open a road but merely to inform them it was now cutting."[14]

Regardless of the clouds gathering over the Creek Nation, the military road from Georgia to Fort Stoddert was opened in November of 1811. The effort by the U.S. Army provided an occasion for Josiah Blakeley to remark on the spectacle of soldiers at work. A native of Connecticut, Blakeley came to Mobile in 1806, bought what is now called (and spelled) Blakely Island in 1807, and in 1813 founded the now-defunct town of Blakeley on the Tensaw River, south of Fort Mims. Writing from the Mobile District on February 12, 1812, he said, "During this last winter the United States army, which had long been wholly idle in this country, has made roads and bridges . . . from Fort Stoddert to the State of Georgia."[15] Meager military records list some of the personnel involved in the various road-building efforts. The applicable "Register of Officers" shows, among other entries:

Capt. Matthew Arbuckle, September 25, 1811, cutting a road to Georgia;

1st Lt. William F. Ware, September 25, 1811, cutting a road to Georgia;

STATE OF GEORGIA.

By his Excellency *David B Mitchell*

Governor and Commander in Chief of the Army and Navy of this State and of the Militia thereof.

all to whom these presents shall come, or whom the same may concern. . . . . Greeting:

KNOW YE, that the bearers hereof *Messrs Isaac Jackson & Lawrence Moore from Anson County North Carolina have*

my permission to travel through the *Creek* Nation *they* taking special care to conduct *themselves* peaceably towards the Indians, and agreeably to the laws of the United States.

In testimony whereof, I have hereunto set my hand and caused the Executive Seal of the State to be affixed thereto.

Done at the State-House in MILLEDGEVILLE, the *6* day of *may* in the year of our Lord one thousand eight hundred and *eleven* of the Independence of the United States of America the thirty-*fifth*

BY THE GOVERNOR.

James Rousseau
Secretary

PASSPORT THROUGH THE CREEK NATION

This Georgia passport was signed by David B. Mitchell, the governor of the state, whose name was given to the Federal Road fort on the west bank of the Chattahoochee. The document gave Messrs. Isaac Jackson and Lawrence Moore, from Anson County, North Carolina, permission to pass through the Creek Nation. Such passports were often issued to traders seeking state approval for dealing with the Indians. (Reprinted, by permission, from Dorothy Williams Potter, *Passports of Southeastern Pioneers.* [Baltimore: Gateway Press, 1982], p. 285)

2d Lt. Evert Bogardus, September 25, 1811, cutting a road to Georgia;

Capt. Edmund P. Gaines, September 15, 1811, designating a road to Baton Rouge;

Capt. William Lawrence, October 18, 1811, opening a road to Tennessee (along with 1st Lt. Robert Peyton, 2d Lt. Robert Cherry, and 2d Lt. Hezkiah Bradley, November 10, 1811).

Col. Leonard Covington was detached for duty with Captain Arbuckle's and Wilkinson's companies on September 29, 1811, and with Captain Campbell's and Lawrence's companies on October 28, 1811, evidently inspecting and supervising the road construction to Georgia and to Tennessee.[16] From this list it appears that Captain Arbuckle was in command of the troops and responsible for "cutting the road to Georgia," in part along the route previously surveyed by Luckett, and was under the general supervision of Colonel Covington.

The road built by the military was intended to be sufficient for moving supply wagons, cannons, and men on horse and foot. The type of construction was similar to other military roads connecting Nashville, Natchez, and other critical locations in the West. A recommendation from Secretary of War Henry Dearborn to Wilkinson in New Orleans in 1803 outlined general specifications, with a special order relating to the watercourses. According to Dearborn a military road should be opened "not exceeding sixteen feet in width and not more than eight feet of the sixteen to be cut close to the ground, and smoothed for passengers. . . . The great object is to have a comfortable road for horses and foot passengers, and instead of the expense of cutting a wide road, it is more important that the swamps and streams should be causewayed and bridged."[17] The water hazard was also recognized in a law passed by the Mississippi territorial legislature on March 1, 1805. It stipulated that public roads should be at least twenty feet wide, causeways at least twelve feet wide with a drain on each side, bridges twelve feet wide, and all tree stumps cut within six inches of the ground.[18]

The overriding irony of the military road building is that, although it looked toward one war, it was the major cause of another.[19] To be sure, the problems with the Creeks had a long foreground, as several histories have detailed. Although the Federal Road sparked the Creek

War of 1813–14, the root of the conflict involved a clash between two incompatible cultures. Even Hawkins's efforts to civilize the Indians, to encourage them to grow cotton and to teach them crafts, increased the hostility by creating a division between nativist Creeks, who wanted to practice the old way of life, and those attracted to the new. A century of trading, intermarriages, and treaties produced factions and provided fertile ground for the agitations of Tecumseh. Influenced by the British at Detroit, the famous Shawnee chief, whose parents had lived among the Creeks, came in October 1811 and addressed five thousand warriors at Tuckabatchee. In an hour-long speech he appealed to the Muscogees to restore their tribe's reputation for bravery. He admonished the Creeks to send the intruders "back where they came, upon a trail of blood." He raised the image of the white man who plows over the tombs of the Muscogee dead and "fertilizes his fields with their sacred ashes."[20]

Tecumseh's shrill rhetoric struck a chord among Creeks able to read the times. The conversion of the horse path into a road for wheeled vehicles was already increasing the traffic through their territory. Hawkins reported that, between October 1811 and March of the next year, 233 vehicles and 3,726 people had passed his Indian agency on the Flint River, heading west.[21] In response, the hostile Creeks, called the Red Sticks, were cultivating the established alliances.

Operating in the background of the conflict were the Spaniards at Pensacola, who were also providing a base for the British trading company of John Forbes & Company, successor to Panton, Leslie & Company and John Leslie & Company.[22] Mail taken by the Indians on the federal post road had been delivered to the Spaniards at Pensacola; in addition, post riders had been attacked and shot, horses killed, and horses and provisions stolen.[23] U.S. sympathizers had sent word that a party of Indians under Peter McQueen and High-Head Jim (also known as Jim Boy) had been furnished powder and shot by the Spaniards and were making their way back to the territory of the Upper Creeks. To stop the distribution of military supplies, Col. James Caller of Washington County, Mississippi Territory, the senior officer of the frontier, summoned local militia, about 180 men, and on July 27, 1813, encountered the party at Burnt Corn, just south of the federal military road.[24]

Caller's men, among them Sam Dale, later to become an Alabama hero, drove off the Indians but were distracted in their efforts to divide the military spoils. Indians in the swamps along Burnt Corn Creek launched a counterattack, made loud with war whoops, and succeeded in scattering the whites. When his men could not be reassembled, the commander himself, according to one report, wandered in the woods for a week. Two accounts disagree on the number of Americans killed and wounded; but whether it was two or five killed, or ten to fifteen wounded, the victory was significant for the Creeks. It showed that a smaller force of Indians, even if taken by surprise and armed for the most part only with clubs, bows and arrows, and the ancient battle cries, could defeat the whites. The victory gave new authority to the fanatical prophets and encouraged Creeks still angry over the surprise attack to look to another target west on the Federal Road.

Fort Mims, established before the Creek War of 1813–14 on the east bank of the Alabama River at Mims' Ferry, near where Luckett had begun his survey, was one of a line of stockades that would become critical points for soldiers, and later travelers, on the Federal Road. It was a plantation house palisaded to protect settlers, especially those south along the Tensaw River.[25] Although an attack by a large body of Red Sticks was anticipated, the commander of the fort, Daniel Beasley, was poorly prepared; on the morning of August 30, 1813, the day of the assault, in which he would be killed, Beasley prepared a dispatch for his superiors, discounting the plausibility of reports that a local plantation was already "full of Indians committing every kind of Havoc." The Creeks attacked at noon, firing into the fort through portholes that had been cut too low. Sand interfered with closing the main gate, and the Indians entered before it could be shut. Led by William Weatherford and Paddy Welsh, a prophet whose magical protection against bullets proved ineffectual, the Creeks by midafternoon had succeeded in massacring the defenders. A burial party sent to Fort Mims three weeks later found 247 white men, women, and children dead. It is estimated that from 20 to 40 whites escaped. The bodies of about 100 warriors were also found.

In October 1813, Brig. Gen. Ferdinand L. Claiborne, brother of territorial governor W. C. C. Claiborne, set out from St. Stephens with an expedition of Mississippians to seek out the Upper Creeks. The

SAM DALE AND THE CANOE FIGHT

This frontispiece engraving from an 1860 biography of Sam Dale shows the Indian fighter in solo combat with hostile Creeks. In the actual Canoe Fight, which took place on the Alabama River in 1813, Dale joined with James Smith, Jere Austill, and a slave named Caesar in a spectacular victory over nine Indians. Dale and the others were a part of an expedition led by Gen. Ferdinand Claiborne sent out to drive the Creeks from the Alabama River valley after the Battle of Burnt Corn and the Fort Mims massacre. General Claiborne's brother, William Charles Cole Claiborne, was the territorial governor, and the general's son, John Francis Hamtramck Claiborne, was the author of the Dale biography. (Reprinted, by permission, from the Alabama Department of Archives and History, Montgomery)

campaign got an early boost and Alabama history its most celebrated tableau in the Canoe Fight. A party under Claiborne consisting of Sam Dale, Jeremiah Austill, James Smith, and a black slave named Caesar fought a band of Creeks hand-to-hand between boats in the Alabama River and killed nine, before spectators from each side, and none in the Claiborne party suffered serious injury.

After creating a base at Fort Claiborne, in Monroe County, about forty miles north of Fort Mims, on the road that led from St. Stephens across Clarke County to the Federal Road, the general left a supply point at Fort Deposit farther up the road and advanced to the Holy

Ground, near the mouth of the Pintlala on the south side of the Alabama River. Indian medicine men considered the site holy because it was defined by a river, two creeks, and a swamp and presumably could not be taken in battle; it was also the headquarters of Weatherford. On December 23, 1813, Claiborne's Mississippians defeated the Indians, killing about twenty-one Creeks and twelve Negroes with the loss of only one American. In the Battle of the Holy Ground, a village of about eighty wigwams and a town of about two hundred houses were destroyed, but Weatherford was not taken. Mounted on his horse Arrow, he leapt down a bluff into the Alabama River and emerged safe and defiant on the opposite bank.[26] On Christmas Day the army left the Holy Ground and returned via the Federal Road to Fort Deposit, Fort Claiborne, and dismissal. They had succeeded in driving Weatherford out of central Alabama; the next concentration of hostile Creeks would be at Horseshoe Bend.

News of the Indian uprising, and in particular of the massacre at Fort Mims, quickened the pulses of Georgians with a long-standing interest in winning more territory. Civilian travel over the new road was arrested, however; in August 1813, the Georgia militia was called out and placed under the command of Gen. John Floyd. Three months later Floyd at his base at Fort Hawkins received a plea from friendly chiefs whose homes were being burned and cattle driven off by hostile Creeks. Their desperation was spelled out in a letter written November 18, 1813, at Coweta and sent by runner:

General Floyd,
    four days we have been surrounded and we have sent you two runners. And we have not heard from you. The main body of Indians is about half a mile from us and there are scouts of them up and down the river about the same distance. They are killing every thing and burning all of the houses, we cant turn out to fight them on account of our women and children. They are more than double our number, and we cannot leave our entrenchments for fear of them getting possession. Now my friend come and relieve us, come night and day. If you don't come soon we will be in a starving situation. If we hear you are coming it will give us a great relief. You have had full time to come. The hostile party are in the open pine woods. If you was here, it is a good place to fight them. If you mean to come fight them, come. If they make off you will have trouble to find them. We only want 1000

of your men we would turn out and fight them. We have sent Tobler
to pilot you to the river. We are your

> Friends
> Big B W Warrior
> William McIntosh
> Little Prince
> Alexr A C Cornells[27]

Ensuing events would prove the immediate logistic significance of
the Federal Road. Responding to the call, Floyd crossed the Chattahoochee on November 24, 1813, and his troops built a stockade a
mile west of the river, twelve miles below the site of Columbus.
Named in honor of the governor of Georgia, David B. Mitchell, it was
to be the first fort west of the Chattahoochee in a series of stockades
about a day's travel apart, erected in an attempt to extend the supply
line beyond the 135-mile distance from Fort Hawkins to the Chattahoochee so that the Americans could remain "within Striking distance of the enemy."[28] Floyd selected Federal Road sites near the
homes of the friendly Indians who had called on him for protection;
these chiefs also had some influence with the Creek Nation. Fort
Mitchell was near the home of Little Prince. Of the others built later,
Fort Bainbridge, in present-day Macon County, was near the home
of Big Warrior; and Fort Hull, also in Macon County, was adjacent
to the lands of Alexander Cornells and his brother Joseph.[29]

By the time of Floyd's campaign the road had been widened; in
several places new routes had been made, so that a network of roads
existed. Although considerable manpower was needed for repairs,
the road was good enough for cannons mounted navy-style on four-
wheeled wagons to pass—an accommodation that would have consequences in the battles to come.

At daybreak on November 29, Floyd's 950 militia with three or four
hundred friendly Indians attacked the village of Autossee, an important center of the Red Stick faction, located north of Tuckabatchee.
Although eleven Americans died and the friendly Indians suffered
heavy losses, about two hundred hostile Creeks were killed, among
them two principal chiefs, and the Red Sticks were routed. The battle
was more closely fought, however, than the lopsided casualty count
indicates. The artillery that was moved over the Federal Road—per-

haps the first to be fired in battle in Alabama—turned the tide for the Americans. Heavy cannon fire into the village was followed by a bayonet charge that put the hostile Indians to flight. Because Floyd had not been able to establish his supply lines, he was unable to pursue the Red Sticks. Injured himself, he had to return to his Federal Road base at Fort Mitchell before making another march into the heart of the Upper Creek country.

The image several histories leave of the Creek Nation during the winter of 1813 is of a country devastated by war. Crops had been destroyed; many Indians had been driven into the swamps; and munitions were in short supply. Although the Americans too were having trouble with supplies (the crops of friendly Indians were also ruined) and there were military squabbles over authority in the territory, the hostile Creeks faced opposition from three sides. Claiborne's troops were active in the south as protection for the lower settlements; the Georgians were regrouping at Fort Mitchell and were soon to be joined by more disciplined, regular army troops from South Carolina; and advancing from the north were the Tennesseans under Gen. Andrew Jackson. It appeared that the stage was set for a last stand.

In January 1814, Floyd, believing that he could move sufficient supplies over the Federal Road, launched another campaign. He was prompted to act quickly because the South Carolinians had not arrived and the six-month enlistment of his state militiamen was to expire February 22. Forty miles west of Fort Mitchell, he established Fort Hull, which was to be his westernmost Federal Road outpost, and encamped there with 1,100 militia and volunteers and 600 friendly Indians. Attempting to penetrate further, Floyd advanced with his infantry and artillery to the west side of Calabee Creek, where his actions were observed by hostile Creek scouts.

A surprise attack before dawn on January 27 at Calabee Creek by about 1,300 warriors under Weatherford, Welsh, William McGillivray, and High-Head Jim resulted in 169 casualties for Floyd's force before the Indians retired from the field of battle. The commander was injured again, and his aide, Joel Crawford, had a horse shot out from under him in the fighting after daybreak.[30] The Creeks had learned at Autossee what death the cannons could deal, and they attacked the artillery, fighting low and close; only after the barrels were lowered

GEN. JOHN FLOYD

John Floyd (1769–1839), a native of South Carolina, was a brigadier general in the Georgia militia when he commanded the Georgia expedition against the Creek Indians. His troops established a series of forts along the Federal Road to serve as their main supply line. Although wounded at the Battle of Autossee, Floyd remained in command until the militia returned to Georgia. Later he served in the Georgia legislature and in the United States Congress. (Reprinted, by permission, from Georgia Department of Archives and History, Atlanta)

MAJ. JOEL CRAWFORD

As a young man, Joel Crawford (1783–1858) was an aide to Gen. John Floyd in the Creek War of 1813–14 and had two horses shot from under him in the battles of Autossee and Calabee Creek. Later in life he served in the Georgia legislature and in the United States Congress and was a member of the commission that established the Alabama-Georgia boundary north of the Chattahoochee River. Fort Crawford in Escambia County was named in his honor; he was a first cousin of the nationally prominent Georgia politician William Harris Crawford. (Reprinted from the Rebecca Crawford Hamilton photo album in the private collection of H. D. Southerland, Jr.)

could any damage be done to the attackers. Floyd's short-term militiamen were not destroyed, but their spirit was broken. One soldier recorded a scene indicating how alien the behavior of the Indian allies could seem to a white American.

> The friendly Indians, who were with us, exercised great barbarity upon the bodies of our enemies slain, on the morning after the battle. They ripped them open, cut their heads to pieces, took out the heart of one, which was borne along in savage triumph by the perpetrators; and strange to tell, cut off the private parts of others. What bestial conduct. One dead Indian was hoisted upon a horse and as he would tumble off, the savage spectators would cry out, "Whiskey too much."[31]

Deep in the Creek country and mindful of his weak supply line, Floyd fell back to Fort Hull with nearly a fourth of his troops sick and wounded. He transferred the command of the fort to Col. Homer V. Milton and marched back to Georgia over the road that had brought him two engagements with the enemy—the first clearly a victory, and the second at best a Pyrrhic victory.

Under Milton, the luck changed. He held the fort until the regular army reinforcements arrived from South Carolina. Sixteen miles east of Fort Hull, during a heavy snowstorm, the South Carolinians built Fort Bainbridge, completing Floyd's plan of Federal Road supply posts within one day's march. In March additional reinforcements arrived from North Carolina, and Milton was able to turn west again, for a deeper penetration into Creek country. In April, his troops built Fort Decatur on the Tallapoosa, opposite Tuckabatchee. The strengthened forces and the more reliable supply line were preparation for an army to come down from the north to deliver the final blow.

Jackson, meanwhile, had been making progress with Tennessee militiamen aware of the threat the Creeks posed to their settlements. A raiding party in the spring of 1812 had attacked a small community on the Duck River, killing a man, a woman, and five children, and holding one woman as a captive for several weeks, until she escaped and was rescued by a white trader. Jackson meant to destroy the Creeks, a motive he carried from military life into his political career.

Just west of Tallusahatchee, after that village had been destroyed

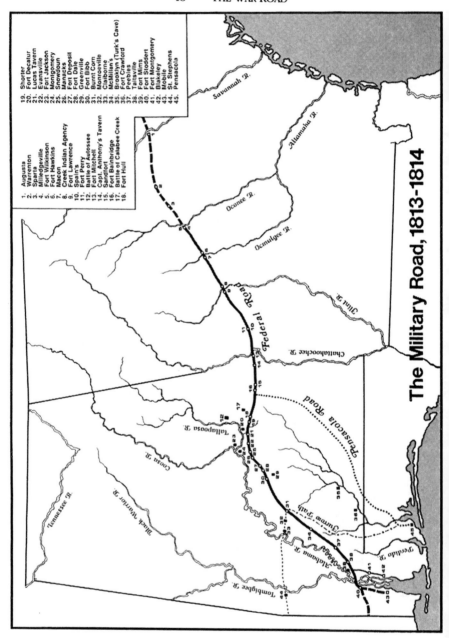

The Military Road, 1813-1814

1. Augusta
2. Warrenton
3. Sparta
4. Milledgeville
5. Fort Wilkinson
6. Fort Hawkins
7. Macon
8. Creek Indian Agency
9. Fort Lawrence
10. Spain's
11. Fort Perry
12. Battle of Autossee
13. Fort Mitchell
14. Capt. Anthony's Tavern
15. Sandfort
16. Fort Bainbridge
17. Battle of Calabee Creek
18. Fort Hull
19. Shorter
20. Lucas Tavern
21. Evansville
22. Fort Jackson
23. Montgomery
24. Snowdoun
25. Manacks
26. Fort Deposit
27. Fort Dale
28. Greenville
29. Fort Bibb
30. Burnt Corn
31. Monrooville
32. Claiborne
33. McMillin's
34. Brooklyn (Turk's Cave)
35. Fort Crawford
36. Peebles
37. Taitsville
38. Fort Mims
39. Fort Stoddert
40. Fort Montgomery
41. Blakeley
42. Mobile
43. St. Stephens
44. Pensacola

by the cavalry of Gen. John Coffee, Jackson built Fort Strother as a holding place for supplies and a point for reinforcement, but before the fresh troops arrived, Jackson decided to attack the fortified village of Talladega. On November 8, he attempted to envelope the town using two columns, but the Red Sticks, fighting more fiercely than Jackson had experienced, found an opening and many escaped. Although about three hundred were killed, many fled, and Jackson was not able to deliver the coup de grace. By March, he had a newer and bigger army and was ready to approach the major encampment of Indians behind fortified breastworks at Horseshoe Bend on the Tallapoosa.

Although badly outnumbered and poorly armed, the thousand warriors from the Upper Creek villages led by Chief Menawa were gathered at the bend to make their stand, with the river behind them as an escape route. On the morning of March 27, 1814, Jackson's artillery opened from the front, shelling continuously for two hours, during which time friendly Indians under Coffee swam the river and cut loose the canoes of the hostile Creeks. A charge by Jackson's troops broke up the Indians' front line, forcing about 300 into the water, where they were killed by Coffee's men firing from the opposite bank. The bodies of 557 warriors were found on the battlefield. Andrew Jackson had scored his major victory.

The significance of the Battle of Horseshoe Bend transcends an isolated conflict with the Indians of the Creek Nation or a history of the Federal Road. It was fought in the context of the War of 1812 and is regarded by at least one historian as a major battle of that war.[32] The British already were landing troops in the South with arms and supplies for the Indians. Jackson had to turn his attention to threats from remnants of the Creeks at Pensacola, but when he returned to the fort named for him and built on the site of the old French stockade Fort Toulouse, near the confluence of the Coosa and the Tallapoosa, he believed that he had rung down the curtain on the Creek Nation.

The shaky treaty intended to formalize the end of the conflict was forced into reality by Jackson's iron will. The terms reflected his antipathy for all of the Indians, even the allies who had fought bravely with the Americans and believed they would be favored. The annexation of 22 million acres of land, however, included the holdings of the friendly Creeks. Hawkins viewed the taking of over half of the Creek Nation as harsh, and the friendly Creeks were embittered, but Jackson shamed and threatened them into signing the Treaty of Fort Jackson on August 14, 1814. The names on the treaty included those of thirty-five friendly chiefs and only one who, perhaps, had been a Red Stick. Jackson's affront to Indian pride drove much of the hostile Creek remnant into unity with their Muscogean relatives, the Seminoles of Florida, who maintained ties with the British.[33] More important, the contemptuous attitude of the United States embodied in the treaty virtually assured that, if this group of Indians could get revenge, it would. Jackson, meanwhile, was free to march down the Federal Road to meet the British wherever they might strike on the Gulf coast, Mobile or New Orleans.

Although the Treaty of Fort Jackson may not have been regarded as binding by Creeks, who felt betrayed, the confederation had surrendered one-fifth of its land in Georgia and three-fifths of its Alabama territory, including all of the land on the Federal Road west of Line, or Okfuskee, Creek. The surveying of the new boundary, visible in part today as the line between Montgomery and Macon counties, was an indication that the United States regarded the entire Alabama River valley as off-limits to the Creeks and open for settlement. The treaty left as a final Creek possession a narrow tract in east Alabama and west Georgia running north and south from the lower Piedmont to the Wiregrass, bisected by the Federal Road.

Except for military travel, movement on the road had come to a standstill during the hostilities of 1813–14; however, the availability of new lands on the fertile watercourses identified in Lieutenant Luckett's "brief delineation" increased the traffic. Although journals wax eloquent in their descriptions of the hazards of travel over roads that were washed out and streams that were flooded, the Federal Road had been widened and improved, and in several places alternate routes over the network were available. Moreover, the development of the forts along the Federal Road created an illusion of security.

The character of the countryside was about to change drastically. Those who passed over the Federal Road would become part of a region in transition, exploding with energy and urgency, with the Creek Indians still in their Nation, not yet vanquished.

4

"ALMOST IMPASSABLE"

Aᴼᴿᴛᴇʀ 1814, A TENUOUS PEACE PREVAILED in the Creek Nation. The Treaty of Fort Jackson officially ended the fighting of 1813–14, but it did not remove the threat of violent death at the hands of vengeful Indians. The British and Spanish, allies of the hostile Creeks and Seminoles, were vanishing. The ratification of the Treaty of Ghent in 1815 concluded the War of 1812, and the United States had navigational rights to the Mississippi River. The Spaniards left Mobile for good in 1813 and ceded the Floridas in 1821. News that the United States had cleared these three obstacles from the path of expansion, opening lands west of the Creek Nation and above the thirty-first parallel, over which Fort Stoddert stood sentinel, made the Alabama and Tombigbee river valleys into magnets for settlers seeking fertile soil and fresh prospects.

Unless these pioneers were in a position to come up the rivers from Mobile, a hard and expensive venture before steamboat travel became common in the 1830s, or to cross the high ridges and move down the Tallapoosa, Coosa, Cahaba, or Black Warrior valleys from the Tennessee, they had a Hobson's choice in roads. The major arteries of the East and North had connections that led eventually to Milledgeville, the last settlement before entering the newly acquired Indian lands and the remaining Creek Indian Territory. Although traders and light travelers from the North probably continued to come through Athens, Watkinsville, and High Shoals, over the postal horse path that was opened in 1806, after 1811 wheeled vehicles probably would have come south through Madison to the new military—now Federal—road at Milledgeville. Those coming from the East would have traveled through Augusta and Sparta to Milledgeville for a replenishment of supplies before entering the most hazardous section of the passage—through the Creek Nation over the same

Federal Road. If the journey proved typical, the road itself would be one of the trials.

In fact, if early nineteenth-century pilgrims had had access to a contemporary vocabulary, they would have remarked in a chorus that the Federal Road made a negative environmental impact. The soils along the upper fringes of the coastal plain are, for the most part, sandy. The road often climbed sandy ridges and was described as rambling "with incredible sandbeds that one would ordinarily not expect to find short of the sea coast."[1] In Russell County, Alabama, the Federal Road was built primarily on Ruston sand or fine sandy loam, Norfolk sand or sandy loam, and Susquehanna fine sandy loam.[2] When vegetation is removed from the surface of these soils and rain follows, the land erodes rapidly, especially on the slopes. Where the road went up or down grades, the pressure of the horses' hooves and the iron bands on the wagon wheels, pulling uphill or braking downhill, disturbed the soil more than on level ground. The next rain washed away even more of the sandy soil. (The soil type was emphasized in the name of General Floyd's breastworks built in this section—Sand Fort, pronounced locally "SAN-fud.") In some such instances on the hills of western Russell County, the old route had been worn down by heavy traffic as much as six or seven feet below the natural ground level, leaving a recessed roadbed. Sir Charles Lyell, the famous British geologist, traveled fifty-five miles on a still-active segment of the Federal Road from Milledgeville in 1846 and remarked that the clearing of the woods, previously level and unbroken, caused the soil to be cut by torrents so that gullies were visible everywhere.[3]

The laborings through swamps and sandbeds found expression in political communications between the new country and Washington on the issue of road and bridge maintenance. In February 1815, as a major wave of emigration was beginning, Congressman William Lattimore from the Mississippi Territory submitted to the House of Representatives a report recommending that the road from Fort Hawkins to St. Stephens be repaired and kept in repair.[4] In 1816, Congress did appropriate five thousand dollars for the road repair, the same amount it had allocated in 1809 and would appropriate again in 1818. More funds were included in two ten-thousand-dollar appropriations bills passed in 1816 and 1818 to repair two roads, the first from Columbia, Tennessee, to Madisonville, Louisiana, and the second from Georgia to Fort Stoddert.[5] When the 1816 appropriations bill was passed, William Harris Crawford, serving briefly as secretary of war, wrote Maj. Gen. Andrew Jackson at Nashville informing him of the ten thousand dollars to be divided equally between the Tennessee-Louisiana road and the Federal Road. "If there are many bridges to be erected the appropriation will be inadequate to the object," he wrote on September 24, 1816. "In that event the employment of a part of the troops may become necessary." Crawford must have sensed that whoever followed him as secretary of war might redistribute the money; he advised Jackson to act quickly, because "as little time should be lost in collecting it as possible."[6] If Crawford did have doubts, they were well founded. John C. Calhoun followed Crawford as secretary of war and decided that all of the funds should be expended on the Tennessee-Louisiana road.[7]

Crawford was a Georgia political leader with strong interests beyond the Chattahoochee, which makes the position he took as secretary of treasury, the next cabinet post he held under President Monroe, surprising, to say the least. In a report to Monroe in December 1817 for transmission to the House of Representatives, Crawford stated that appropriations for opening a road from the frontiers of Georgia to New Orleans were intended principally for the movement of mail through the wilderness, that they were completed "as far as the object for which they were intended required," and that they were then in a condition of maintenance and repair satisfactory to accomplish the mission for which they were built.[8]

The various political exchanges among officials indicate that the Federal Road could be considered, by turns, a mail road, a military road, a national road, or perhaps even a territorial or state road and had such low priority, however considered, that it often went begging. When Israel Pickens, then a North Carolina congressman and chairman of the Committee on Public Expenditures, requested in February 1817 that Calhoun advise him of the status of repairs on the two roads authorized in the ten-thousand-dollar expenditure, he got the roundabout answer that Gov. David B. Mitchell had been appointed to succeed Benjamin Hawkins as agent to the Creeks and that the matter would be in his hands when he assumed the duties of agent.[9] In response to two additional inquiries, Mitchell informed the secretary of war that Reuben Hill had agreed to take on the repair job for five years for five thousand dollars, an inadequate sum, perhaps, since Hill declined to take on the job at all.[10]

Although Calhoun, as secretary of war, had made the Federal Road play second fiddle to the Tennessee-Louisiana route, he had not dismissed its strategic importance. In letters written in March and April 1818, he asked Mitchell about the status of repairs of the road from Fort Hawkins to Fort Stoddert and reported that troops under Edmund P. Gaines, who had risen to the rank of major general, had repaired about ninety miles of the road.[11]

To these letters Mitchell replied in May that the draft of five thousand dollars was insufficient, that the road was 330 miles long, that the swamps were extensive and the bridges decayed beyond repair, that General Jackson had been ordered to send troops to assist but the Seminole War had diverted his attention, that, of two people engaged to build the bridges, one had abandoned the contract and the other had stopped work because of the recent "horrid attack upon Cheehaw."[12] Gaines had been directed to furnish such troops to work on the road as the state of his command would allow, but no troops could be spared. Mitchell was again asked by the secretary of war, twice in August 1818, whether ten thousand dollars would be sufficient, and, if not, what amount would be necessary.[13]

In September Mitchell finally answered, stating that he could get no private citizens of the territory to offer to build bridges between Line Creek and Claiborne because the inhabitants were clearing land and making plantations and no reasonable compensation could detach them from such objectives. He said he was negotiating with a Colonel Barnett for bridges across Persimmon, Calabee, and Keebihatchee (Cubahatchee) creeks. Between Fort Hawkins and the Creek Indian Agency, Hawkins's old place on the Flint River, three bridges would have to be built; between the agency and Fort Mitchell, six bridges; and between Fort Mitchell and Fort Bainbridge, two more. Mitchell projected optimistically that the bridges would be completed by November. In response to Calhoun's final question, he answered yes: the sum of ten thousand dollars was small in comparison to the object, but he did not presume to set a figure.[14]

Not only the condition but also the location of the Federal Road was a cause for correspondence. From Fort Stoddert, Judge Harry

Toulmin of the Mobile District wrote to Calhoun on May 25, 1818, concerning the recent appropriation. He had been in touch with Judge Charles Tait, and they desired a relocation of a part of the road on the east side of the Alabama River. As Toulmin explained the circumstances to the secretary of war:

> When the military opened the roads in this country under the order of General Hampton, our commanding officer here (Col'l Covington) seemed to think he had no discretion but that he was to follow whatever act the convenience of the post rider had induced him to adopt in carrying the mail. ... General Gaines had a way marked out for a road on the east side of the Alabama & Mobile last summer, and plank was sawed for a bridge—over Major Creek—but the Seminole War prevented any further operations.[15]

Mitchell supported Toulmin in a letter to Calhoun, stating that the route Toulmin proposed would shorten the distance and afford a better and drier road by keeping it on the high ground between Fort Bainbridge in Macon County and Fort Claiborne in Monroe and furthermore, to repeat a refrain, that the sum appropriate would not be enough without the help of troops which General Gaines could spare to help relocate the road. The secretary of war approved the change of location on October 19, 1818; likewise he approved a suggestion from Samuel B. Shields of Clarke County on November 16, 1818, that the road between Fort Hawkins and Burnt Corn Springs (he was obviously referring to the section west of Fort Bainbridge) be located along the ridge between the Escambia and Alabama rivers to shorten the distance by fifty to seventy miles and make it easier to maintain.[16]

Laws put the burden of maintaining highways, ferries, and bridges on private citizens. According to an 1805 act of the Mississippi territorial legislature, roads were to be kept twenty feet wide, and bridges and causeways twelve feet, with tree stumps "not to exceed six inches above the ground, and pared round the edges." All free male persons and all male slaves between the ages of sixteen and fifty, with a few exceptions, could be required to work on at least one road for up to six days a year, using privately owned tools. Free males who refused to serve or did not send a substitute and owners who failed to provide slave labor could be fined a dollar a day. Overseers appointed by the court were charged with providing names of the workers and supervising the labor. Those who refused to serve as overseers could be fined forty dollars, but "no person shall be compelled to serve as an overseer of a road more than one year in three." Overseers were allowed to keep half the fines for their own use and required to spend the other half hiring substitutes.[17] When Alabama became a separate territory in 1817, the Mississippi statute was embraced but amended. "All and every person," not exempt because of age or other reasons, could be required to work "ten days and no longer" on roads and "not exceeding twenty days" on bridges and causeways.[18]

Despite the territorial and state laws, the good suggestions from citizens, and the agreements from the central government to carry them out, there is little evidence before 1833 of maintenance or major improvements to bridges, causeways, and adequate roadways— or of anything other than slight shifts in the location of the Federal Road. The Post Office Department continued to use it as a post road, but the principal route for mail to New Orleans remained through Abingdon, Knoxville, Nashville, and Natchez, a distance of 1,380 miles and a travel time of twenty-four days. The shorter route through Athens, Fort Hawkins, and Fort Stoddert to New Orleans had been tried and found to be impracticable because of numerous streams without bridges or ferries (although mail within the South was still transported over this route). In its report to the Senate on December 15, 1824, the Post Office Department admitted that, if a substantial road was made along this route, the mail could be carried in only twelve days. However, there may have been some memory of the defeat Joseph Wheaton had suffered almost twenty years earlier. Postal officials concluded that the old route from Washington City to New Orleans by way of the Natchez Trace, though longer, was safest and best, considering "the present conditions of the roads."[19]

The one major change that did take place came after Congress authorized the opening of a new road through the Creek Indian lands between Line Creek and the Chattahoochee River, connecting with a new covered bridge completed above the falls at Columbus. The $22,000 appropriation of February 20, 1833, created "the Upper Federal Road," which looped through the Creek Nation but on higher ground more easily traveled in wet weather before joining the exist-

ing road beyond Calabee Creek, near the western boundary of the
Creek Nation.[20] This change came late in the life of the Federal Road;
it had been in existence only three years before the Indian removal
allowed other roads through the territory.

Increasing commercial use of the Federal Road did not make it
safer or more secure. Milledgeville was the last stop before entering
the sparsely populated country, and it was the nearest place east for
Alabama planters beyond the Creek Nation to buy goods and supplies. Freight was hauled by wagon from Charleston and Savannah
through Augusta and Milledgeville for sale by merchants in Montgomery, which had begun to develop after the Treaty of Fort Jackson.
For freight haulers and other travelers, the road condition was only
one of the hazards. Attacks by hostile Creeks and Seminoles continued as far north as the Federal Road with a randomness that defied
defense. In March 1818, members of the Ogle (or Ogley) and Stroud
families were killed at Fort Bibb; more were killed a week later, near
the same location by a party led by Savannah Jack, or John Hague, the
half-breed son of a British soldier captured by Indians in Pennsylvania during the Revolutionary War. The Stokes family was wiped out
above Claiborne, after which a military sweep of the area was conducted by Sam Dale and Maj. White Youngs of the Eighth Infantry,
stationed at Fort Crawford.[21]

On March 26, 1818, William Wyatt Bibb, the governor of the Alabama Territory, sent a letter to Big Warrior at Coosada, a village
north of Montgomery, advising him of the military action and calling
for his help in ending the slayings on the Federal Road:

> Friend, I send you this letter to inform you that some of the white peo-
> ple in this territory have been cruelly murdered, and to explain to you
> the things I have found it necessary to do.
>
> On Friday night the 13th of this month, a family consisting of men,
> women, and children, while sitting in peace around their fire, on the
> Federal road about sixty-five miles this side of the town of Claiborne,
> were attacked by a party of red men, and eight killed. The next Friday,
> five men riding quietly along the road, in the same neighborhood
> were fired on, three killed and one badly wounded. These unex-
> pected and unprovoked murders could not be borne. We could not sit
> down, and permit our wives and children to be tomahawked without
> resistance. I have, therefore, ordered our soldiers to find and slay the

hostile party. But I am informed, there are many of your people among us who are our friends; and we know not how to distinguish them from our enemies. They alarm our women and children. When the army meet them, they cannot know whether they are friends or foes, and the murderers themselves will say "We are your friends." In this situation, it is best that your people should go home. They might be killed through mistake, and I should be sorry for it. I have, therefore, ordered that they go from among us immediately.[22]

In his written reply, Big Warrior, who signed himself with his Creek name, Tustenugge Thlucco, addressed Bibb as "friend and brother."

You have sent me a talk. I am glad to hear from you. Our people are, and wish to remain in peace with their white brethren, your people. You say that the blood of your men, women and children has been spilled by red men. I am sorry to hear it. I could not hinder it. Those red men who spilled your blood are none of our people. We are your friends. I am glad that you have taken me by the hand, and called me friend. That you have sent me a talk. You say that your warriors are out. You are friendly in giving me that notice. I know that all red men are alike in appearance. Your warriors, therefore, cannot tell the good from the bad. They cannot distinguish between friend and foe. Those hostile men are like the Wolf. They creep and sculk until they can spill blood.—They frighten my people, as well as yours. I have sent for my hunters to return to our land; all may not have had notice. I shall in three days send one of my warriors, Barney Riley, to you, to aid and assist in giving what few hunters may be among you notice that they must return. I want to see you that we may talk together, and not mistake each other.[23]

Neither the road conditions nor the terror inspired by the sporadic attacks stopped traffic on the Federal Road. Hostile Indians were a small minority of a red population that had been taking on white ways and learning a new method of scalping. Under the 1805 Treaty of Washington, the Creeks were allowed to provide "houses of entertainment" at suitable places on the horse path for the accommodation of travelers with the "prices of entertainment for men and horses" to be regulated by the Indian agent or at prices usual among white people. After the military road replaced the horse path in 1811, and after the erection of forts during the Creek War of 1813–14, more "stands" were created, often on or near the fort sites. These way stations became stagecoach stops, relay points for post riders, inns, and taverns, and they were situated about sixteen miles apart, considered the average day's travel for foot traffic. Most often run by an Indian with a white partner, the stands usually charged exorbitant prices for poor meals and insect-riddled beds, a kind of gouging the Indians learned to repeat wherever they could extort high ferry and guide fees.

This practice started soon after Indians were given the rights under the Treaty of Washington, and it continued as long as the road was part of their territory. A typical reminiscence is that of Margaret Ervin Austill, the wife of Jeremiah Austill, who in 1811 as a young child left with her family from Washington County, Georgia, bound for Louisiana. Entering the Nation, they felt strength of numbers after being joined by other families, also with their bands of slaves. The company experienced the earth trembling that Tecumseh had predicted during his recent trip to Tuckabatchee; even the Indians' faces were "pale with fear and horror." The Creeks recovered quickly enough, however, to exercise the authority granted under the treaty. "Then the rain set in, not a day without rain until we crossed the Alabama; there were no roads, and mud and water, large creeks to cross with slender bridges made by the Indians, which they demanded toll at high price for every soul that crossed a bridge, and often rather than pay, the men would make their negroes cut trees and make a bridge, which gave the Indians great anger, and they would threaten us with death." Remembering her family's ordeal, Mrs. Austill believed they would have been killed if her uncle, Daniel Eades, who had been stolen by the Indians as a boy and knew their language, had not told the Creeks "they were fools, that they were nothing, and could never whip the whites, but their Nation would be destroyed." The toll may have been avoided because the prophetic uncle also brandished a long sword his father had worn in the Revolutionary War.[24]

Continuous complaints about the high charges had reached the secretary of war in Washington by at least as early as 1817. In response, Calhoun requested that Indian agent Mitchell and one or more chiefs designated by the Creek Nation fix the fees for public houses and ferries annually, as set forth in the treaty. In 1818, Bolling Hall, a Virginian and a veteran of the Revolution who had served as a Georgia congressman from 1811 to 1817 before moving to Alabama, complained about the condition of the road and the exorbitant prices for corn, forage, and ferriage. For Hall, the Federal Road was his only land connection to the east, and he requested that the high charges be justified or reduced.[25] Although Hall may have had standing in Washington because of his political ties, there is no evidence that the prices were regulated officially.

By the early 1820s, the road was sufficient for stagecoach travel, although, as the published narratives testify, often only marginally so. Earlier for-hire passage had been on wagon teams put in service by Sam Dale, who had been a trader with the Indians before he became their foe; he also hauled deerskins and Indian goods eastward to export at Savannah. The first stagecoach route was established by Maj. James Johnston, a Scotsman who operated the inn at Fort Mitchell, and Lewis Calfry, who lived at Fort Hawkins. The route extended to Montgomery, with one trip per week, and Johnston's was the first stage to bring the mail to Montgomery in April 1821. By 1823, the trips had increased to two a week. Later that year James Beddo put on competing vehicles between Fort Mitchell and Montgomery, and in 1826, Hugh Knox, whose stage and stop would figure prominently in at least one travel narrative, ran three stages between Milledgeville and Montgomery. In 1830, he was operating the stages between Milledgeville and Columbus and had made a rest stop in between at his home at Knoxville.[26] According to one account, before 1840 three stage lines operated on the Federal Road between Columbus and Montgomery, the "Mail Line," the "Telegraph Line," and the "People's Line."[27]

Travel southward started in 1826, when Patrick Byrne of Baldwin County joined with Maj. James Johnston of Montgomery County and Ward Taylor of Butler County to form the Montgomery-Blakeley stagecoach line. An advertisement by Johnston in the *Mobile Commercial Register* of June 1, 1827, stated that the Alabama and Georgia stages left Montgomery on Monday, Wednesday, and Friday at four o'clock and arrived at Milledgeville early on the following Thursday, Saturday, and Monday. According to the advertisement the three-day trip offered good horses, suitable carriages, excellent road condi-

The Subscriber,

HAVING obtained the mail contract from Milledgeville to Montgomery, Alabama, will commence running a Line of Stages between these two points, on the 20th inst. three times a week.—The public may rely on the punctuality and faithfulness of the discharge of their duties. They have made such arrangements as will remove all possibility of disappointment. Their stages and horses shall be of the best kind. They rely on a liberal public to sustain them in this undertaking.

Hugh Knox & Co.

Milledgeville, April 25.
⁂ The Montgomery Republican, Cahawba Press, Mobile Register, Constitutionalist, Georgian, Lang's Gazette, New-York, will publish the above weekly for three months, and send their accounts to   H. K. & Co.
May 12, 1826.   30 p

Alabama and Georgia

STAGES,

WILL leave Montgomery every Monday, Wednesday, and Friday morning, at 4 o'clock· and arrive at Milledgeville early on the morning of the following Thursdays, Saturdays, and Mondays.

Good Horses and suitable Carriages have at great expense been provided — The excellent condition of the roads, and the convenient stands established throughout, render this as pleasant and is expeditious a route as any in the Southern States.

The attention of Travellers is respectfully solicited by

The Proprietors.

⁂ The *Mobile Commercial Register* and the *Louisiana Advertiser* will insert the above four times, and forward their bills to this office for payment.
June 1, 1827.

STAGECOACH ADVERTISEMENTS

The punctuality and faithfulness of the best stages and horses and arrangements to "remove all possibility of disappointment" claimed by Hugh Knox in 1826 and the "excellent" road conditions advertised in Major Johnston's appeal for passengers in 1827 emphatically were not confirmed by those who rode over their lines or by the journal keepers riding any other Federal Road stages. The conditions were so bad, in fact, that stages often overturned, and passengers learned to sway in unison to keep the vehicles balanced. Ward Taylor & Co. also advertised in 1830 in the Montgomery *Alabama Journal* that very commodious stages, with the very best horses and only sober, skillful drivers, ran three days a week between Montgomery and Mobile. (Reprinted from *Alabama Highways,* May 1827, p. 5, and *Alabama Journal,* November 12, 1830, p. 4, both in Samford University Library, Birmingham)

tions, and convenient stands; furthermore, the trip was over "as speedy and pleasant a route as any in the southern states."[28] In 1839, William Kitchen of Mobile had become partner with Ward Taylor in a new stage line with several routes, including Mobile to Montgomery. At one time they owned four six-passenger coaches. Kitchen and Taylor also claimed to have two hacks, seven carts, and 199 horses, pastured at intervals of sixteen to eighteen miles along their stage routes.[29]

The five stagecoach models available in the United States during that period were the heavy Cumberland, the egg-shaped Trenton of 1818, the Troy, the old Concord, and the 1828 Concord.[30] The heavy vehicles of iron and wood had open windows that in winter could be covered with a canvas or an oilcloth flap. The coaches were usually nine-passenger three-seaters, the middle seat fitted with a broad leather strap for leaning back on and reserved for the women along.[31] Some stages were for mail and carried only six passengers, and occasionally a venturesome passenger would ride on top with the driver. The body of the coach was suspended from springs by straps, which produced a rolling motion that made some passengers seasick.[32] If roads were bad enough, up to six horses might be hitched as a team, which could be changed at the stops. At the word of the driver, passengers swayed left or right, or even leaned out like small-craft sailors to keep the coach from tipping over—though not always successfully. The speed averaged only four or five miles per hour, because of the delays at post offices and the breakdowns.[33] At one way station in Butler County, a pair of greased, tilted rails functioned as a jack; as horses pulled the coach, or as men pushed it, the axles would slide up on the slick rails, lifting the coach off the ground to allow for lubrication or a change of wheels.[34]

A usual fare was one dollar for every eight or ten miles, but competition eventually brought it down. In the late 1830s, when the "Mail Line" had the monopoly over the ninety miles from Macon to Columbus, the fare was twenty dollars. That was cut in half by a second line, and halved again, to five dollars, when a third line was put in service. The price war escalated to cut-throat scale when the first two lines dropped their fares to a dollar and the third, attempting to kill off both competitors, offered free transit and free dinner with champagne at the hotels. The loss-leader tactic did not succeed; the three lines formed a cartel and adopted a uniform fare of ten dollars per ninety miles.[35]

By the 1830s, advertisements for stage lines were common, and printed schedules, showing waybills—or mileages from a central location and between stops—were available. The puffery in promises of "pleasant" and "expeditious" journeys was deflated in detail by journal-keeping passengers. John H. B. Latrobe, a lawyer and son of the famous architect Benjamin Latrobe, en route from New Orleans

AN AMERICAN STAGECOACH

The American Mail Stage in which Capt. Basil Hall journeyed deserved a place in his travel accounts, and so he made this black-and-white drawing, accompanied by a colorful description of the conveyance. Its springs were of hide, and, Hall said, "Everything about it is made of the strongest materials. There is only one door, by which the nine passengers enter the vehicle, three for each seat, the sufferers placing themselves on a movable bench, with a broad leather band to support their backs. . . . The baggage is piled behind, or is thrust into the boot in front. They carry no outside passengers— and indeed it would try the nerves as well as the dexterity of the most expert harlequin that ever preserved his balance, not to be speedily pitched to the ground from the top of an American coach, on almost any road that I had the good fortune to travel over in that country." (Basil Hall, *Forty Etchings from Sketches Made with the Camera Lucida in North America in 1827 and 1828,* 4th ed. [Edinburgh: Cadell, 1830], plate no. 40)

back to his practice in Baltimore in early December 1834, opted to take the full Federal Road stage trip through Alabama rather than face "the probability of great detention" in the steamboat ride from Mobile to Montgomery.[36] Leaving behind a prosperous and accommodating city and armed with a flask of brandy to dilute the "wretched water" of the road, he took the steamboat *Emmeline* across to Stockton, a new town, to catch the stage; on the way he stopped at Blakeley, "a village pregnant with Cholera & yellow fever." In the detailed account of Latrobe's long trip, the three days on the Alabama portion of the Federal Road stand out as his passage through the deepest wilderness, natural and human. The stage he boarded on the night of December 7 was better than he had expected; in place of a window one door had a piece of slashed canvas, and the other sash was "deficient in the glass." Latrobe's sarcasm did not dull his perception. Flaming pine knots in gratings mounted on arms beside the coach provided "a most brilliant illumination to our road extending far on either side into the recesses of the forest." When the passengers walked ahead to avoid an upset, Latrobe looked back to see "the carriage dashing along the road with its strange lamp gear leaving a long train of smoke behind it spangled with sparks from the pine and giving the boles of the trees as they received and then lost the red glare of the light the appearance of tall spectres dancing in the gloom." When the travelers, among them two slave traders, stopped for breakfast, they laughed at how the lightwood (called "lightard") smoke had "converted" them into Negroes. They washed, had breakfast at a cabin in a scanty clearing, and survived a neck-risking race for many miles between the stage and a two-horse phaeton.[37]

At Claiborne, named for Latrobe's father-in-law, Gen. Ferdinand Claiborne, he sat down with "an odd set of folks, all cotton worshippers, for they talked of nothing else, thought of nothing else, and no doubt dreamt of nothing but long & short staple and twenty cents per pound." At night the boorish slave traders slept on the corn fodder on the floor of the stage, leaving Latrobe an entire seat for his bed. Hungry at Greenville, he was less than pleased again, "hog and hominy and cornbread being still the preponderant bill of fare." The six-passenger stage moved over a good dry road, through gigantic pines and tracts of oak and hickory acknowledged not to be the best in Alabama "by any means."[38]

After a brief stop in Montgomery, Latrobe's stage entered the ninety-mile stretch to Fort Mitchell. A quiet country doctor came aboard for a short ride; he "snored like an elephant when asleep & also eructated most unpleasantly during his dreams." Kicks in the shin were necessary to make him more suitable company. At Line Creek, reached at 2 A.M. on the third night from Mobile, the passengers had to stand by a huge fire, roasting their front and back sides "alternately like geese in the process of cooking," while the stage drivers—"lords paramount in this country"—took their time changing horses.[39]

At the breakfast stop, a house called Durants, run by a white man married to a half-breed Indian, Latrobe was served by two good-looking "quadroon" girls. At the dinner stop, past Fort Hull and probably on the site of Fort Bainbridge, he spied a well-dressed woman "with a neat foot that would have passed muster anywhere and with a carriage and tournure [figure] more than ordinarily good." He struck up a conversation with this "flower planted among the forests of the Creek nation" and found that she had given up civilized society for a handsome but worthless husband. She had, however, made her peace with the new country. She told Latrobe, "To be sure, these Indians are great thieves and leave one no peace of one's life. They kill the cows, steal the poultry, and are very devils when they can get drink." Still, she said, "when one's content, that's enough." Latrobe thought she was a coquette and "the prettiest thing I had seen for three hundred miles." Before leaving Alabama, he had more familiar sights to record—encampments of white emigrants for points west and gatherings of Indians in preparation for their removal in the same direction.[40]

Two years later, in 1836, when James D. Davidson, a Virginia lawyer, was returning from a trip to Alabama to settle some business for a client, he took note of the perils. "Stage Traveling! . . . Loss of sleep—hard jolts—rough fare—upset stages—Mud—wind & Cold." One story he heard about travel in the Creek Nation contributed to his sleepless journey eastward into Columbus:

Last night I passed over the ground where the *Stages were attacked* during *last year* by the Indians, and the *Driver, passengers, & horses killed.* One of the Contractors, who owns this line was in the Stage with me, and gave a full account of the affair. The first stage was attacked during the night on its way from Columbus to Montgomery. The Driver & two passengers were killed, and some of the horses. The next morning the Stage left Montgomery for Columbus, and was attacked about twilight before it reached the scene of the previous night. The Driver put whip to his horses, which had already begun to run off, and kept them in the road. They came suddenly upon the other stage and dead horses lying in the road, which frightened them. They turned suddenly and upset the Stage, which was full of passengers. The passengers all escaped. As I passed the bones of the dead men and the horses were pointed out to me.

He summed up his impressions by associating hard traveling with the state; "Home! Sweet Home! Alabama! O how I would bless thee, were I once clear of thy domains."[41] In 1839, as the Federal Road was being steadily replaced by other roads and means of travel, claims were made that a four-horse stage could make the 192-mile run from Montgomery to Blakeley in forty-three hours.[42] Also in 1839, Franz and Clara von Gerstner (he an Austrian railroad engineer who had built a railroad in Russia) made the trip from Macon to Montgomery by "coach and horses" in forty and a half hours.[43]

Whatever the means of travel, direct references to the road throughout its history rarely vary from the comment of Israel Pickens, the former North Carolina congressman and future Alabama governor, who took up duties as register of the land office at St. Stephens in the early part of 1818. He wrote that he had returned to the territorial capital "from Carolina after a tedious and unpleasant journey with my family over the almost impassable road which leads from Georgia here."[44] Yet, the road was passable, and articulate journal keepers were already chronicling the section it was helping to transform.

5

PASSING STRANGERS

HARDLY HAD THE FEDERAL ROAD OPENED before it became an avenue for curious travelers venturing into the Old Southwest to write prose portraits most often meant to enlighten and entertain readers in the East and in Europe. As passers-through, they turned sharp eyes on the land, the flora and fauna, the manners (or lack of them), the racial mix, the food and lodgings, and, always, the Federal Road, which functions in the writing both as a narrative thread and a silent character, rarely praised and never personified. What the travelers described along this road has contributed to the formation of a national and international reputation, a largely unfavorable regional image that exists to this day; yet, they also developed the stereotypes of the grotesque, the humorous, and the fantastic, and of human beings with a capacity for honor and heroism, which set the tone for the great works of Southern literature to come. A sampling of travel narratives beginning in 1811, the year the Federal Road was opened, shows how the new country appeared to strangers bold enough to endure the hardships of travel and to report their experiences. As superior, often supercilious observers, they entered a section considered by many to be unmapped, unsettled, and uncivilized and found it in many places beautiful, bursting with energy, and promising, though, for many, several rungs down the cultural ladder from themselves and their readers.

A composite view left by thirty years of travel narratives reveals a Federal Road divided into three distinct sections. Travelers departing westward, or to be more accurate, southwestward, entered a first section, about 120 miles long, beginning at the Oconee River crossing near Fort Wilkinson and Milledgeville, from 1804 to 1868 the state capital, and ending at Fort Mitchell, about twelve miles down the Chattahoochee from Columbus, which was founded in 1827. When the Federal Road opened, only the eastern end of this section, which ran generally on the fall line of rivers flowing from the Appalachian chain across the coastal plain, was in Georgia; treaties in 1821, 1825, and 1826 made the whole section part of the state. A second segment of about 90 miles passed directly through the Creek Nation and remained under the influence of the Indians until their removal in 1836. This section was cut along a ridge westward from Fort Mitchell, located just south of the old Indian village of Coweta, to Creek Stand, before entering the long succession of streams and swamps ending at Line, or Okfuskee, Creek. Mileage and routes of travelers across this section varied after the bridge across the Chattahoochee River was completed about 1833. Some travelers still took Joseph Marshall's ferry across to Fort Mitchell and continued westwardly along the original Federal Road. Others crossed the bridge about ten miles upstream and traveled the Upper Federal Road to the westerly junction of the two roads near Calabee Creek. At the Line Creek boundary travelers entered a third section, roughly 130 miles long, through lands ceded in the Treaty of Fort Jackson. At Evans's way station, they could take a branch for Montgomery, which began to develop in 1817.

The main Federal Road turned southward along the divide between the Alabama and the Conecuh-Escambia rivers to a spot near Burnt Corn, where the whites' surprise attack on the Red Sticks had backfired in 1813. There those whose destination was St. Stephens, Alabama's territorial capital from 1817 to 1819, took a right fork, which led to the Alabama River ferry at Claiborne and through Clarke County to the Tombigbee. The main Federal Road continued to Mims' ferry, or Fort Mims, in upper Baldwin County, a few miles below the junction of the Alabama and the Tombigbee rivers. Travelers for Fort Stoddert could take a ferry across a cut-off between the rivers, about twelve miles; those for Mobile could continue to Blakeley, where a ferry carried them across the estuary into the port. When steamboat travel became common, many travelers went by water from Montgomery to Mobile.

Over this long journey and over the twenty-five most active years of the Federal Road, the travelers wrote about a world changing hands and colors, from red to white, with black completing the polychromatic scheme. The racial lines that were blurred when British,

French, and Spanish white men moved and intermarried among the Indians remained blurred when runaway slaves entered the section. Some became slaves of the Creeks, but others moved south to join and intermarry with the Seminoles; some of those who had been slaves of the Indians fared better than they would have under their white masters, a point made by more than one British traveler. The Indians were regarded both as besotted victims of the whites and as noble but doomed savages. The likelihood of settlements on the route succeeding and growing into cities was based on the fleeting perceptions of the travelers. Many of the places mentioned in the writings have disappeared; aware of the instability of the frontier, one journal keeper made an early note of towns that were "juvenile but decaying."[1]

It is obvious that many of the writers had negative expectations they were happy to have fulfilled, but most of the narratives are replete with surprises. In addition to the detail and anecdote collected along the way, there was the road itself, which inspired its own stream of prose. Details taken from various accounts and reordered geographically, from east to west, reveal how the road was changing—almost never for the better—and how the adventures and spectacles reported by the travelers define the transformation of the region.

In 1825, when the party traveling with Lafayette left Milledgeville, the marquis's secretary, Auguste Levasseur, stated that they knew they were leaving on a journey across a vast country between Georgia and Alabama that was without roads, towns, and almost without inhabitants; it was the territory of the Creek Indians, "which civilization has blighted with some of its vices but without deterring them from a wandering and savage life." The road—the French visitor does deign to use the term—was like a gully or fissure; both Lafayette and Levasseur were so uncomfortable that they thought the carriage might be torn to pieces at any time, and they followed on horseback.[2]

Other travelers, earlier and later, reported a less hazardous start. In December 1817, Peter A. Remsen of New York, who had made twenty thousand dollars selling whiskey to the U.S. Navy and was off on a jubilant journey to seek a second fortune speculating in cotton in Mobile, wrote in a diary (published 101 years after his death in 1852) that the soil west of Milledgeville on the Federal Road was

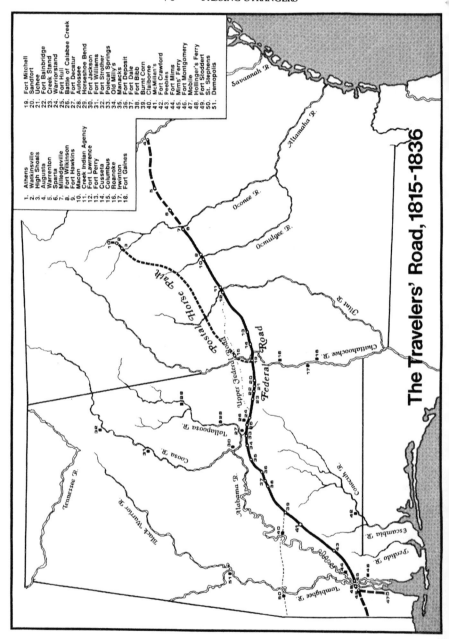

1. Athens
2. Watkinsville
3. High Shoals
4. Augusta
5. Warrenton
6. Sparta
7. Milledgeville
8. Fort Wilkinson
9. Fort Hawkins
10. Macon
11. Creek Indian Agency
12. Fort Lawrence
13. Fort Perry
14. Cusseta
15. Columbus
16. Roanoke
17. Irwinton
18. Fort Gaines
19. Fort Mitchell
20. Sandfort
21. Uchee
22. Fort Bainbridge
23. Creek Stand
24. Warriorstand
25. Fort Hull
26. Battle of Calabee Creek
27. Fort Decatur
28. Autossee
29. Horseshoe Bend
30. Fort Jackson
31. Fort Williams
32. Fort Strother
33. Polecat Springs
34. Old Milly's
35. Manacks
36. Fort Deposit
37. Fort Dale
38. Fort Bibb
39. Burnt Corn
40. Claiborne
41. McMillan's
42. Fort Crawford
43. Peebles
44. Fort Mims
45. Mims' Ferry
46. Fort Montgomery
47. Mobile
48. Hollinger's Ferry
49. Fort Stoddert
50. St. Stephens
51. Demopolis

The Travelers' Road, 1815-1836

sandy, the timber pine, and the country poor.[3] Thomas Hamilton, an English author of Scottish descent who headed west in April 1831, described a route through "almost unbroken pine forest," over a road so sandy "the wheels sank half-way up to the axles."[4] For Adam Hodgson the experience was more pleasant. This Englishman gave a detailed, interesting, and extensive account of his travels through the Creek country in March and April 1820. About thirty miles after leaving Milledgeville for Fort Hawkins, he passed acres of peach trees in full bloom, several settlements, several wagons, and many groups of slaves going from the Carolinas and Georgia to Alabama and Mississippi. Fort Hawkins, a small quadrangle of buildings that had been of importance in the Creek War of 1813-14, was significant to Hodgson because it included a house of entertainment for travelers.[5] By December 1825, five years later, the old fort on the Ocmulgee near Macon was deserted when the party of Karl Bernhard, the duke of Saxe-Weimar Eisenach, passed. On a road that was described as sandy and uneven, the Germans came to the Ocmulgee, crossed on a ferry, and spent the night in a new tavern on the other side.[6]

When William Gilmore Simms made his second trip over the Federal Road in 1831, seven years after his first, he not only noted the changes but also had read Karl Bernhard's account. In a series of travel letters published in a Charleston, South Carolina, newspaper under the title "Notes of a Small Tourist," Simms recounted an incident unreported in the German duke's journal. Bernhard thought he had booked an entire stagecoach out of Milledgeville, apparently not realizing that no seat could be fully secured until the fare was paid. He arrived at his carriage to find, in one of the best seats, a local traveler "wrapped up in his fearnought, and snoring like a buffalo, in all the elysian beatitude of a first nap."[7] The indignation of the German aristocrat was met with a "lesson in republicanism" from the stage driver, "a sturdy Southron," who offered to whip the duke in a fair fight and to take on the governor himself when Bernhard threatened to appeal to a higher authority.[8] On the second trip, Simms continued his reflections on the now-dead William McIntosh, called Thle-Cath-Cha, or the Broken Arrow. In a full-length portrait of McIntosh in a Macon public house, Simms saw a man tall and gaunt, unsatisfactory as a model, with a face expressing "less of dignity than low cunning."[9]

When Anne Royall, an opinionated American writer, left Milledgeville for Macon, about 1830, she traveled in one of Hugh Knox's
stagecoaches through a world of flowers. She exulted particularly
in the Cherokee roses that ran rampant by the roadside and in the
large fields of cotton, rye, wheat, and barley. The ferry across the
Ocmulgee at Macon had by this time been replaced by a bridge,
and Mrs. Royall entered a city she found to be flourishing and
wealthy, "a polite town of astonishing growth."[10] The next day she
traveled through piney woods and sparsely settled land and dined at
Knoxville, which consisted of one house—Knox's. Although the Federal Road had passed a short distance south, Knox had it rerouted
past his house for a meal stop and a change of horses.[11] Between Fort
Hawkins on the Ocmulgee River and the old Creek Agency on the
Flint River, the Federal Road crossed the divide separating waters
flowing into the Gulf of Mexico from those flowing into the Atlantic.
On the Flint, the first river of the Gulf watershed, the Creek Indian
Agency had been established by Hawkins shortly after he took over
as agent in 1796. It became a haven for early travelers, among them
Lorenzo Dow, the fiery circuit-riding preacher who spent a night
there with Hawkins in 1805 and again, accompanied by his wife,
Peggy, in December 1811. Both kept journals that were later published—his having in its title the keyword *cosmopolite*, hers the
more fitting *vicissitudes*.[12] In 1813, General Floyd established Fort
Lawrence on the bank opposite the agency.

When Adam Hodgson passed through the agency in 1820, he
stayed at a log dwelling that was memorable because over a door had
been draped two rattlesnakes, one of them seven feet long, with
twenty rattles. However fearsome that serpent might have been, it
does not, as a later narrative showed, take the prize for largest in the
travel accounts.[13]

Eight years later, when Capt. Basil Hall of the Royal Navy and his
wife, Margaret, came to the agency, they found a contrast to promising Macon. On March 27, 1828, while their carriage was being repaired in Macon, they had washed clothes, bought sheets, and
shopped, in wise anticipation of what the road beyond would deny
them. The next day, while traveling to the old Creek Agency on the
Flint, they crossed a ferry and innumerable fords where bridges had
been but were no longer serviceable, an indication that the trickle of

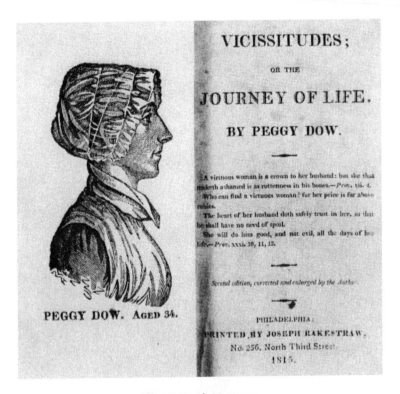

VICISSITUDES;

OR THE

JOURNEY OF LIFE.

BY PEGGY DOW.

A virtuous woman is a crown to her husband: but she that maketh ashamed is as rottenness in his bones.—*Prov.* xii. 4.
Who can find a virtuous woman? for her price is far above rubies.
The heart of her husband doth safely trust in her, so that he shall have no need of spoil.
She will do him good, and not evil, all the days of her life.—*Prov.* xxxi. 10, 11, 12.

Second edition, corrected and enlarged by the Author.

PHILADELPHIA:
PRINTED BY JOSEPH RAKESTRAW,
No. 256, North Third Street.
1815.

PEGGY DOW. AGED 34.

PEGGY DOW'S MEMOIRS

On his tenth trip into the wilderness, Lorenzo Dow was accompanied by his wife, Peggy, who aptly named her part of the travel narrative *Vicissitudes*. Lorenzo's account was entitled *God, Man, and the Devil*. . . . The Dows endured the hardships of the wilderness, spread their Christian message, and recorded what life was like along the newly opened Federal Road. In addition to seeing death and other travails along the road, Mrs. Dow also saw a Tombigbee River that was "as clear as a crystal." (Courtesy of the Brantley Collection, Samford University Library, Birmingham)

funds from Washington when Mitchell was the Indian agent had apparently not been sufficient to keep the bridges in repair. The Halls' resting place that night was a one-room hovel with no windows but with abundant light and air through the open logs around the room and the loose planks on the floor. For supper they had the rice, chicken, and tea they had bought in Macon. Also, they furnished their own sheets and put up a mosquito curtain made for them in Savannah. Mrs. Hall, whose letters are published separately from her husband's journal under the ironic title *The Aristocratic Journey*, wrote that, without the mosquito netting, "we could not possibly have sat, for the mosquitoes and flies exceeded anything I ever saw."[14]

Bernhard had described the agency in 1825 as being a group of about twenty log houses and some Negro huts on the left bank of the Flint River, the right bank being in the Creek Nation.[15] The next year, 1826, the land along the Federal Road between the Flint and the Chattahoochee was ceded to the United States.[16] The same Flint the Halls crossed on a ferry in 1828 still was not bridged as late as January 1846, when Sir Charles Lyell took the stage out of Macon; he found a sandy road often obstructed by fallen trees that had to be gone over or around, with deep ruts from wagons heavy with cotton to be loaded on the railroad for Savannah. The passengers had to shift to the high side of the stagecoach from time to time to prevent it from turning over.[17]

Not only was the location of the road over the poor pine-barren soil changed slightly from time to time, but the location, ownership, and names of the stage stops and taverns also changed. For example, Hodgson left the Flint River early on March 23, 1820, and, after twenty-eight miles, arrived at noon for lunch at Spain's Inn, where the landlord was a white man and his partner an Indian chief. In late December 1825, Bernhard rode twenty-eight miles westward after crossing the Flint River on a ferryboat to the lonely plantation of Mr. Currel, formerly of Virginia. Currel had "habits of intoxication" like the Indians; his plantation consisted of log huts through which the wind blew so hard no lamp could burn; and there was no ceiling in the room. However, Bernhard had a good supper of "excellent venison" and was surprised to discover, in such a place, the works of Shakespeare.[18]

Nearby was Fort Perry, another supply base built by General Floyd's troops in the fall of 1813. The road from there ran southwest and then west along Upatoi Creek to Cusseta, and again west about a mile along lowlands to the Chattahoochee River. Cusseta, in 1825 a town of about one hundred houses, was a center for the Lower Creeks and was a friendly "White Town"—in contrast to Coweta, about seven miles upstream on the opposite bank and a hostile "Red Town."[19]

On crossing the Chattahoochee River, there was a change in the environment, and the traveler entered the second section of the old Federal Road. In the early days, crossing the river was accomplished by taking the baggage and people over in an Indian canoe and swimming the horses alongside in several trips. In 1811, Peggy and Lorenzo Dow arrived on the west bank before sunrise, but the boat was gone. It was almost noon before they were safely across and on their journey eastward.[20]

Lafayette's party, led by the general, his son George Washington Lafayette, and the secretary, Levasseur, crossed the Chattahoochee in grander—maybe the grandest—style. Leaving the east bank on March 31, 1825, in Joseph Marshall's ferry, they were greeted by battle cries coming across the water and saw throngs of Indians waiting for them. Fifty costumed warriors waded out to the ferry and placed Lafayette in a sulky, "not willing, as they observed, that their father should step on wet ground."[21] They pulled the sulky by ropes up the steep embankment for ceremonies welcoming the "boy wonder" of the Revolution, who now was sixty-eight, a plump and, from all accounts, cordial man, dressed in yellow pantaloons, a buff vest, and a blue broadcloth coat. The entire assembly of Americans, Indians, and Frenchmen knelt for a prayer by the Reverend Isaac Smith, formerly an aide to Lafayette.[22] Smith was superintendent of the Asbury School and Mission, one mile north of Fort Mitchell, which was organized to teach Indian children reading, writing, and other white skills. This first school in the Chattahoochee Valley was opened in 1822 and closed in 1830, when a large portion of the tribe was removed to the West.[23]

The Creek that Levasseur recognized as a chief was Chilly McIntosh, the twenty-eight-year-old son of William McIntosh, the chief of the Lower Creeks, whose support of the Americans had earned him the rank of general. Levasseur saw the melancholic expression on the young McIntosh's face, surprising in one whose "limbs were perfect, his physiognomy noble," and concluded after a conversation that "his mind had been cultivated at the expense of his happiness."

> He appreciated the real situation of his nation; he saw it gradually becoming weaker, and foresaw its speedy destruction; he felt how much it was inferior to those which surrounded it, and was perfectly aware

that it was impossible to overcome the wandering mode of life of his people. Their vicinity to civilization had been of no service to them; on the contrary, it had only been the means of introducing vices to which they had hitherto been strangers; he appeared to hope that the treaty which removed them to another and a desert country, would re-establish the ancient organization of the tribes, or at least preserve them in the state in which they now were.[24]

There was good reason for Chilly McIntosh's foreboding. He and his father had signed a treaty at their home in Indian Springs in February, ceding even more of the Creek lands, and had been condemned to death by a council of the Upper Creeks. Within a month of the meeting with Lafayette, the elder McIntosh was executed at his home, and the younger barely escaped the same fate.[25]

Before resuming their tour over the Federal Road, the guests of the Nation were treated to an Indian ball game, described by Levasseur in all its formality and violence. Its star was Chilly McIntosh, who followed the entourage across the Creek lands, where Indians assisted at the stream crossings and sights were pointed out by Gen. Thomas S. Woodward; the travelers crossed Line Creek, and Chilly McIntosh continued with them to Montgomery, where he attended the festivities, dressed as a white man.[26]

Fort Mitchell, on the west side of the Chattahoochee, came in for mixed reviews over the years. Built by Floyd as one of his supply bases in 1813, it also served as a procurement and a supply point for Gen. William McIntosh's brigade of Indians camped at Fort Scott, located on the Flint near its junction with the Chattahoochee, during the Seminole War of 1817–18.[27] In late 1817, the Indian "factory," or trading house, was moved from Fort Hawkins on the Flint to Fort Mitchell, but it was abandoned in 1820.[28] Little Prince, a chief of the Lower Creeks, owned half-interest in the tavern at Fort Mitchell from 1811 to 1824. After 1820, Capt. Thomas Anthony from Philadelphia ran it. By 1825, the tavern was being kept by Thomas Crowell, brother of the Indian agent, Col. John Crowell, and was known as Crowell's Tavern. When Thomas Hamilton visited the fort in 1831, he found it to be like a rat trap—hard to get into, and still harder to get out of. Hamilton spent a week waiting for transportation and saw enough of the military presence to be highly critical. Discipline was lax, the

Sunday dress parade slovenly, and desertions a weekly occurrence. Karl Bernhard spent New Year's Eve night at Crowell's and was "accommodated with freer circulation than would have fallen to our lot in a German barn." By 1830, the tavern had changed hands again and was being run by Maj. James Johnston, co-owner of the stagecoach line and the mail carrier for the route between Milledgeville and Montgomery in the 1820s; it was renamed Johnston's Hotel.[29]

One spot of ground near Fort Mitchell had a special, if limited, use. Because the land was outside of Georgia, not strictly within a military base, and on land claimed both by the Creeks and, after 1832, by the state of Alabama, argument could be made that, in this territory of disputed jurisdiction, laws prohibiting dueling could not be enforced. On January 25, 1828, Thomas Edgehill Burnside, an uncle of the Union general Ambrose E. Burnside, was killed by George Walker Crawford in an "affair of honor" involving an insult to Crawford's father published anonymously in an Augusta newspaper. Though not the author, Burnside, a promising young lawyer, assumed responsibility. He was buried in the Crowell cemetery at Fort Mitchell, and Crawford, who was Georgia's attorney general at the time, went on to become governor.[30] On January 22, 1832, Maj. Joseph T. Camp killed Gen. Sowell Woolfolk in a duel resulting from a disagreement in Milledgeville, where both served in the legislature. The *Columbus Enquirer* reported that Woolfolk was "shot through the breast, and expired in a few seconds"; Camp took a bullet in the abdomen, "but fortunately for him without entering the hollow." The newspaper regretted that "the talents, worth, and chivalry of our country should be subject to such a barbarous custom." Camp was later killed on a Columbus street, but his slayer was not prosecuted because Camp had the first chance and was known as a crack shot.[31]

Before the Federal Road was made passable for stagecoaches, horseback riders crossed the Chattahoochee at Benjamin Marshall's or Kennard's, about ten miles north of Fort Mitchell, near where Columbus was established later. Thomas Stocks used this crossing returning on a scouting expedition for prospective settlers in 1819. Though not learned or prolix, he was precise. His account includes "way bills," mileage between points over an old horse path running northeast from the river to the homes of Samuel, Joseph, and James Marshall, Scott's Ferry, Monticello, Madison, and to Stocks' home, just southwest of Athens.[32] By March 1820, the Indians had a ferry at the Chattahoochee, a river Adam Hodgson found "beautiful." He was ferried over by Indians, who sang responsively in a boat song, but their dress frightened the horses.[33]

Captain and Mrs. Hall found warmth and cheer at Crowell's Tavern when they arrived on the morning of March 31, 1828, the agent greeting them with breakfast and a blazing fire in his comfortable house. They drove their carriage up the west bank of the Chattahoochee and crossed back over on the ferry to tour Columbus, which had been laid out, with lots to be sold the following July. While the future citizens were waiting for the land, they built an early version of the mobile home, which Hall described as being "on trucks—a sort of low, strong wheels, such as cannon are supported by—for the avowed purpose of being hurled away when the land should be sold." Shrewd carpenters had also built about sixty house frames on speculation and had them lying on the ground, precursors of modern prefabrication, ready for assembly "at the call of future purchasers."[34]

In her brief passage through Columbus, probably in 1828 or 1829, Anne Royall, surely the most effusive and mercurial of the tourists, called the city "the Savannah of the west!" Her account, unlike those of the European travelers, often reads like advertising to excite emigration, but she does not gloss over the perils of travel. From Columbus she hired a private coach to take her to the crossing at Fort Mitchell, hoping to avoid Hugh Knox and "the insolent ruffian who had taken some liberties" with her in Knox's stage. She crossed the Chattahoochee in a ferry, and the carriage soon became stuck in the mud. After a while, with help from a passing gentleman, it was pulled from the quagmire; Mrs. Royall found at Crowell's a large airy house with a long piazza and was privileged to spend the night with excellent service in a "little hut" adjoining the tavern. After being insulted by Fort Mitchell soldiers, whom she characterized as a "parcel of paltroons," she boarded one of Captain Walker's stages, whose drivers, horses, and coaches were advertised as exceeded by none, only to find that the drunken lout she had sought to avoid was also a passenger for the trip to Montgomery. She teamed up with the driver, who had been instructed to look after her, and with a delicate gentleman named Mathews for protection until she could reach the safety of friends in Montgomery and the steamboat *Herald* for the river journey to Mobile.[35]

The humor Mrs. Royall often seemed too indignant to catch was not lost on Sol Smith, an actor-producer-director who traveled from Montgomery to Columbus with his troupe in the spring of 1832. In his autobiography, published in 1868, Smith offers anecdotes in the style of Old Southwest humor, which had burst upon the nation in 1835 with the publication of Augustus Baldwin Longstreet's *Georgia Scenes*. Smith's stories indicate that the material for such fiction was flourishing in Columbus. His company, traveling in barouches with baggage accompanying in a large Pennsylvania wagon, crossed the river from the Creek Nation and was happy to enter "Georgia! generous hospitable Georgia!" When Smith announced on Sunday, May 20, that his play would open the following Thursday, the follow-up question "Where?" was answered, "In the New Theatre." In yet another comment on the skill and speed of Columbus carpenters, Smith remembered a newspaper's reporting the following:

EXPEDITION—A theatre, 70 feet long by 40 wide, was commenced on Monday morning last by our enterprising fellow-citizen, Mr. Bates, and finished on Thursday afternoon, in season for reception of Mr. Sol Smith's company on that evening. A great portion of the timber, on Monday morning, waved to the breeze in its native forest; fourscore hours afterward, its massive piles were shaken by the thunder of applause in the crowded assemblage of men.[36]

In fact, the weekly *Columbus Enquirer* of May 19, 1832, did run an advertisement from Smith announcing that "a fashionable comedy and a popular farce" would open on May 24 in a "temporary theatre that will be fitted up in this place."[37] A guarded review published the following Saturday did not mention that the farce had gotten out of hand. "In a new house, one got up in a week, and on new boards, to which the performer has had not time to become accustomed, it must be expected that he will commence under some restraint if not embarrassment. This was the case, no doubt, in a measure, on Thursday evening. Notwithstanding, we do the dramatis personae but niggard injustice when we say that their execution was above mediocrity."[38]

In his sketch, entitled "Unusual Ceremonies in the Temple of the

Sun," Smith told who some of these "dramatis personae" were, and how they contributed to his embarrassment in a production of *Pizarro*—intended as neither a comedy nor a farce. As extras to play the Peruvian army, he hired twenty-four Creek Indians, who furnished their own bows, arrows, and tomahawks; each was paid fifty cents and a glass of whiskey, but unfortunately the whiskey was consumed in advance of the performance. First, the Indians shouted before their cue and started to dance but were quelled. When Smith, then, in the role of High Priest of the Sun, began his song, he found he was not alone. The Indians started to hum, and when the play's chorus joined the strain, it was outdone by "the rising storm of *fortissimo* sounds which were issuing from the stentorian lungs of the savages." Smith believed he was hearing war songs and seeing battle dances; the Indians flourished knives and tomahawks, and after the curtain was finally dropped they continued in fine voice. When they returned the next night for a second performance, their services were declined.[39]

In April 1831, the stage carrying William Gilmore Simms mired down near Fort Mitchell and was pulled out by a "tribe of Indians" directed by one of their slaves, whose authority and status prompted a long discourse from Simms on which race was the master in the peculiar relationships between Negroes and Indians. He also told the story of a chief named Tuskina, who, rather than use the formality of the post office to send a letter, decided to stop the stage. When the driver of the stagecoach—which carried, in addition to mail, the "wooden shoed rope dancer," Herr Cline—put the whip to his horses, the Indian sprang forward and seized the reins. Tuskina was tried at Mobile, Simms said, and fined one hundred dollars.[40] The stories, whether fact or fiction, that Simms heard in his travels over the Federal Road, together with his direct observations, figured in three "border romances"—*Guy Rivers: A Tale of Georgia* (1834), *Richard Hurdis; or, The Avenger of Blood: A Tale of Alabama* (1838), and *Border Beagles: A Tale of Mississippi* (1840). In the poem "The Indian Village," published in 1839 and addressed to pioneers, Simms made a specific reference to the full length of the Federal Road:

Nature and freedom! These are glorious words
That make the world mad. Take a glimpse at both,

Such as you readily find, when, at your ease,
You plough the ancient military trace,
From Georgia to the "Burnt Corn" settlements.[41]

When Simms returned to Alabama in 1842 to speak at the University of Alabama, the road—over which nobody apparently traveled "at ease"—was not the sole route through the Creek Nation, and the South Carolina writer had become one of the country's leading men of letters.[42]

In 1832 and 1833, the first bridge, wooden and covered, was built across the Chattahoochee at Columbus, and most of the traffic was diverted from Fort Mitchell to the Upper Federal Road, which ran from a few miles west of Fort Perry through Columbus and Tuskegee to its junction with the older road, near Calabee Creek.[43] Before Harriet Martineau, an English writer, left Columbus on the covered bridge, she had experienced a change of attitude. Approaching by stage in April 1835, she had heard stories about attempted murders and the thwarted abduction of a young lady. She arrived to find the town swarming with Indians, but they were "fair and friendly"; the squaws formed a contrast to the young white woman who presided over the breakfast table, "with her long hair braided and adorned with brilliant combs, while her fingers shone in pearl and gold rings." The Indian women were barefooted, whereas the men who walked before them wore embroidered leggings and had pouches and white fringes dangling from their clothing "like grave merry-andrews." Martineau found gentlemanly men on the city's three principal streets, good houses, and five hotels; she summed up Columbus as "a thriving, spacious, handsome village, well worth stopping to see."[44]

Across the river there was another story. The driver stopped to talk to a woman who spoke "almost altogether in oaths." Although the Englishwoman does not mention the place, the stage was passing through Sodom, the earliest name of the village which later became Girard and finally Phenix City. It had become infamous for drunkenness, debauchery, and prostitution, but Harriet Martineau had little light in which to see any of this evil. Her stage left at seven on the evening of April 10, 1835, and soon was on a Creek Nation road "as bad as roads could be." The patient passengers became skillful in shifting their weight to keep the coach level. When they stopped for breakfast at a log dwelling, there was neither basin nor towel for washing up, although a tin dish was finally presented. Although the Federal Road through the Creek Territory was "extremely bad," nature provided a spring parade—violets, mayapple, buckeye, blue lupine, iris, crow poison, and sourwood. But the grandest, the most exquisite of all, the "queen of the flowers," was the honeysuckle of the southern woods, the wild azalea, with its globe of blossoms larger than a lady's hand. Less solace was to be found in the human presence. Through her stage window Martineau saw slaves, who, when asked where they were going, answered, "Into Yellibama." In the most degraded class of Negroes, she never saw "in any brute an expression of countenance so low, so lost."

The Columbus that Harriet Martineau left behind offered another, more ironic sight to Sir Charles Lyell eleven years later. When he arrived in 1846, the last detachment of five hundred Indians had been removed, and waterpower had been installed to operate new cotton mills, which employed white labor and no slaves.[45]

For travelers on the Federal Road while the Creeks still could claim it, the first stand, inn, or tavern was located about three miles west of Fort Mitchell at the junction of the Big and Little Uchee creeks at "Uchee Bridge," or "Natural Bridge," not one of the grand wonders of nature but a place where the streams passed under rocks, leaving a fording spot in dry weather. In March 1820, when the party of Adam Hodgson arrived at Uchee Bridge over a Federal Road that "though tolerable for horses would with us be considered impassable for wheels," he stayed in a log cabin without windows and supped with a host, whom he does not name, and several "unwashed artificers and unshaven laborers." A few days before, the host had killed a panther within twenty yards of the house; for his English readers, Hodgson defined the cat as not a "true panther" but a puma of a uniform tawny color. In Choctaw country, farther west, he "started" two panthers, which "bounded from us with a sort of careless independence."[46] In March 1825, when General Lafayette stopped at Natural Bridge, the tavern was called Crabtree's and was run by Haynes Crabtree.[47]

Fourteen or fifteen miles west of the Chattahoochee was Sand Fort, the earthworks erected by General Floyd's army in 1814 and, from 1825 to 1836, the site of Royston's Inn, which served as a rendezvous and defensive position during the Indian troubles of 1836.[48]

About five miles west of Sand Fort was located a stage stop called Uchee, and ten miles beyond was Fort Bainbridge, yet another of Floyd's stockades, on the Macon-Russell county line.[49] It was located near the intersection of the Federal Road and the Three-Notch Road to Pensacola. After the Creek War of 1813–14, Capt. Kendall Lewis, a native of Maryland, a lieutenant of scouts under Benjamin Hawkins, and a captain of one of the Georgia regiments in the War of 1812, operated the Lewis Tavern at Fort Bainbridge. Just before the Battle of New Orleans, Lewis delivered twenty-two boxes of military supplies to Maj. Gen. William Carroll near the city; later he was appointed commissary of purchases by Colonel Brearley and served at Fort Mitchell as assistant commissary of purchases between February and May of 1818. In the First Seminole War (1817–18), he fought in Gen. William McIntosh's brigade under Colonel Lovett. His wife was a Creek, the daughter of his silent partner, Big Warrior. Lewis operated the tavern from about 1816 to about 1827; he applied at the Creek Indian Agency on June 6, 1855, for bounty land in the territory west of Arkansas, claiming to be "an adopted Creek Indian, aged seventy years."[50]

About Lewis and his tavern much was reported. Adam Hodgson reached Fort Bainbridge on May 26, 1820, and discovered a tavern with an efficient headwaiter from "one of the principal inns in Washington." But he was most taken with Lewis, whom he found "to unite great mildness and intelligence" with a love of solitude so ardent "that he lately removed his stand from the most profitable situation, because there was a neighbor or two within four miles." Hodgson went hunting with Lewis about sunset; after going about two miles, they killed a gray fox that had been treed by hounds in the same way the panthers were hunted. In the course of the excursion, Lewis told Hodgson about Indian government and civil customs and about the deleterious influence of the whites, especially in their introduction of whiskey, the bane of the Indians.[51]

Five years later, in 1825, when Lafayette's party passed through, Big Warrior had been dead three weeks. Karl Bernhard, the German duke, arrived at Fort Bainbridge ten months afterward, on Sunday, January 1, 1826, after his chilly New Year's Eve sleep at Fort Mitchell and after walking the last four miles. The bad road through sandy soil had proved too much for his carriage; in a narrow place it had tipped to the side on which Bernhard was riding and turned over for the eighth time. Earlier in the day, he had "crossed two small streams, the Great and Little Uchee, on tolerable wooden bridges," and by nightfall he found the day's reward. At "Lewis' handsome house," the best found in the Creek country, they had a sumptuous dinner: soup of turnips, roast beef, a roast turkey, venison with sour sauce, roast chickens, and pork with sweet potatoes.[52]

Margaret Hall, who spent the night at Lewis's Tavern on April 1, 1828, also described the facilities as excellent, despite the cold weather, talking, and snoring, which kept her awake most of the night. The road, if it might have been called that, lay through the heart of the forest and was marked out by slashes on the trees. According to her, the available houses of accommodation were about thirty miles apart (the actual miles were probably less) and were so uncomfortable that the travelers were eager to get an early start each morning and "just as desirous at the end of the day to quit the carriage."[53] Eventually, dirt got into everything, even their food.

By the end of the decade the tavern was operated by Mrs. Harris and was sometimes called "Mrs. Harris' Hotel." Anne Royall reported staying the night in Fort Bainbridge at a "large and elegant tavern and well kept" by Mr. and Mrs. Harris. A Mrs. Bird personally gave her a cup of coffee the next morning, even though the departure was at about 1 A.M.[54]

When the English author and geographer George W. Featherstonhaugh (whose four-syllable surname is pronounced, in British English, "Fanshaw") came through eastbound in January 1835, the stand was called "Cook's Tavern." Cook was described as a "cheerful dissipated sort of fellow," whose wife was very respectable; they provided the company with a "tolerable clean supper and separate beds." Cook was a collector of natural curiosities, and he showed Featherstonhaugh the stuffed skins of three "diamond rattlesnakes" hanging on the porch of his tavern. The largest measured seven feet ten inches long and thirteen and a quarter inches around.

Featherstonhaugh's account, which is entitled *Excursion through the Slave States*, takes note of the strain and anxiety of the pioneers, in sharp relief against the laurel-lined streams and graceful pine hills through which they were passing.

> This day we met an almost uninterrupted line of emigrants, with innumerable heavy and light wagons. Some of them got stuck fast in the deep bottoms, and the men around them were pulling, hauling, whipping, and cursing and swearing to get them out; there were also some light carriages, indicating a better class of emigrants. . . . As we advanced they all inquired if the road was not better ahead; and our answer generally was, "Keep up your spirits and you'll get through."

That day, Featherstonhaugh estimated, his party met 1,200 people, black and white, on foot; later thay passed at least a thousand slaves on foot and numerous heavy wagons carrying black women and children.[55]

Three miles west of Fort Bainbridge, also on the ridge forming the Chattahoochee-Alabama watershed, was Creek Stand, where a tavern and at one time a post office were located.[56] The road in that section was known locally as "the old stage road." Sampson Lanier opened a tavern at Creek Stand in 1832, the same year the new bridge at Columbus began to funnel traffic into the Upper Federal Road. To attract travelers, Lanier used advertisements in the *Columbus Enquirer*—one of which was certain to prove the power of negative suggestion. Lanier claimed to welcome fair competition, but he objected to malicious and unfounded rumors about his tavern. He insisted that his house was neat, his tables abundantly supplied, and his charges moderate, and he assured satisfaction to all who called at his house.[57]

Warriorstand, a stage stop five miles west of Creek Stand, was the residence of Big Warrior, chief of the Upper Creeks from about 1805 until his death in 1825. West of his stand, near Fort Hull, Big Warrior had built a large racetrack that was widely known throughout the area.[58] In 1832, Sol Smith and his theatrical troupe stopped twelve miles west of Columbus at Elliott's, where the landlord had caught many fish in a trap the night before (he claimed to have caught as many as three hundred in one night) and served them an excellent fish dinner. At Warriorstand the food in "this then uncivilized country" was not abundant, nor were the lodgings pleasing. The landlord, identified by Smith as "Black Warrior," was out hunting, and his wife gave the humans "lenten fare" but fed the horses well. The beds were infested with fleas and bedbugs, for which accommodations enormous charges were exacted.[59]

The combination of tavern and racetrack at Big Warrior's was no doubt similar to one Sol Smith must have seen in his travels through the Creek Nation in 1832. In a sketch entitled "The Consolate Widow," Smith displays the skills and the literary sensibility of the Old Southwest humorist.

Between Caleba Swamp and Lime [Line] Creek, in the "Nation," we saw considerable of a crowd gathered near a drinking-house, most of them seated and smoking. We stopped to see what was the matter. It was Sunday, and there had been a quarter race for a gallon of whisky. The first thing I noticed on alighting was the singular position of one of the horses of the party. He was kneeling down and standing on his hinder feet, his head wedged in between the ends of two logs of the grocery, and was stone dead, having evidently ran [sic] directly against the building at full speed, causing the house partially to fall. About five paces from the body of the horse lay the rider, quite senseless, with a gash in his throat which might have let out a thousand lives. As I said, most of the crowd were seated and smoking.

"What is all this?" I inquired. "What is the matter here?"

"Matter?" after a while answered one in a drawling voice, giving a good spit, and refilling his mouth with a new cud. "Matter enough, there's been a quarter race."

"But how come this man and horse killed?" I asked.

"Well," answered the chewing and spitting gentleman, "the man was considerably in liquor, I reckon, and he run his hoss chuck agin the house, and that's the whole of it."

"Has a doctor been sent for?" inquired one of our party.

"I reckon there ain't much use of doctors here," replied another of the crowd. "Burnt brandy couldn't save either of 'em, man or hoss."

"Has this man a wife and children?" inquired I.

"No children, that I knows on," answered a female, who was sitting on the ground a short distance from the dead man, smoking composedly.

"He has a wife, then?" I remarked. "What will be her feelings when she learns the fatal termination of this most unfortunate race?"

"Yes," sighed the female, "it was an unfortunate race. Poor man! he lost the whisky."

"Do you happen to know his wife? Has she been informed of the untimely death of her husband?" were my next inquiries.

"Do I *know* her? Has she been informed of his death?" said the woman. "Well, I reckon you ain't acquainted about these parts. I am the unfortunate widder."[60]

Also near Fort Hull was the land of the Cornells, an extended family of mixed blood that had participated in the fighting against the Red Sticks. Alexander Cornells's name was on the letter written from Coweta in 1813 pleading with Floyd for relief. When Peter Remsen came through in 1818, the home of one of the Cornells was the first he had seen in forty-five miles.[61] He wrote that the man had a clean farm, many Negroes, and a wife who was part Indian. The stop Featherstonhaugh found near that location in 1835 was called McGirt's and was owned by a white man who lived in a "filthy, Indian-looking place" and served a breakfast so "disgustingly bad" the Englishman could not eat it. Wrote Featherstonhaugh, "This man said he expected every night to have his throat cut, which induced me to tell him that if it would be any consolation, he might be quite sure they would not touch his victuals." Then Featherstonhaugh put himself and his acerbic wit into the private conveyance hired for sixty-five dollars to take him from Montgomery to Columbus. That day he forded forty to fifty streams, swollen by rains, and saw at least one thousand slaves, "all trampling on foot and worn down with fatigue."[62]

Cornells's and McGirt's stops were near Persimmon Swamp, a mile wide and dreaded for the causeway and the bridge that seemed never to be in repair. Remsen described the road through the swamp as "almost impassable" and "equalled by none."[63] When Featherstonhaugh entered it from the east in 1835, he found a broken-down log bridge, dangerous in spots; but he had the rare good fortune of having a group of well-behaved Indians to guide him across, and he paid them liberally.[64]

The last big swamp before Line Creek was at Calabee Creek, where Featherstonhaugh had also found a mile-long causeway of logs and brush "so dislocated by the incessant passage of wagons and the rise

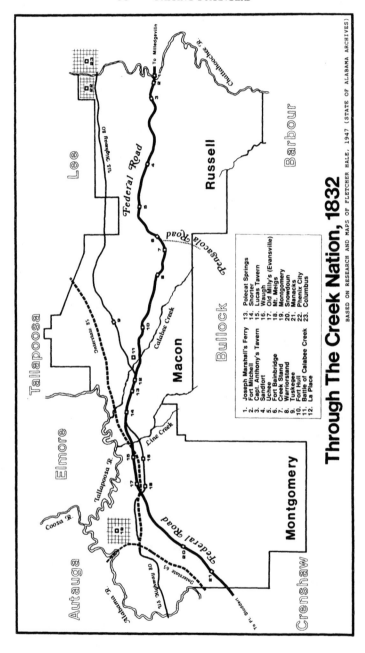

Through The Creek Nation, 1832

BASED ON RESEARCH AND MAPS OF FLETCHER HALE. 1947 (STATE OF ALABAMA ARCHIVES)

1. Joseph Marshall's Ferry
2. Fort Mitchell
3. Capt. Anthony's Tavern
4. Sandfort
5. Uchee
6. Fort Bainbridge
7. Creek Stand
8. Warriorstand
9. Tuskegee
10. Fort Hull
11. Battle of Calabee Creek
12. La Place
13. Polecat Springs
14. Shorter
15. Lucas Tavern
16. Waugh
17. Old Milly's (Evansville)
18. Mt. Meigs
19. Montgomery
20. Snowdoun
21. Manacks
22. Phenix City
23. Columbus

of waters" that he doubted the carriage could make it across. Although the Irish comedian Tyrone Power does not mention the stream by name, the mileage in the account of his harrowing thirty-two-hour trip from Columbus to Montgomery of December 1834 points to Calabee Creek. Power came to the swamp at dusk, after having been on the road since the previous midnight. His narrative includes a description of a woman of questionable virtue who boarded the stage in Sodom with her "protector," later referred to as her "proprietor." They passed an abandoned Fort Mitchell and had a good meal in Tuskegee; they were also moved from a dry stage to a wet one and finally to a "mail box," a simple flatbed wagon with four erect sides into which was dumped baggage, mail, and passengers. Rain and darkness fell simultaneously, and the party had to dismount and walk across a bridge a quarter-mile long, each passenger carrying a small lightwood torch, which the rain soon extinguished. Fortunately for them, they encountered a courteous Indian guide whose large torch did not go out. The deliverance made Power forget his discomfort, and he claimed the scene was the most vivid in his memory.

> Let the reader imagine a figure dressed in a deep-yellow shirt reaching barely to the knees, the legs naked; a belt of scarlet wampum about the loins, and a crimson and dark-blue shawl twisted turban-fashion around the head; with locks of black coarse hair streaming from under this, and falling loose over the neck or face: fancy one half of such a figure lighted up by a very strong blaze, marking the nimble tread, the swart cold features, sparkling eye, and outstretched muscular arms of the red man,—the other half, meantime, being in the blackest possible shadow; whilst following close behind, just perceptible through wreaths of thick smoke, moved the heads of the leading horses; and over all, flashed at frequent intervals vivid lightning; one moment breaking forth in a wide sheet, as though an overcharged cloud had burst at once asunder; the next, descending in zigzag lines, or darting through amongst the full pines and cypress trees; whilst the quick patter of the horses' hoofs were for a time heard loudly rattling over the loose hollow planks, and then again drowned wholly by the crash of near thunder.

Power claimed he was so overcome with gratitude that he offered the Indian a flask of cognac, which was politely but adamantly refused, making the guide an anomaly in such narratives, in which the drunken Indian is usually a stock character.[65]

At "Kalebah Hatchee," which may have been Cubahatchee or Calabee, after three or four days over corduroy roads, Sol Smith and his theatrical troupe in December 1832 reached a flooded swamp where the bridge had been swept away. It was estimated that ten thousand people were waiting for the flood to subside. No one had passed for several days, and the woods were red with campfires. Indians were abundant, begging for whiskey. Sol and his company, to the surprise of all, went from tent to tent, singing and rehearsing choruses for their opening in Montgomery. The Indians repaired the bridge during the night, and Sol connived to get his teams over the first thing next morning, notwithstanding the impatient push of two thousand others anxious to cross.[66]

Although the white settlements near the Creek Nation were getting larger and white traffic over the road was constant, activity of the Indians as late as 1827 indicated how much they still adhered to old customs. On April 2 of that year, Captain and Mrs. Hall were at "Captain Triplett's Cabin . . . within twenty seven miles of Montgomery." On the morning of April 3, their journey was delayed long enough for Captain Hall to see an Indian ball game and to regret that he had not brought his camera lucida along so that he could sketch the action. The Halls were still able to reach Montgomery before dark.[67]

Between Calabee Creek and the Creek Nation boundary, near Shorter, was the Pole Cat Springs Indian Agency, which functioned from about 1805 to 1836, adjacent to which was a tavern operated by Capt. William Walker, the husband of another of Big Warrior's daughters. His tavern was open from about 1816 to 1836, when Shorter was an important crossroads, at the junction of the Federal Road west, the Tuckabatchee road north, and a Fort Jackson road northwest. For twenty years westbound travelers found Captain Walker's tavern to be the last white residence in the Creek country.[68]

Line Creek, beyond which lay the third section of the Federal Road, was a landmark mentioned by most travelers, and not simply because it was the dividing line created by the Treaty of Fort Jackson. Westbound travelers expected, and usually found, the roads better and the prospects of civilization more pleasing. Peter Remsen did not have immediate good luck, however; he crossed the fifty-yard-wide creek on a "charming warm day" in January 1818 but felt the commercial chill in the hearts of white people on United States land, "who from all appearance were Christians." They sold him corn for three dollars a bushel and "good sailor's grog" for four dollars, outrageous prices that put Remsen "out of all conceit of Christianity."[69]

The demand for corn, grog, and other commodities had to increase as the traffic became heavier. The travel narratives frequently note the flocks of people who were headed west. Two years after Remsen, the Englishman Hodgson, as he approached Line Creek, was impressed with the crowds and the various vehicles he had seen that day gathered on the banks of streams. "We usually found a curious collection of sans soucis [literally, "without care"; probably a light, open conveyance], sulkies, carts, Jersey wagons, heavy wagons, little planters, Indians, Negroes, horses, mules, and oxen; the women and little children sitting down frequently for one, two, or three, and sometimes for five or six hours, to work or play, while the men engaged in the almost hopeless task of dragging or swimming their vehicles and baggage to the opposite side."[70]

The crossing of Line Creek, at times on a ferry pulled by ropes, was an occasion for travelers to look back over their shoulders and express gratitude. Margaret Hall may have been pardonably overstating when she said that her company in 1828 found the road in Alabama to be, in comparison with the one in the Creek Nation, "quite perfect."[71] In another encomium, Karl Bernhard called it "really good."[72] After a long night of struggling over the Federal Road to get to Line Creek, in a carriage sometimes ankle-deep with water, guided by Indians with torches over ruts, crevices, stumps, and fallen trees, Thomas Hamilton in 1831 brought the long litany of complaints to an emphatic *amen*. "I have had occasion to say a great deal about roads in these volumes, but I pronounce that along which our route lay on the present occasion to be positively, comparatively, and superlatively the *very worst* I have ever traveled in the whole course of my peregrinations."[73]

Signs of civilization also lifted the spirits of the travelers. As early as 1819, Thomas Stocks came through on horseback and remarked on the rich level land of James Abercrombie's plantation, between Line Creek and Evans's stop on Milly's Creek, four miles west.[74] In

1826, Bernhard described an Alabama soil that was fertile enough for the lush vegetation along the Line Creek, where he saw oaks of all descriptions and the magnolia, whose towering presence impressed most of the strangers. Shortly, the road brought sights of cotton plantations, two-story houses with piazzas and balconies, cotton gins—in general, marks of cultivation everywhere.[75] Two or three years later, Anne Royall, her eye sharp for evidence of prosperity, exclaimed over the rich soil and the large plantations of cotton, corn, and sugar cane. After her passage through the Creek Nation, she rejoiced to be in the wealthy state of Alabama, "not only wealthy but the handsomest in the Union."[76]

Perhaps the best-known tavern, and certainly the best preserved and the most fully documented, was located just west of Line Creek at Waugh. On January 6, 1821, in the first issue of the *Montgomery Republican*, Walter B. Lucas announced that he had taken over the well-known stand on Line Creek that had been run by James Abercrombie since about 1818.[77] Lucas, one of the earliest settlers in Montgomery County, continued to run his mercantile business in Montgomery, and his wife, Eliza, ran the tavern. At one time Lucas also had a large gin and a general store at Line Creek. Lucas's Tavern was a four-room frame building with a long central hall; its most famous guest was Marie-Joseph-Paul-Yves-Roch-Gilbert du Motier, the Marquis de Lafayette, whose large entourage stopped there on April 2, 1825. According to Gen. Thomas S. Woodward, writing in 1859, "Everything was done up better than it ever will be again. . . . Such a cavalcade never traveled that road before or since."[78]

The Federal Road continued west from Line Creek and Waugh to Evans's Tavern, which had been previously known as Milly's Tavern. It was located on Norcoce Chappo Creek, later called Milly's Creek, named for the widow of a British soldier, who ran a toll bridge and a tavern at the site and later married Evans.[79] The tavern is mentioned in the account of Aaron Burr's arrest and return to Virginia in 1807 for trial, and it must have been in operation until about 1820. At Milly's, or Evans's, the Federal Road turned southwest to Snowdoun, but most of the stagecoaches and travelers continued west through McLaughlin's and Mount Meigs, two or three miles from Lucas's, to New Philadelphia, which later became Montgomery, sixteen miles from Evans's.

LUCAS'S TAVERN BEFORE REMOVAL
Before its restoration in Montgomery's Old North Hull Street Historic District in 1980, Lucas's Tavern remained in its original Federal Road setting, between U.S. 80 and Interstate 85 near Mount Meigs. It had seen its best days during the 1820s and 1830s as the first stop after the ordeals of travel from Columbus or Fort Mitchell through the Creek Nation. The most famous guest of the tavern was Lafayette, who stayed one night in April 1825. (Photograph by Scott Photographic Services, Montgomery)

Not all the accounts of travel through this stretch are as glowing as Mrs. Hall's or Mrs. Royall's. In 1835, Harriet Martineau's carriage was blocked at the ford of a creek by an emigrant's carriage; when a gentleman tried to help her across a footlog in the deceptive moonlight, she lost her footing and fell waist-deep into the creek.[80] Featherstonhaugh's trunks went underwater, and the carriage floor had eight inches of water before he arrived at McLaughlin's, described as fourteen miles east of Montgomery, in 1835.[81] The next year Phineas Taylor Barnum, twenty-six years old at the time, organized his first touring company and traveled from Columbus to Montgomery. The day before he set out, "the mail stage had been stopped and the passengers murdered, the driver alone escaping." The news was an unrecognized omen: Barnum had fun along the journey, particularly playing a practical joke on an Italian actor who claimed to be unafraid of Indians, but he apparently did not make much money in Montgomery, and his troupe went to Nashville and disbanded.[82]

After the Federal Road turned southwesterly at Evans's Tavern, there were fewer stops, and because so many travelers went on to

Montgomery, where they caught a steamboat for Mobile, less has been reported about the final section of the road. In fact, of the Federal Road narratives found for study, only three describe a journey over this major portion of the road, going toward Fort Stoddert. Latrobe's 1834 journal dealt primarily with the stagecoach and passing sights; more detailed descriptions of the countryside came from Hodgson, who kept a journal of his travels in 1820, and from James Stuart, a Scotsman who closely observed manners and morals when he came through ten years later.

Ten miles south of Montgomery, after the Federal Road crossed Hunter Road and Catoma Creek, was Snowdoun, where Bonham's (sometimes Bonum's or Bonam's) was located. Although the road through this prairie land was generally good, it offered rough going along low ground. Adam Hodgson traveled from Evans's Tavern to Bonham's over a "wretchedly bad road" through thick clay in which his horses got stuck, through entangling trees and vines, and through several swamps.[83] When James Stuart was traveling to Bonham's seeking a breakfast, his driver preferred a ford to a bridge, and the result was a flooded, almost swamped, carriage. They met a whiskey wagon, and the driver offered them a free drink, but it was too early in the day for the journal keeper. Stuart had to demand a breakfast from the reluctant Mrs. Bonham, whom he described as "the worst-tempered American female" he had encountered in his three years of travel. The tavern, erected in 1820, had one room to hold family, guests, the stagecoach driver, and Mrs. Bonham's fury.[84]

The fare was better at Colonel Wood's, the next stop down from Bonham's, although Wood and the stage driver sometimes kept the passengers waiting until they came back from hunting. Wood, whose honorary military title was bestowed by neighbors, who depended on him for protection should the "Creeks rise," served not only good food but also an excellent beer brewed from molasses. Recovered from his bout with Mrs. Bonham, Stuart thought the country more beautiful than that east of the Chattahoochee; he was able to appreciate splendid specimens of oak, tulip, poplar, chestnut, sycamore, magnolia, redbud, dogwood, catalpa, plum, and crab apple; wild turkeys were abundant, and the venison was better than it was in the north.[85]

Southwest of Colonel Wood's the next stop was Sam Manack's

house, on Pinchony Creek. The first licensed tavern in Alabama, it operated for paying guests from about 1803 to 1816 and was mentioned by Lieutenant Luckett in the notes for his road survey in 1810. Lorenzo and Peggy Dow stopped there soon after the road had been cut and the trees notched to guide the travelers.[86] In 1820, four years after Manack had moved out, Adam Hodgson came to a solitary log house in the woods after crossing two bad swamps. The host's talkative daughter made breakfast and could not contain her surprise at seeing Hodgson's white servant. Although she was "of the poorest class of emigrants" and was living in "a log house pervious to the weather in all directions," when Hodgson told her that in England black and white servants ate at the same table, she replied that she had rather "fight a funeral than eat with a black."[87]

Down from Manack's in Butler County was Fort Dale, established by Sam Dale after the Stroud-Ogle killings of 1818 as a defense against the hostile Indians led by Savannah Jack. In 1820, only a few palings were left, but the site was on a flourishing plantation, five miles north of Greenville and ten miles southwest of General Claiborne's Fort Deposit. The landlord in 1820 had a library, and among its volumes Hodgson spied the Bible, the Koran, a hymnal, *Nicholson's Encyclopedia*, Sterne, Burns, Cowper, Coelebs, Camilla, and *Acts of the Alabama Legislature*. Hodgson did not recognize the "intelligent" landlord as Sam Dale himself, the Alabama hero and member of the legislature.[88]

After about 1823, the tavern at Fort Dale closed, and travelers came to Maj. Ward Taylor's tavern at Greenville. When James Stuart stayed there in 1830, nothing was very comfortable, and the only mattress a meager featherbed. Taylor operated one of the stagecoach lines, and Price was a driver for the fifteen-mile run to Price's Hotel, which he owned, near Butler Springs. Mrs. Price, who was born a Fraser on the Isle of Skye, had an excellent breakfast laid out, but she would not serve Stuart until her husband, who was tending the horses, could sit down with them. She had lived in South Carolina for a long time before coming to Alabama, where the climate was healthier and her husband better paid but where there was a "want of schools for her children." Mrs. Price, like William Gilmore Simms, was able to get in a published last word to a travel writer. As it turned out, she had read, "and with no small disapprobation," Capt. Basil Hall's *Trav-*

els in North America, published the year before. Returning Hall's volley, she said he knew nothing of American manners.[89]

In 1820, Hodgson left Fort Dale and traveled twenty miles to his night's lodgings at Murder Creek. During the day he had heard tales of the Ogle-Stroud slayings two years before; after he learned that the creek's ominous name came from another massacre fifteen years earlier, he was afraid to stay in the lone cabin in "the deep glen."[90] His fearful visions were dispelled by the close company in the one-room dwelling in which the narrator, his servant, five other travelers, and the host couple slept.[91]

The mileages recorded by Hodgson and Stuart may not have been exact or correct, but if Stuart is accurate, the next stop for him in 1830 was near the Claiborne road turnoff. Burnt Corn was actually about a mile or two north of this road, which led to a ferry across the Alabama and the road across Clarke County to St. Stephens. Stuart wrote that, when he left Price's, he rode thirteen miles to Cocker's for a change of horses and then sixteen miles farther to Longmyre's Tavern. Stuart found that Mrs. Longmyre was respected by her neighbors because of her knowledge of medicine, demonstrated by her skill in nursing one of the young stage drivers back to health after an attack of fever.[92]

In that vicinity in 1820, Hodgson spotted a fingerpost of wood fastened to a tree and pointing down a grass path; on it was written "To Pensacola." This was probably the "Furrow Path" used by the Red Sticks when they were moving supplies from the port north in 1813. As Hodgson passed through, he encountered "a very pleasing family in the middle of the forest" that regretted leaving Georgia because the manners of their new neighbors were "rough and ill suited to their tastes"; however, the family was optimistic because Sabbath laws were being enforced and because a free public school had opened, offering Latin and French and paying its master seven hundred dollars per annum.[93]

Before Stuart left the Federal Road, his stage took on a new driver, Elisha Lolley, who paid no attention to the baggage, acted as if he were lord of the road, and was as rude and uncivil as possible. Sixteen miles down the road a stop was put to his profanity by Duncan MacMillan (also McMillan), a Scotsman who had settled in the area about 1820. Stuart was pleased to meet MacMillan, a native of Argyle who was able to greet him in Gaelic, as was his American-born wife, and was impressed particularly by the piety of the family; through a thin-wall partition he was able to hear them at their evening prayers.[94] But Stuart's bad luck with stage drivers was not over. At the next tavern, run by a Mr. Peebles, a planter whose house, furniture, and food showed education and culture, Stuart had another breakfast, and the stagecoach acquired a more lawless driver, named Symes, who left Stuart to hold the reins for thirty-five minutes while he had an assignation with a woman he kept in a hidden cabin not far from the road. When Symes returned and asked Stuart for advice, he was told to marry the girl, but he said her family was beneath his, and he could not disgrace himself. Stuart condemned the driver not for immorality but for "leaving the whole southern mails at the mercy of a stranger."[95]

The refinement Stuart found at Mr. Peebles's indicates how much the country had changed in a decade. In 1820, Adam Hodgson and his servant had traveled a solitary road through the area; he slept one night in blankets under the trees and recorded the effects of a hurricane or tornado that had ripped up the forest. Benighted and fearful of alligators, they saw winking lights that turned out not to be the cottage windows they were hoping for but lightning bugs, the first Hodgson had seen. On April 2, 1820, he had breakfast at the home of a man who had lived on a farm for fifteen years and who claimed to have two thousand head of cattle, but there was no milk or butter to serve. A bearskin was drying in the sun at his place; seven miles south, Hodgson saw, and knew to recognize, a recently stuffed panther; and at the next home was one of his final sights on the Federal Road—a fresh rattlesnake skin.[96]

Ten years later, Stuart found that the spirit of temperance and order embodied in the MacMillan family was also reflected in the policies of Mrs. Mills, who ran the next tavern down from Mr. Peebles. She was an intelligent lady who allowed no whiskey in her home, but she expected that she had to serve wine on special occasions, and Stuart considered her a good influence on the neighborhood. The family raised food for the table, and her Indian gamekeeper kept her supplied with venison and turkeys.[97] Ten miles farther was McDavid's Hotel, a two-room house with a dog-trot between. Here travelers could wash their face and hands in a pewter basin and dry on a roller towel before dining on the abundant supply of excellent pork. Another good hotel, Judge Burns's, was located five miles north of Blakeley. In 1830 the road in the vicinity was still a track of stumps, one of which stopped Stuart's carriage, and was not to be traveled by night.[98]

About twenty miles down the Federal Road from Burnt Corn Springs, near Taitsville, the road forked, with its southwesterly branch leading to Blakeley and the westerly branch leading to Fort Mims and the Alabama River ferry. Both Hodgson and Stuart were bound for Mobile and took the road to the ferry at Blakeley. Hodgson got to the ferry and headed across the bay on a Sunday morning, hoping to find a Protestant church. He was disappointed and wrote that, "to the disgrace of Protestant America, no place of worship is established here, except a Catholic Church, built by the French or Spanish." The ferry was large enough to accommodate six horses; it transported carriages, wagons, and people, among them Indians with deer hides to trade in Mobile, and was operated by John Fowler from 1823 to 1828.[99] When Stuart reached the steam ferry at Blakeley for the twelve-mile trip to Mobile, his Federal Road experiences with stagecoach drivers extended to the ferry crew, which he characterized as careless and profane.[100]

The travel accounts of the Federal Road that ended, literally, when Hodgson and Stuart took the branch for Blakeley do not constitute a complete picture of the lower Federal Road. By 1814, Fort Stoddert had fulfilled its use as a guardian of the thirty-first parallel, and its military personnel were moved to Mount Vernon; after 1819, St. Stephens had been replaced by Cahaba as the Alabama capital. Conspicuously absent from the accounts of Hodgson and Stuart—indeed, missing from all but one of the other accounts studied as well—are first-hand experiences of violence, particularly of robberies.[101] In 1818, Thomas Stocks had all of his provisions stolen somewhere between Fort Hull and Fort Bainbridge in Macon County, and he was doubtful of travels back to Athens.[102]

The Federal Road was, in fact, ripe for robbers. For a few months, at some time between 1811 and 1818, one of them, the nationally notorious highwayman Joseph Thompson Hare, operated with his partners out of Turk's Cave, near Brooklyn, in Conecuh County, Alabama, about forty miles from the Federal Road. The cave was twenty feet

wide, nine feet long, and twenty feet high and was located in the cleft
of a rocky hillside covered with grapevines and bushes. The robbers
approached the cave from the hilltop and let themselves down to the
opening on a ladder made of the vines. In a popular confession apparently dictated while he was in prison, Hare said that the cave was
located "near a track that led to the *Gold Mines*," an obvious reference to the road. The woods were also bountiful; Hare and his ac-
complices killed deer and turkey and shot a wolf which had prowled
into their cave seeking fresh meat. "He sprung seventeen feet down
from the rock, but we put two balls into him as he jumped," said
Hare.

One of his partners was married to a Spanish girl and spoke
French and Spanish. From a Pensacola hotel "where he had put up
at," he returned with good biscuits and better news about a gentleman from "Old Spain" who would shortly be passing over the road
carrying a good deal of gold. After checking out the party, in particular their weapons, the robbers painted their faces red and went to
the road to Baton Rouge—the Federal Road. Hare, the courtly leader,
described their method.

> We came up to them, and passed them ten or fifteen paces, when we
> suddenly wheeled round, and presenting our rifles told them we were
> highway robbers, and that if they made any resistance or offered to
> run, until they had delivered up their money to us, we would stop
> them with powder and ball. . . . I would not suffer them to speak to
> each other whilst I was robbing them, as I did not understand their
> lingo, and was afraid of some scheme. We got forty weight of gold
> from this company of five; and twenty-eight dollars in silver. We did
> not take their watches, nor rob their waiter. My share of this robbery
> amounted to two hundred and thirty-three doubloons ($3,728). As we
> left them, one of the Spaniards said to the other, that we were Amer-
> ican devils.

This robbery took place about forty miles from the cave, and one
hundred twenty miles from Pensacola. After two months in the hide-
out, the robbers had made $26,700, and Hare's portion was $9,009.
But what to do with it? "I thought that it was time for us to leave our
cave," Hare said, "and go on to some civilized place, where we could
enjoy our money, for we had made enough to satisfy us."[103]

ROBBERY ON THE FEDERAL ROAD

Joseph Thompson Hare and his fellow highwaymen operated for a while from a cave near the Federal Road. This engraving from an account of the famous robber's deeds shows him confronting the rich Spaniard whose party has come up from Pensacola before turning west for Louisiana. Given the court records of Hare's trial and conviction, his description of the Federal Road exploits have the ring of credibility. (Reprinted, by permission, from the Rare Books and Manuscripts Division, New York Public Library, Astor, Lenox, and Tilden Foundations)

Not permanently, however. Hare was caught—"white-handed," as it were—on March 11, 1818, after he and two other men had robbed a mail wagon before daylight that morning on the road between Baltimore and Havre-de-Grace, Maryland. They had tried the face-painting ruse, this time using black instead of red, but the driver observed that they had forgotten to blacken their hands. They had the driver tied to the wagon, and as they tore through the letters searching for money, they apologized to him and gave him ten dollars "to buy bitters." The highwaymen were caught in a clothing store at about 10:30 P.M. while they were buying blue and scotch-plaid frock coats, pantaloons, and hats to replace their muddy garb. Sad for them, a constable walked in, recognized them as suspicious strangers, and questioned them about the mail robbery. Daggers, pistols, and bills from far-flung locations were sufficient evidence for arrest. One robber left behind a pair of his pantaloons, stuffed with money, but before departing, a clerk testified, he "seized my right foot by laying his on it, knocking me with his left elbow, and showing me with his eyes the place of deposit; leave the goods, said he, I will call for them." But he never did. Prosecuted in federal court by William Wirt, the U.S. attorney general who had unsuccessfully tried another traveler on the Federal Road, Aaron Burr, nine years earlier, Hare and his fellow highwaymen were found guilty on all counts and sentenced to die. In prison, Hare offered up for print his own travel narrative, from his birth in Philadelphia to his crimes on the Natchez Trace and the Federal Road as well as in New Orleans, Philadelphia, New York, and, finally, Maryland. On September 10, 1818, on a Thursday morning in Baltimore, 1,500 people watched him hang.[104]

Hare's story adds one vital tessera to complete the mosaic of the travel journals. Most of the writers came and left as strangers, apparently glad to shake the dust or scrape the mud off their feet at Columbus, Montgomery, or Mobile; nevertheless, writing as aristocrat and commoner, European and American, man and woman, they have provided enough sharp, accurate glimpses of the Federal Road to leave a fuller picture of pioneer transportation. Despite their occasional condescension and criticism of the people and places, most of the narrators convey an affection for the sundry characters and the raw settlements; the writers too seem flushed with the excitement of seeing an entire section of the country at the moment of its birth. The common sore point for all was the road; in these accounts "stumped," "swamped," and "benighted" take on full, concrete meaning. Even allowing for the embellishment needed to impress upon readers the perils of travel in a distant land, their comments about the hazards of the road are enough to make one wonder why anyone reading or hearing of raging floods, monstrous sandbeds, rickety log bridges, dangerous causeways, overpriced lodgings, lousy beds, ill-tempered hostesses, disgusting food, immoral stagecoach drivers, and insulting, sometimes sordid companions—not to mention hostile Indians, wolves, panthers, bears, and giant vipers—would come to this new country as anything other than adventurous writers. Or, to put the matter another way, to wonder what manner of people might set out on the Federal Road seeking a new home.

6

SOJOURNERS AND STATEHOOD

F LOODING, THE TERM SO OFTEN USED to describe the status of streams in the Creek Nation, also aptly describes the rush of pioneers over the Federal Road. In August 1800, the white and black population of the portion of the Old Southwest that became the state of Alabama was 1,250; in June 1830, the state census revealed 309,527 residents; and ten years later the number had leapt to 590,756.[1] Settlers were flocking into the section over more than one route, but the major thoroughfare for the lower Mississippi Territory was the Federal Road. Passing over the narrow track through the woods were emigrants from the East propelled by the promise of fertile lands beyond the Creek Nation, purchasable on easy terms. This westward thrust of settlement was evident as soon as the military road was opened. Benjamin Hawkins's report that, in the six months between October 1811 and March of the following year, 233 vehicles and 3,726 persons had headed west past his Indian Agency on the Flint River was merely an indication of the first wave of emigration.[2] By 1817, the movement was described by James Graham, with an italicized misspelling that further emphasizes how the phenomenon in North Carolina resembled a plague. "The *Alabama Feaver* rages here with great violence and has *carried off* vast numbers of our Citizens. . . . There is no question that this *feaver* is contagious . . . for as soon as one neighbor visits another who has just returned from Alabama he immediately discovers the same symptoms which are exhibited by the one who has seen alluring Alabama."[3]

In a rhetorical pronouncement worthy of Thomas Paine and ringing with unconscious irony, Benjamin John McKinley of Alabama justified the exodus by declaring, "It is better to be a tenant on rich land than a landlord on poor; it is better to be a free man in the West than a slave to a manufacturer in the East."[4] One reason given for the lack of population growth in North Carolina was the mass migration from 1820 to 1840, when many of the best citizens left "to the enrichment of Alabama and Mississippi."[5] Not coincidentally, this twenty-year span also was the high-water mark of the Federal Road, over which these "best citizens" and many more of lower social status were streaming into the section.

They came walking ("riding shank's mare," it was often called), or with their worldly goods in hogsheads fitted with trunnions and axles so that the whole barrel could be pulled by horse or hand, or in the variety of vehicles, from light carriages to crude wagons, described by the travelers. Although a few had the dreams and the means for setting up plantations along the fertile watercourses, most fit the description of Mississippi pioneers in William Faulkner's *The Hamlet*.

> [They came] in battered wagons and on muleback and even on foot, with flintlock rifles and dogs and children and homemade whiskey stills and Protestant psalm books. . . . They came from the Atlantic seaboard and before that, from England and the Scottish and Welsh Marches, as some of the names would indicate. . . . They brought no slaves and no Phyfe and Chippendale highboys; indeed, what they did bring most of them could (and did) carry in their hands. They took up land and built one- and two-room cabins and never painted them, and married and produced children and added other rooms one by one to the original cabins and did not paint them either. . . . Their descendants still planted cotton in the bottom land and corn along the edge of the hills.[6]

The attitudes and fortunes of those coming over the Federal Road to settle in the new territory ran the register, as three examples will demonstrate.

In 1811, Peggy Dow was returning eastward over the recently opened road, its trees still "fresh marked" to serve as guides, with her husband, Lorenzo, a Methodist evangelist, who was raising his voice on this, his tenth trip through the wilderness. After crossing the Alabama River at Fort Mims, they met land seekers who had just faced one of the sadder consequences of early travel, though with a reaction that startled Mrs. Dow.

Rolling Hogshead of Early Settler

Some settlers unable to afford better vehicles put their worldly goods in barrels, or hogsheads, into the ends of which had been fixed trunnions, housings into which axles could be fitted. These were pulled by horses or oxen or by hand into the new country. (Drawing by Charles J. Hiers)

We came across a family who were moving to the Mississippi—they had a number of small children; and although they had something to cover them like a tent, yet they suffered considerably from the rain the night before: and to add to that, the woman told me they had left an aged father at a man's house by the name of *Manack* one or two days before and that she expected he was dead perhaps by that time. They were as black almost as the *natives,* and the woman seemed very much disturbed at their situation. I felt pity for her—I thought her burthen was really heavier than mine. We kept on, and about the middle of the day we got to the house where the poor man had been left with his wife, son, and daughter. A few hours before we got there, he had closed his eyes in death—they had lain him out, and expected to bury him that evening; but they could not get any thing to make a coffin of, only split stuff to make a kind of a box, and so put him in the ground!

I thought this would have been such a distress to me, had it been my case, that it made my heart ache for the old lady. But I found that she was of that class of beings that could not be affected with any thing so much as the loss of property; for she began immediately to calculate the expense they had been at by this detention—and I do not recollect that I saw her shed one tear on the occasion.[7]

Better luck followed the cheerful family of Gideon Lincecum, a frontiersman who wrote about traveling from the Ocmulgee over the Federal Road.

My father loved a border life, and the place he had purchased on the Ocmulgee, as the people had already commenced settling on the opposite side of the river, was no longer looked upon as a border country. He sold his place and was soon equipped and geared up for the road, and so was I. I had been reared to a belief and faith in the pleasure of frequent change of country, and I looked upon the long journey, through the wilderness, with much pleasure.

Our company consisted of my father and mother and eight children, with six negroes; Joseph Bryan, my brother-in-law, and his wife and two negroes; my wife and me and two small sons and two negroes. We had good horses and wagons and guns and big dogs. We set out on the 10th of March, 1818. I felt as if I was on a big camp hunt.

The journey, the way we traveled, was about 500 miles, all wilderness, full of deer and turkeys, and the streams were full of fish. We were six weeks on the road, the most delightful time I had ever spent in my life. My brother Garland and I "flanked it" as the wagons rolled along and killed deer, turkeys, wild pigeons and at nights, with pine torches, we fished and killed a great many with my bow and arrows, whenever we camped on any water course. Little creeks were full of fish in that season.[8]

Lincecum settled in the log-cabin village of Tuscaloosa in 1818, in the wildest, least-trodden, and most "tomahawked country" along the Tombigbee system, and expressed his energy as a jack-of-all-trades.[9] He had confidence that he could provide for his family, "for I was as strong as two common men and could do anything from cutting and splitting fence rails to fine cabinet work." Moreover, in mercantile action he "was familiar with all the duties from the lumber house to the counting room."[10] The frontier restlessness caught up with Lincecum eventually, and his door could have been marked "G.T.T.," as were those of other Alabama settlers who had gone to Texas.

In 1829, when Benjamin Porter came from South Carolina with his young wife to settle on the Alabama River ten miles above Claiborne, they had the all-too-normal Federal Road experiences—frights from "half-naked savages and beastly Negroes" maddened with rum, "unjust exactions" by Creeks at the many toll bridges, and unfair prices for corn, charged by the whites beyond Line Creek. But worst of all was the pierced illusion when he got to his destination.

> We had an uncle in Monroe, an early settler, to whose mansion we were hastening. We indulged in golden dreams of his appearance and that of his house. We pictured him a portly, well-looking old man; and his homestead the very abode of comfort. A large white house, piazzas and green blinds floated before our eyes; and amidst the toils and privations of our long journey, we rioted, as we neared his home, upon the vapors of benevolence which rose from his face, and the savory smells from his kitchen. But alas, for our round-bellied uncle, and the white house and green blinds; alas for the fat turkeys and old hams! We found our uncle a small man, with a very lean girdle—his house was a rail pen, full of squalling, mischievous babes, and snapping bull puppies; and our supper a rasher of bacon with boiled greens.[11]

With a hatchet, saw, old plane, and chisel, Porter made a "not contemptible bedstead, table, and arm chair" from a large poplar, but he learned an even more important lesson from "the manufacture of children." As Mrs. Porter was approaching her first confinement, he engaged an old midwife in Claiborne, ten miles away, and was "continually swimming the two large creeks" between his house and the town in anticipation of the delivery. Since the Porters were novices, the good nurse charged them thirty-five dollars and made Porter give her a receipt for the receipt she had given him. After that well-documented initiation Porter learned what the going price was, "and my other children have cost only five dollars a head for being introduced into the world."[12]

Porter also learned firsthand how the patriotic residents regarded state laws pertaining to road work. "I was summoned and, of course, went. I toiled for three days with slaves in the hot sun. The whites who were also summoned sat under the shade and talked and laughed. I was so young and foolish that it never occurred to me that one required to perform a public duty could neglect it. I injured my

fentatives, and one copy of the journals of the Legislative Council.
GABRIEL MOORE,
Speaker of the House of Representatives.
JAMES TITUS,
President of the Legislative Council.
Approved, the 3d day of February, 1818.
WM. W. BIBB,
Governor of the Alabama Territory.

—

AN ACT

To amend the Laws now in force respecting public roads.
Sec. 1. *Be it enacted by the Legislative Council and House of Representatives of the Alabama Territory, in General Assembly convened,* That it shall hereafter be lawful for the overseer of any public road, if he deems it necessary, to require all and every perfon, or perfons refiding within his precinct, and not exempted from such service by law, to work on faid road ten days and no longer; except when bridges and

causeways may require repair, and in that cafe as long as may be neceffary for that purpofe, not exceeding twenty days.
Sec. 2 *And be it further enacted,* that hereafter the overfeer of any public road fhall be liable to be fined on prefentment, at the discretion of the Jury trying the fame, if the road of which he is overfeer fhall have remained out of repair for the period of twelve days at any one time, provided fuch overfeer have any notice thereof.
Sec. 3. *And be it further enacted,* that hereafter when any delinquent fhall be returned to a juftice of the Peace, by the overfeer of a public road, and it fhall become neceffary to iffue procefs againft fuch delinquent, fuch procefs fhall be iffued, and all further proceedings carried on in the name of the Territory; and if the profecution fail, the coft fhall be adjudged as in other Territorial cafes: and the court may, if it appear that the return has been made, or the profecution commenced by fuch overfeer from malicious motives, tax him with coft.

ALABAMA TERRITORIAL ROAD WORK ACT

In addition to revealing the state-of-the-art printing done at St. Stephens in 1818, these passages excerpted from the territorial code of Alabama show what was required of citizens eligible to do work building and maintaining roads. Despite the stern language in the code, there is little evidence that it was strictly enforced. (Courtesy of the Brantley Collection, Samford University Library, Birmingham)

reputation very seriously by working, instead of sitting in the shade!"[13]

Although the main attraction for these settlers was the opening of the land, assuming ownership was not a simple matter, because of legal entanglements and shady sales practices. Joseph Glover Baldwin, a Virginia lawyer best known as the author of *Flush Times of Alabama and Mississippi,* one of the standard works of Old Southwest humor, described the unlimited opportunities for young attorneys. The fiction he wrote in the new country was grounded in fact; the litigation growing out of the Indian claims to land under treaties, the preemptive rights of settlers on public lands, and the various land sales all provided a field for unbridled speculation. Land was bought and sold on credit, and often that land had defective title. The carelessness of public officials and a varied assortment of frauds prompted a circus of lawsuits. In light of the treaties and the actions by local officials, Baldwin was not indulging in hyperbole when he wrote of the "swindling of Indians by the nation! . . . Stealing their land by the township."[14]

To acquire a land title involved clearing prior claims through French, British, and Spanish grants and settlement, surveying the land, and selling the land, all by the United States government. France relinquished the region to the British in 1763. Spain's possession south of the thirty-first parallel was confirmed by Britain and the United States in 1783, but Spain claimed that West Florida's north boundary extended from the mouth of the Yazoo on the Mississippi River due east to the Chattahoochee (32° 28'). In 1795, Spain recognized the claims of the United States to all lands above the thirty-first parallel, but later claimed all of West Florida up to the Yazoo-Chattahoochee line. Spanish troops were not ordered south of this line until 1799.[15]

In a division of the region, Tennessee became a state in 1796, with its southern boundary fixed on paper but not on the ground. The central portion of the southern boundary of the state of Tennessee was established by Thomas Freeman on October 12–15, 1807, at a point north of Huntsville, Alabama, and later extended east and west.[16] In 1798, the Mississippi Territory was formed from the land ceded by Spain in 1795, framed east and west between the Chattahoochee and the Mississippi rivers, on the north by the Yazoo-Chattahoochee line, the old northern boundary claimed by Spain, and on the south by the thirty-first parallel, above which was built Fort Stoddert in 1799. Cessions within this territory gradually increased the domain of the United States. State claims by South Carolina and Georgia were surrendered in 1787 and 1802, although the South Carolina cession was dubious and the Georgia cession was subject to certain stipulations and payments. These lands were formally added to the Mississippi Territory in 1804. Lands south of the thirty-first parallel and west of the Pearl River were made part of the Orleans Territory in 1810, and those between the Pearl and Perdido rivers were joined to the Mississippi Territory in 1813. In 1816, both the Chickasaw and Choctaw ceded lands west of and adjacent to the Creek cession of 1814, opening even more land for survey and settlement.[17]

The cession of Georgia's claims to its western lands raised a particular set of complications. The agreement required the validation

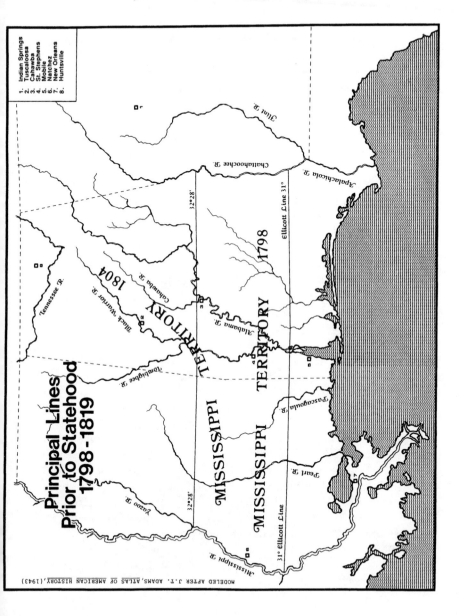

Principal Lines
Prior to Statehood
1798-1819

1. Indian Springs
2. Tuscaloosa
3. Cahawba
4. St. Stephens
5. Mobile
6. Natchez
7. New Orleans
8. Huntsville

MISSISSIPPI TERRITORY

MISSISSIPPI

MISSISSIPPI

1798

1804

Ellicott Line 31°

31° Ellicott Line

32°28'

32°28'

Tennessee R.

Black Warrior R.

Cahawba R.

Tombigbee R.

Alabama R.

Pascagoula R.

Pearl R.

Yazoo R.

Mississippi R.

Chattahoochee R.

Apalachicola R.

Flint R.

MODELED AFTER J.T. ADAMS, ATLAS OF AMERICAN HISTORY, (1943)

of all British and Spanish titles by persons residing on the land in 1795 as well as the removal of Indian claims of title to all land in the state of Georgia, as soon as practicable, at reasonable prices. A board of commissions for lands east of the Pearl River was set up in 1803; it met at Fort Stoddert, heard claims, and adjourned in 1805. Needless to say, overlapping titles and inconsistent practices were common. Some settlers had their prior titles confirmed, others were donated their land because of long possession, and still others were given first priority to purchase the lands to which they claimed preemptive rights; a century of litigation of land-title claims followed.[18] The Yazoo claims, arising from Georgia's spurious sale of lands west, were settled when Congress issued $8 million in scrip that could be used in purchasing land.

The presence of land, money, and buyers and the absence of clear lines of authority created an ideal climate for speculators seeking a quick profit and a rapid turnover. They made down payments, hoping for a sale before the next payment came due, and some public officials used knowledge gained through their office as a basis for personal speculation and profit-splitting contracts.[19] To this day, the term *land-office business* refers to the frenzy of trade inspired by these frontier conditions.

The process that ended in so many conflicts had had a more orderly beginning. In accordance with the Land Ordinance Act of 1785, all lands in the Mississippi Territory to which Indian titles had been extinguished were to be surveyed into townships and subdivided into half-sections. In 1807, land offices were set up at St. Stephens and Huntsville. The St. Stephens base line (east and west) was established substantially along the Ellicott line (the thirty-first parallel), and the principal meridian (north and south) ran through St. Stephens. The Huntsville base line was established along the southern boundary of Tennessee, and the principal meridian ran through Huntsville. Lands surveyed from these points of reference were to be sold for a minimum of two dollars per acre, payable over a four-year period, and cash discounts were allowed for those with currency in hand. The first sales were made at St. Stephens on December 26, 1806, but no sales of Tombigbee land were made until September 2, 1811.[20]

Overseeing this imposition of the European and American system of land division on the new territory were military surveyors. Although the survey of these public lands by the U.S. government was begun by Maj. Thomas Freeman in 1807, progress was interrupted by the Creek Indian War of 1813–14. Freeman had been the surveyor of the Mississippi Territory, but Gen. John Coffee, close friend and able second to the then politically powerful Gen. Andrew Jackson in the War of 1812, was also a surveyor and desired employment as such. William H. Crawford, secretary of the treasury, was impatient to have these surveys completed and in March 1817 had Coffee appointed surveyor general of public lands for the northern portion of the Mississippi Territory. Freeman continued to survey, north from the St. Stephens principal meridian, the area which on December 10, 1817, became the southern portion of the Alabama Territory. Location of the Federal Road is shown on section and township plats of government land surveys which crossed the road and were made after its completion in 1811. Freeman completed the survey of the southern portion before Coffee finished the northern part and stopped with regular sections at a line running east and west through Fort Williams, one of Jackson's forts built during the Creek War of 1813–14, located southwest of Sylacauga on the Coosa River. Coffee later completed the survey south from the Huntsville principal meridian and tied into Freeman's northern line with fractional sections. The division between these two surveys (Huntsville and St. Stephens) is called the "Coffee-Freeman Line." In 1818, Coffee's authority was extended to all of the Alabama Territory and Freeman's to the state of Mississippi.[21] (One vestige of the military system still present in both states is the use of the term *beat* for Alabama and Mississippi voting districts.)

The tremendous influx of settlers, some coming through Huntsville but most entering the southeastern portion of the Mississippi Territory over the Federal Road, had a great influence on the changing sectional and political situation and on the issue of whether the territory should be one state or two—and, if two, where the dividing line should be. From the onset of emigration, two population centers developed, one near Natchez on the Mississippi, the other on the Tombigbee. The Mississippi settlement was larger, grew faster, and dominated the early government; it was deaf to the pleas of the Tombigbee settlement for more adequate protection against the Indians and better representation in governmental affairs. The Tombigbee people requested separation into two states to prevent domination by the Mississippi River settlers, who were benefiting from the single-government system. Some time after Georgia's western lands were added to the Mississippi Territory, George Poindexter, the territorial delegate in Congress, proposed division by a line running due east from the mouth of the Yazoo—the same 32° 28' line used to form the initial northern boundary of the Mississippi Territory—with the entire southern part admitted as the state of Mississippi. Settlers in Madison County, Alabama, above the proposed line, where the population center at Huntsville was growing, favored Poindexter's plan because it would separate them from control by the Mississippi settlement, but the Tombigbee settlement vigorously attacked the proposal. In 1812, the proposition passed in the House of Representatives, but the Senate recommended postponement to study division along the line of the Tombigbee.[22] In 1815, the new territorial delegate, Dr. William Lattimore, favored admission as one state. The House passed a single-state bill after receiving a petition from the territorial legislature, but the issue quickly became national. Southern senators wanted as many slave states as possible, and the Senate followed their lead, rejecting the act of the House.

A more local balance-of-power controversy developed as the Tombigbee country began to fill with settlers. The eastern portion soon was more populous than the Natchez-Washington area, and the capital of the single state could be moved east to St. Stephens. Realizing the shift, the Mississippi settlement desired immediate statehood, over the protests of Judge Harry Toulmin, Col. Sam Dale, and others of the Tombigbee settlement. By December 1816, a committee of the House of Representatives was unanimously in favor of a division, with the western portion admitted as a state and the eastern portion given territorial status. Although the southern boundary of Tennessee would be a horizontal line, where to draw the vertical line was still at issue. Some wanted the Pascagoula River and others the Mobile-Tombigbee as the line. Charles Tait, then a U.S. senator from Georgia, and others favored a compromise line in between, which was acceptable to Judge Toulmin. That issue resolved, the Alabama Territory was formed in March 1817, and Mississippi became a state in December of the same year.[23]

The settlers coming from Georgia over the Federal Road had great influence on the timing of the division and the location of the line between Alabama and Mississippi, and their politics had much to do with the survey and sale of lands. Commissioner Josiah Meigs, who corresponded with U.S. Postmaster Gideon Granger about the horse path and who had served from 1801 to 1810 as president of the University of Georgia, directed Thomas Freeman to give priority to surveying the better lands along the Alabama River. These were placed on sale in 1817—not at the Alabama land offices, but at Milledgeville. This scheme made buying the land easy for the friends of the political kingpin William H. Crawford but impracticable for settlers in the territory. After the best lands had been sold at Milledgeville, the land office was moved to Cahaba, and later a land office was opened at Sparta in Escambia County.[24]

The debt to Crawford traveled with the Milledgeville settlers over the Federal Road. Their patron had been elected U.S. senator from Georgia in 1807, when he was thirty-five years old. He was elected president pro tem in 1812, and the next year he left the Senate to accept President Madison's appointment as minister to France. In 1815, Crawford returned to serve a few months as secretary of war and then as secretary of the treasury under Madison and Monroe.[25]

Crawford's position in the state and the nation gave him great influence in early Alabama appointments to public office. As one historian has summed it, "Crawford was in control of public office and put his friends into office whenever he could."[26] William Wyatt Bibb, Bolling Hall, Charles Tait, and George M. Troup all served in the United States Congress with Crawford.[27] Bibb resigned as senator in 1817 because of the protests over his voting to increase the salaries of senators; Tait likewise came under fire but remained in the Senate until Alabama became a state in 1819 to make certain the dividing line was west of the Mobile-Tombigbee river system. Bibb was appointed governor of the territory in 1817 and was elected first governor of the state in 1819. Tait, who had recently moved to Wilcox County, was appointed judge of the Federal District Court, with jurisdiction over all of Alabama, when the court was formed in 1820.[28] Hall, who had served as representative from Georgia from 1811 to 1817, moved to Alabama and became a member of the Crawford political machine. He settled on a plantation in a part of Autauga County

WILLIAM HARRIS CRAWFORD

William Harris Crawford (1772–1834), from his position in Washington, greatly influenced patronage in the Mississippi and Alabama territories and in the state of Alabama, though he was never a resident. He was United States senator from Georgia, 1807–13; minister to France, 1813–15; secretary of war, 1815–16; secretary of the treasury, 1816–25; and unsuccessful candidate for president in 1825. The Crawford, or Georgia, machine finally gave way to the North Carolina faction. (Reprinted from Rebecca Crawford Hamilton photo album in the private collection of H. D. Southerland, Jr.)

ISRAEL PICKENS AND WILLIAM WYATT BIBB

William Wyatt Bibb (right) and Israel Pickens (left), travelers over the Federal Road from Georgia and North Carolina, respectively, represented two factions of settlers. As part of the William Harris Crawford machine, Bibb (1781–1820) was among the early leaders who helped Georgians get preferential treatment in land purchases and in appointments to federal offices. Pickens (1780–1827), who was the spokesman for the plain people, also had authority as register of the land office at St. Stephens. Both served in Congress before coming to Alabama. Bibb was the territory's and the state's first governor. Pickens was the state's third governor and was in office in 1825 when Lafayette made his famous journey across Alabama. (Reprinted, by permission, from the Alabama Department of Archives and History, Montgomery)

that became Elmore County and sent his wagons back over the Federal Road to Milledgeville for supplies.[29]

Opposing Crawford was Israel Pickens, whose tenure in the Congress (1811–17) coincided with Hall's. He came to Alabama from North Carolina, over the "almost impassable" Federal Road to become the register for the Mississippi Territory land office at St. Stephens in 1817. Waging political warfare as a spokesman for the plain people, he became the third governor of Alabama, serving from 1821 to 1825. He also served a few months as senator in 1826; he died the following year and was buried in the family cemetery near Greensboro in Hale County, Alabama.[30]

Although politics most often becomes the stuff of recorded history, a more representative settler than either Pickens or Hall was the

Reverend Joshua Wilson, a Revolutionary War soldier and a Methodist minister who purchased land at the St. Stephens office in 1815 but did not move his family until 1817. At the age of fifty-seven, he took his wife, children (some grown and married), slaves, livestock, wagons, carriages, and household possessions over the Federal Road and settled at Gainestown, in Clarke County, three miles from the Alabama River. His descendants became prominent in Clarke County affairs.[31]

Though the mails were not reliable, even after the postal horse path was widened into the Federal Road, new post offices were being created to serve the settlers. The location and dates of establishment point to where the population was growing and when. Many new post offices were created on and near the Federal Road just after July 1818. Some of the earlier post offices, postmasters, and dates of first return, as indicated in the National Archives' first returns from postmasters prior to July 1818, included:

New Orleans	Blaise Cenas	October 1, 1804
Fort Stoddert	Edmund P. Gaines	April 1, 1805
Fort Stephens	Joseph Chambers	July 1, 1805
Milledgeville	Thompson Bird	October 1, 1806
Ocmulgee Old Fields	Jonathan Halstead	April 1, 1807
Tensaw	John Pierce	April 1, 1808
Creek Agency	Benjamin Hawkins	January 1, 1810
Mobile	James B. Wilkinson	July 1, 1814
Coweta	Joseph Marshall	April 1, 1815
Fort Jackson	Walter R. Ross	October 1, 1815
Fort Claiborne	Andrew Mitchell	July 1, 1816
Fort Mitchell	Daniel Hughes	April 1, 1818[32]

Mail between Washington and New Orleans continued to be carried via Natchez until 1826, when a contract was made to carry the mail via Georgia. About that time the steamboats and stagecoaches, being more reliable, supplanted the individual mail riders on horseback. This use of the Federal Road contributed to the gradual decline in national importance of the Natchez Trace.[33]

Although there are no accounts indicating that the many waters along the Federal Road parted to allow Christian pilgrims to pass with unmoistened feet, zeal was not dampened. Churches were springing up across the region, and religion, as some of the travelers noticed, exerted a civilizing influence. Especially worthy of note is the growth of churches along the lower section of the Federal Road, the most sparsely populated outside of the Creek Nation. At Fort Dale in Butler County, the Town Creek Baptist Church was organized in 1819 or 1820, and the Friendship Baptist Church in 1821. In Conecuh County, three Baptist churches had been organized by 1821: the Bethany Baptist Church, on Old Stage Road; Olive Branch Baptist Church, at Gravella Station; and the Brooklyn Baptist Church, in the vicinity of Turk's Cave, where the highwayman Joseph Thompson Hare had hidden while engaged in his own preying. The Belleville Baptist Church also was located in Conecuh County, and the Alabama Baptist Convention, founded in 1823, met there in 1827.[34] The Methodists were not far behind: Abner McGehee made a home in southern Montgomery County about 1822 between Catoma and Pintlala Creek, near the Federal Road, and soon thereafter built the Hope Hull Methodist Church. The Reverend James King was a Methodist minister at Burnt Corn from about 1821 to 1834. By 1819, three conferences—the Tennessee, Mississippi, and South Carolina—were furnishing preachers for the Alabama circuits, and the Alabama Methodist Conference was organized in 1832.[35]

Because of the access provided by the Federal Road, Alabama grew at a rate of more than 1,300 percent between 1810 and 1820, much faster than either Mississippi or Louisiana. Although Alabama had less population than Mississippi in both 1800 and 1810, its population exceeded that of Mississippi in the period 1820 to 1850, and also exceeded that of Louisiana in the period of 1830 to 1850.[36]

The steady growth of a dominant, white population in the section, with its own customs, religions, and ingrained animosities against the Indians, made assimilation with the Indians out of the question. The early practice of white soldiers and traders who married Creek women and produced half-breed offspring that might partake of both white and Indian ways came to an end. It had begun as early as 1717 at Fort Toulouse, at the junction of the Coosa and the Tallapoosa, which became the site of Fort Jackson in 1814.[37] The French commander, Captain Marchand, and an Indian woman named Sehoy, frequently called Princess Sehoy and referred to in genealogical charts as "Sehoy I" because of the name repetition, were the parents of a daughter, Sehoy II. Sehoy I was a member of the dominant Wind Clan of the Upper Creeks, and her children became leaders of the Creek Nation. Sehoy II married first a Tuckabatchee chieftain (or, according to one account, a Scotsman, Malcolm McPherson) and had Sehoy III, who married first a Colonel Tate and became the mother of David and John Tate. After Tate's death, she married Charles Weatherford, a Scotsman, and became the mother of William Weatherford, or Red Eagle, an architect of the massacre at Fort Mims, who surrendered to Andrew Jackson after the Battle of Horseshoe Bend and lived out his life as a planter in Monroe County, Alabama. Sehoy I, who had first married Captain Marchand, had a second husband named Lachlan McGillivray; to that union three children were born: Sophia, who married Benjamin Durant; Janet, who married LeClerc Milfort; and Alexander McGillivray, who died in 1793 and was the last chief to dominate the entire Creek confederation.[38] William Weatherford's daughter Betsy married Sam Manack, who operated a stand below Montgomery and whose name appears in many accounts. Their son David, who spelled his surname Moniac, was the first Indian to graduate from West Point. He was a brave, well-considered man, who easily passed for white, and was killed in the Second Seminole War—fighting against troops under the command of a halfbreed who passed for Indian, Osceola.[39]

Another arabesque story of assimilation, marked by tragedy and significant in a study of the Federal Road, was that of the McIntosh family. John McIntosh, son of Lt. Benjamin McIntosh and Catherine McIntosh, married Margaret McGillivray; they were the parents of Capt. William McIntosh, a Tory during the Revolution. Capt. William McIntosh lived among the Creek Indians with his two wives, one of whom was the mother of Chief William McIntosh—who signed the Treaty of Washington in 1805 and later died because of a treaty. An earlier McIntosh, John McIntosh Mohr (the final name indicating "great" or "large"), had sailed from Inverness, Scotland, on October 18, 1735, in the *Prince of Wales*, commanded by Capt. George Dunbar with some two hundred Highlanders, including about fifty women, and had settled New Inverness, which became Darien, the county seat of McIntosh County, Georgia. His son Lachlan was a brigadier general in the Continental Army in the American Revolution. He is also famous in Georgia for having killed Button Gwinnett, a signer of the Declaration of Independence, in a duel near Savannah on May 12, 1777. With John McIntosh Mohr had come two cousins, John and Roderick, sons of Brigadier William McIntosh of the Jacobite Uprising of 1715. These two McIntoshes settled at McIntosh Bluff on the Tombigbee River, near where Aaron Burr was captured in 1807; both were captains in the British Army. On a trip back to Scotland, Catherine, daughter of Capt. John McIntosh, married a British officer named Troup; she returned to McIntosh Bluff for the birth of her son, George M. Troup, destined to be the governor of Georgia from 1823 to 1827, when Creek-Georgia relations were critical.[40] To complete a sketch that is better than the plot for a historical romance, George Troup was governor when his first cousin William McIntosh, who signed several treaties, was killed in an act of tribal retribution at his home in Indian Springs, Georgia, on April 30, 1825.[41] Chief-General McIntosh had, simultaneously, three wives, one of whom, Eliza Grierson (raised by the Hawkins family), was the mother of Chilly McIntosh, whose melancholia and insight into the problems of Indians was detailed by Lafayette's secretary in 1825.[42]

Another contrast to the later Federal Road settlers was Abraham Mordecai (also Mordacai), whose life also deserves longer treatment. He was born in Pennsylvania in 1755 of Jewish and German descent. After settling on the Flint River to become a trader, he was employed to negotiate for the ransom of white captives held by the Indians. Sometime between 1785 and 1789, he moved to Line Creek, where he erected a house that stood there until 1812. Mordecai's place was near "Old Milly's," the tavern site east of Montgomery, not far from where the Federal Road made its southwesterly turn. Mordecai carried on an extensive trade in furs and skins, which he conveyed on packhorses to Augusta, Pensacola, Mobile, and New Orleans, assisted by the Indians. Between 1802 and 1804, Mordecai built the first cotton gin in the Mississippi Territory, just below the junction of the Coosa and Tallapoosa rivers, and sold his cotton in New Orleans for as much as thirty-three cents a pound. His left ear was cut off—according to Brannon because his horse had eaten some of the Indians' corn, but according to Pickett because of an amorous affair with a pretty married squaw. The removal of an ear was, in fact, a traditional punishment for adultery. Mordecai was also beaten, and his gin was later burned, yet he remained loyal to the American cause.

GEORGE M. TROUP

The life of George M. Troup (1780–1834) represents two perspectives on dealing with the Creek Indians. While Troup was governor of Georgia, his first cousin, Chief William McIntosh, was killed by his fellow Creeks after signing the 1825 Treaty of Indian Springs. Troup was born at McIntosh Bluff on the Tombigbee to Catherine (or Margaret, in some genealogies) McIntosh Troup. The McIntosh family, like the Weatherford, Cornells, and Manack/Moniac families, represented the several generations of white-Indian intermarriages that occurred before the rush of white settlers over the Federal Road after 1811. (Reprinted, by permission, from the Georgia Department of Archives and History, Atlanta)

Mordecai's wife was described as "considerably darkened by the blood of Ham," an allusion to Negro blood. Mordecai served as a guide for General Floyd and joined in the battles of Autossee and Calabee Creek; in 1814, he returned to the Creek Nation with his family, which represented several races. A true settler, he refused to move to Arkansas in 1836 at the time of Indian removal.[43]

By the time the Federal Road had developed into a pioneer thoroughfare, the Indian traders with their international loyalties had either disappeared or lost their influence. In 1798 and 1799, Benjamin Hawkins had surveyed the white population of the Creek Nation and reported the names of some Indian traders and their families. He listed names and occasionally the nationality: Christopher Heinckle, a German; Christian Hagle of Germany; Richard Baily, an Englishman; Nicholas White of Marseilles; Michael Elhart, a Dutchman; Patrick Lane of Ireland; John Townshend, an Englishman; Timothy Barnard, an interpreter; Captain Ellick; Stephen Hawkins; Obediah Low; Joe Marshall; Zachariah McGive (or McGirth); John McLeod; John O'Kelley; William Pound; John Proctor; James Quarles; James Russell; and others.[44] Several of the later traders entered the Creek Nation under passports issued by the state of Georgia.[45]

Many of the children and grandchildren of the Indian intermarriages entered the American mainstream and became prominent citizens. Their Indian relations, who had been a majority in the early 1800s, were far outnumbered by whites by the start of the third decade. The total Creek population in 1825 was 20,653, with 10,703 in the Upper Nation and 9,950 in the Lower Nation.[46] By the time removal of the Indians was increasing in May 1833, the Upper Nation population was 14,142 and the Lower Nation 8,552, a total of 22,694.[47] The widening gap between the populations of the two nations points to the increase of white settlements in the Lower Nation and demonstrates that settlers were more critical than soldiers in reducing the Indian population. By the start of the 1830s, whites must have outnumbered Creek Indians in Alabama by at least a quarter million.[48]

Into the hands of these settlers was passing the fate of the section. Observing the people who had come over the Federal Road and the natural resources at their disposal, an English traveler in 1839, James Silk Buckingham, saw the new country's potential and what might

keep it from being realized. "It will equal, if not surpass, the very fin-
est part of England or France; and if well and wisely governed, be as
happy a country, as it is sure to become a rich and productive one.
Nature has done everything to make it so; and if it fails, it will be the
fault of its institutions or its inhabitants."[49] Even if the pioneers struggling to make their homes in the newly opened country could have
heard Buckingham's charge, with its tone of admonition more au-
dible to twentieth-century ears, they probably would not have taken
his magisterial view or have been so objective about their mission.
They were busy getting the land cleared not only of trees but also of
what many considered the last obstacle to progress and peace of
mind—the Indians.

7

Two Ghosts

A COVERLET WOVEN ON A LOOM by Sarah Ann Stephens, an early settler in Chambers County, Alabama, in what had recently been the Creek Nation, memorializes the Indian wars in woolen yarns dyed with poplar and oak bark into lavenders and earthen browns, in configurations of strong double-walled stockades defined against a white cotton background.[1] The Chattahoochee valley artifact is historically symbolic for more than its materials, colors, or pattern. The last days before the migration of the Creek Indians and the fading of the Federal Road were marked also by an interweaving of the forces and the people that played prominent roles in the transformation of western Georgia and Alabama. Familiar elements in a struggle dating at least from the opening of the horse path in 1806 reappear to complete the design: tensions between Creek factions and between whites and Indians generally; the conflict over national and states' rights; the peace treaties that brought war; the claims to land entitlements that brought bloodshed and lawsuits; a standing cast of characters—Andrew Jackson, Little Prince, Big Warrior, Menawa, William and Chilly McIntosh, William Walker, David Moniac, Jere Austill, Matthew Arbuckle, and Edmund P. Gaines; and the Federal Road itself, with all of its ruts, swamps, and sandbeds, still the agent of intrusion. To be sure, other factors, political, economic, and technological, also figured in the disappearance of the Federal Road as the nineteenth century progressed, but none was as important as the removal of the Indians.

By the start of the third decade of the century, it was evident that no permanent peace was likely between the Creek Nation and the United States government; the civil strife that had been a prelude to the First Creek War, in 1813–14 was destined to turn outward once more in what early historians were fond of calling "depredations" against the whites, whom the Indians regarded as the true predators. One sign that the smoldering hostilities would erupt again came in 1825, when William McIntosh, the Creek-Scottish chieftain-general who fought with the Americans against both the Red Sticks and the Seminoles, signed his fifth and final treaty with the United States. He had been a principal signatory of the first Treaty of Washington (1805), ceding lands to the Ocmulgee and granting rights for a postal horse path; the Treaty of Fort Jackson (1814), ceding lands in the Alabama and Tombigbee river valleys; the Treaty of the Creek Agency (1818), ceding a parcel of land in lower central Georgia; and the first Treaty of Indian Springs (1821), ceding the lands from the Ocmulgee to the Flint.[2] He presumed to speak for the entire Creek confederation and even opened his own road through the Indian territory; it was advertised in the Tuscaloosa *American Mercury* as having been built by General McIntosh through the upper part of the Creek Nation. Estimated to be 118 miles long, the road ran from the Coosa River opposite Shelby County, Alabama, to Fayette County, Georgia, with stops at James Kelly's, a Colonel Hawkins's (the Indian agent had died in 1816), and General McIntosh's place at Indian Springs. The newspaper reported that "not long since three wagons have traveled this road, heavy loaded, and came through with the greatest ease."[3] After McIntosh signed away even more Creek territory, moving the boundary westward to the Flint in the 1821 Treaty of Indian Springs, leaders of the Creek Nation became alarmed; at a council of Tuckabatchee in May 1824, a law was passed forbidding further sale of tribal lands, under penalty of death.[4]

Meeting later in 1824 with federal commissioners at Broken Arrow, south of Fort Mitchell on the Alabama side of the Chattahoochee, the Indians heard that the president of the United States had "extensive holdings beyond the Mississippi" that might be exchanged for their land. The Creek chiefs' response, as recorded by the Americans, showed reasoning grounded in experience.

Ruin is the almost inevitable consequence of a removal beyond the Mississippi, we are convinced. It is true, very true, that "we are surrounded by white people," that there are encroachments made—what assurances have we that similar ones will not be made on us, should we deem it proper to accept your offer, and remove beyond the Mis-

sissippi; and how do we know that we would not be encroaching on
the people of other nations?[5]

Sensing that the faction led by McIntosh favored the removal, one
of the U.S. commissioners, Duncan G. Campbell, reopened the treaty
negotiations at McIntosh's place. Not only were Big Warrior and Little
Prince, chief of the Creeks, absent as a protest against the authority of
McIntosh, they had given him warning of the tribal sanction. Campbell pressed the negotiations, and on February 12, 1825, McIntosh,
whose actual authority was as chief of the Lower Creeks, and his son
Chilly, merely a town chief, signed the second Treaty of Indian
Springs. It ceded lands from the Flint to the Chattahoochee in ex-
change for $400,000 and lands of "like quality, acre for acre, west-
ward of the Mississippi."[6] McIntosh was tried in absentia by the Creek
council and convicted. Big Warrior died on March 8, 1825,[7] and Little
Prince, acting as principal chief of the confederation, ordered Mc-
Intosh's execution. A party of more than a hundred horsemen under
Chief Menawa, who had led the Creeks against Jackson at Horseshoe
Bend, descended on McIntosh's home at dawn on April 30, 1825.
They burned it and killed McIntosh, carrying his scalp back to Tuckabatchee as a return of the order of execution. His son Chilly escaped; the many intermarriages had taken most of the red from his
skin, and he was allowed to slip out unrecognized with the white residents of the house.[8] The fate of the Creeks, which was the real reason for the sadness described by Lafayette's secretary a month
earlier, was about to be realized; in 1828, as Major Chilly McIntosh,
he led the initial contingent of Lower Creeks in their removal to the
West.[9]

The 1825 Treaty of Indian Springs gave all of the present state of
Georgia to the Americans.[10] When President John Quincy Adams
found that it had been negotiated with only a few Creeks, he ordered
a new one drawn up in 1826, ceding only all lands east of the Chattahoochee and a tract of land west of the Chattahoochee but within
the state of Georgia. Adams contended that the new treaty, the second Treaty of Washington, was a valid cancellation of the 1825 treaty.
Gov. George Troup did not recognize the cancellation and claimed
state jurisdiction over all lands contained within the boundaries of
Georgia. The dispute was not settled until yet another treaty was

WILLIAM MCINTOSH AND CHIEF MENAWA
Depending upon the point of view, William McIntosh (1775–1825) was either a martyr or a betrayer. As a chief of the Lower Creeks, he signed many treaties granting Indian territory to the United States; as a soldier in the American cause, he fought against hostile Creeks and Seminoles and earned the rank of general. McIntosh lived a life reflecting both his white, Scottish ancestry and his Indian blood. After he signed a treaty in 1825, a Creek council ordered his execution; it was carried out by Indians under Chief Menawa (c. 1776–c. 1836), who had led the Creeks in the Battle of Horseshoe Bend. These photographs were made from portraits done by Washington artist Charles Bird King when Indian chiefs were visiting Washington to sign treaties during the 1820s and 1830s. (Reprinted, by permission, from the National Anthropological Archives, Smithsonian Institution)

signed at the Creek Agency on November 15, 1827.[11] These subsequent treaties did not reduce the tensions between the Upper Nation and the Lower Nation, or calm the anxieties of Creeks who sensed what was coming.

Adams's new treaty squeezed the Indians into an even smaller area of east Alabama and northwest Georgia, closing them off from other traditional homelands.[12] The Indians Harriet Martineau saw on the streets of Columbus in 1835 had been present since the city was founded in 1827. Dislocated and often desperate, they came across the Chattahoochee during the day by the hundreds, sometimes thousands, but were banned from the Georgia side after dark. Residents of Columbus regarded them as a band of beggars and drunkards whose "object was to get something to eat or steal."[13]

The final drama took another turn when the Creeks' old nemesis, Andrew Jackson, became president. If he had not effectively rung down the curtain on the Creek Nation at the Battle of Horseshoe Bend, he would do so by supporting new legislation and by interpreting the existing treaties—particularly the term *removal*—to the benefit of his frontier constituency. Soon after his inauguration, Jackson stressed that the Creeks should migrate as soon as possible.[14] On May 28, 1830, Congress passed the Indian Removal Act, providing for the exchange of lands with the Indians and for the removal west of the Mississippi. Jackson then proved that the iron will he had displayed in Alabama in negotiating the Treaty of Fort Jackson had not softened. After the Creeks protested the removal act, the president granted them an audience "on the condition that they would be fully empowered to negotiate in conformity with the wishes of the Government."[15]

With the signing of the third Treaty of Washington, on May 24, 1832, the Creeks surrendered all tribal lands east of the Mississippi. In return they were promised removal at the expense of the United States and given subsistence in their new home for one year. The treaty provided for allotments of a half-section (320 acres) to each orphan and head of a family, and a section to each of the ninety tribal chiefs and town headmen, with 16,000 acres to be sold for the benefit of the tribe.[16] Out of a total of 5,200,000 acres credited to the Indians, 2,187,200 acres of the Creek Nation were reserved for them. The census taken on May 1, 1833, to fulfill the provisions of the 1832 treaty revealed 14,142 Creeks in the Upper Nation and 8,552 in the Lower Nation, with heads of families totaling 6,557. Squatters and intruders on Indian lands could also be removed, although, as subsequent events demonstrated, physical force from either the United States or the Indians themselves might be required. Often, fraudulent certification to land speculators went unprosecuted, which aggravated matters and prompted the Creek Council to inform Secretary of War Lewis Cass that, "instead of our situation being relieved as was anticipated, we are distressed in a ten-fold manner."[17]

In 1833, the issue of who held authority over the land exploded in

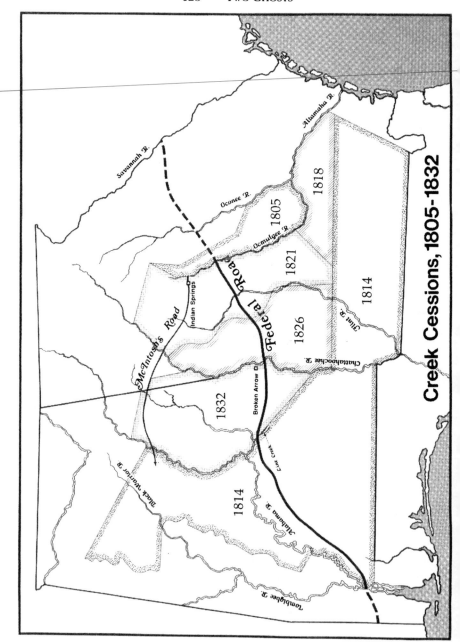

Creek Cessions, 1805-1832

the Hardeman Owens incident. Owens had moved into the Indians' territory as one of the commissioners sent by the Alabama legislature to organize Russell County, one of nine to be created from the Creek Nation.[18] Under the treaty of 1832, however, all whites on the land before the survey was completed were intruders, and the Land Act of 1807 provided procedures for their removal. Alabama officials led by the pro-Jackson governor, John Gayle, did not believe the federal statutes would be enforced. Moreover, Cass had answered Gayle's inquiry on the matter by stating that white persons not bothering Indians or who had not forced Indians off any land could stay until the survey was completed—a violation of the treaty but one that Gayle took for official policy.[19] In response to complaints from the Indians, a deputy U.S. marshal, Jere Austill, who had gained fame with Sam Dale and others in the Canoe Fight twenty years earlier, was sent with a detachment of Fort Mitchell soldiers to evict intruders, even those settling under the aegis of the state of Alabama. Owens, who, according to some reports, had robbed Indian graves and taken one hundred acres of good land from Indians, said he would die before leaving. He mined his house with gunpowder, invited Austill in, and fled out the back door. Austill had been warned and was not in the house when the powder went off. After Owens was caught, he drew a gun on the soldiers, and one of them killed him. For those siding with Gayle, Owens became a martyr.[20]

The Fort Mitchell commander, Maj. James McIntosh, aware of the mob mentality, refused to surrender the soldiers to Russell County authorities. After an appeal to Jackson by the state's congressional delegation, Francis Scott Key, a skillful Washington lawyer as well as author of the "Star Spangled Banner," was sent by the president to Fort Mitchell to adjust the differences. Key also did not trust the higher county officials, but he persuaded McIntosh to agree to a bond giving officers responsibility for bringing to trial the soldiers who had been witnesses and the one who had fired the gun.[21] The issue began to cool further after it was announced that the survey would be completed by January of the following year, and after Lt. Col. J. J. Abert, the engineer supervising the survey, showed settlers in advance where the Indian reserves were. For his part, Key ordered that no Indian could sign away his land rights for less than $1.25 an acre. At Tuscaloosa he charmed the governor's wife (Sarah Haynesworth Gayle described him in her journal as a "man of much intelligence—a lawyer of high standing—a man of honor—a *poet* and a Christian) and attempted to calm Gayle.[22] The soldier who shot Owens did desert, as McIntosh had feared he would; but Gayle's feathers were still ruffled over the treatment in Washington, and he promoted resolutions, which were artfully tabled, denouncing removal of the settlers.[23]

The tensions reflected in the Hardeman Owens incident had flamed up also in the confrontation between soldiers and intruders of Irwinton, formerly the Creek village of Ola Ufala, and now the city of Eufaula. Whites drove off the Indians, burned their homes, and erected a village of log houses, which was incorporated as Irwinton in 1831. A federal marshal sent to evict the intruders in 1832 had to call for help from a detachment of Fort Mitchell troops. After the whites were forced out, their town, like the Creeks', was burned.[24]

The settlement of jurisdictional questions was cold comfort to the Creeks. With voluntary emigration already underway and removal by force imminent, hostilities escalated into what is called the Second Creek War, or the Creek War of 1836. In their last struggle, the Creeks attacked whites and the Indians and half-breeds who favored the treaty of 1832. The alarm among the whites resulted in the formation of the Columbus Guards in 1835. Whites were murdered, homes burned, and stages plundered; by 1836, about two thousand citizens from rural areas sought protection in Columbus.[25] Smaller, makeshift forts were also built where settlements had started after the 1832 treaty; the ruins of one may still be observed south of the railroad crossing of Cusseta, Alabama, northeast of Opelika. The U.S. Army was ordered into the section, and Gen. Thomas Jesup commanded both Alabama volunteers and more than 70 friendly Creeks under Jim Boy.

The pathos and terror of transition were recorded by Dr. Jacob Motte, an army surgeon from South Carolina, who described a "journey into wilderness" and a Federal Road more threatened with violence than it had been since Floyd's campaign in 1813–14. He arrived at Fort Mitchell on July 4, 1836, "a day of feasting and celebration throughout the Union," in time to see "the emigrating party of hostile Indians."

It was a melancholy spectacle as these proud monarchs of the soil were marched off from their native land to a distant country, which to their anticipations presented all the horrors of the infernal regions. There were several who committed suicide rather than endure the sorrow of leaving the spot where rested the bones of their ancestors. One old fellow was found hanging by the neck the night before he was to leave Fort Mitchell for the West, preferring the glorious uncertainty of another world to the inglorious misery of being forced to a country of which he knew nothing, but dreaded every thing bad.[26]

When his party got to Montgomery, one of the Indians escaped and found a knife too dull to cut his throat, but with both hands he "forced it into his chest over the breastbone, and by successive violent thrusts succeeded in dividing the main artery, when he bled to death."[27]

Dr. Motte was ordered to Tuskegee but stalled until he could travel with a military escort because "it would be running the risk of almost certain death to attempt the journey alone." Along the Federal Road, he observed the same destruction he had seen recently at Roanoke, in Stewart County, Georgia. In Alabama he saw "new made graves, where the murdered travelers had been hastily buried beside the road," and a road blocked in one spot by "half-burnt remains of stages and wagons that had been pillaged by the Indians."[28] The bones of men and horses from a similar attack in 1835 were pointed out to the Virginia lawyer James D. Davidson during his harrowing night ride into Columbus in 1836.[29] In one place Dr. Motte witnessed the sight of a Federal Road filled with coffins, scattered by Indians who had attacked the wagons sent out to bring in the dead for burial.[30]

At Creek Stand, Dr. Motte also met David Moniac, "the lieutenant of the escort," who introduced Motte to his father, Sam Manack, "a venerable old Indian." Until that moment, Motte had thought the officer was white. Motte then heard the romantic story of the West Point graduate's two lives, as an Indian who "ranged with native freedom over the woods and plains" and as an officer who showed "gratitude to the government which had fostered him in his youth."[31]

There were enough Creeks left for Motte to observe their ways and hear their speech, which he attempted to record and to form into a grammar. Ordered to join troops at the burned-out village of

Irwinton, he was not able to secure an escort; the fear of "straggling parties of hostile Indians" had caused the settlers to vacate the countryside, leaving Motte with only his "good steed" for a companion. He saw moccasin prints, but was never fired on; and he had the good fortune of coming upon a happy company of flatboatmen, most of them black, as soon as he reached the Chattahoochee. Since the vessel was in the service of the United States, the captain welcomed the army surgeon aboard, provided him with fish-and-bacon chowder served from a tub and coffee from a hand basin, and gave him his mosquito bar to sleep under. Motte made it in to Irwinton "without the occurrence of any further moving incidents by either flood or field."[32]

As Motte was writing, Indians were already on the "trail of tears," called, with accuracy, "one of the blackest stains upon American history,"[33] and a "betrayal of the five civilized tribes."[34] Although U.S. troops were present to assure the eventual removal of the Indians, contractors hired by the government have borne most of the blame for the atrocities. Many of the Creeks, particularly Lower Creeks, came from points east and south to Montgomery, where they were gawked at by the whites. After a brief stay, they went down the Alabama by steamboat and sailed into the Gulf of Mexico for New Orleans. Eventually they went up the Mississippi, or, if the water was high enough, up the Arkansas River to Little Rock, and by land to Fort Gibson. Some traveled overland to Muscle Shoals on the Tennessee River and then went most of the remaining way by steamboat; still others went overland by foot and wagon all the way to Memphis.[35] On every route, the toll in human life was heavy. The boats chartered by the contractors were described in a September 22, 1837, letter from one official as "rotten, old, and unseaworthy"; Indians were crowded aboard in "cabins offensive to every sense and feeling" and kept in a "state unfit for human beings." At Profit Island Bend in the Mississippi, the steamboat *Monmouth* sank, drowning 611 Indians, of which 311 were from Alabama. Four of the children of Jim Boy, who had led the friendly Creeks fighting with General Jesup, were among the victims.[36]

Creeks not departing of their own will or in chains had the option of joining the Seminoles in a war that was an extension of the outbreak of 1836. The fighting in Florida dragged on until 1842, increasingly remote from the Federal Road. On November 15, 1836, six days after he was promoted to major, David Moniac was killed at Wahoo Swamp, leading U.S. troops against Indians fighting under Osceola.[37] Another familiar figure from the Federal Road, Capt. William Walker, a company commander at Fort Decatur during the War of 1812, Big Warrior's son-in-law, keeper of the tavern at Pole Cat Springs for twenty years, and operator of a stage line between Montgomery and Columbus, died at Apalachicola, Florida, on October 20, 1836, while in command of a regiment of Creek warriors under General Jesup.[38] Edmund Pendleton Gaines, a captain at Fort Stoddert when the horse path was being surveyed in 1806, the officer in charge of investigating unreliable mail deliveries, and whose troops helped to maintain the Federal Road, was Major General Gaines, under the command of Gen. Winfield Scott, in the Second Seminole War.[39] Another familiar name from the earlier days is that of Matthew Arbuckle; the captain whose troops were "cutting a road to Georgia" in 1811 was the general who received the Indians when they arrived in Fort Gibson and Fort Scott in Arkansas, after their long ordeal.[40]

The war that continued in Florida was the Creeks' last protest over the invasion and the failure of the United States to uphold the spirit of the 1832 Treaty of Washington. The 1832 treaty also gave the Creeks the right to tribal self-government; in an understatement of duplicity, it did not "compel any Creek Indian to emigrate, but they shall be free to go or stay, as they please."[41] Whatever pleasures the Creeks might have derived from their limited independence in Alabama were weighed against the increasing conflicts with the swelling numbers of whites and their habit of exploitation. The Creeks were easy prey for the unscrupulous, especially since whiskey was available.[42] The climate for violence was created over the years by the whites' behavior toward the Indians generally, not simply in their perpetration of land frauds. When Lafayette's party came through in 1825, his secretary saw how an Indian desperate for whiskey was treated by a Federal Road merchant.

> The evening of our arrival at Line Creek, I went into a store to make some purchases, and whilst there, an Indian entered and asked for twelve and a half cents worth of whiskey. The owner of the shop re-

ceived the money, and told him to wait a moment, as the concourse of buyers was very great. The Indian waited patiently for a quarter of an hour, after which he demanded his whiskey. The trader appeared astonished, and told him if he wanted whiskey he must first pay him for it. "I gave you twelve and a half cents a few moments since," said the Indian. The poor wretch had scarcely pronounced these words, when the trader sprung forward, seized him by the ear, and assisted by one of his men, brutally turned him out of the shop. I saw him give the money, and was convinced of the honesty of the one and the rascality of the other. I felt strongly indignant and notwithstanding the delicacy of my situation, I would have stept forward to interfere, but the whole scene passed so rapidly that I hardly had time to say a few words. I went out to see what the Indian would do. I found him a few steps from the house, where he had been checked by his melancholy emotions. An instant afterwards, he crossed his arms on his breast, and hurried towards his own country with rapid strides. When he arrived on the margin of the stream, he plunged in and crossed it without appearing to perceive that the water reached above his knees. On attaining the other side, he stopped, turned around, and elevating his eyes toward heaven, he extended his hand towards the territory of the whites, in a menacing manner, and uttered some energetic exclamation in his own language. Doubtless, at that moment he invoked the vengeance of heaven on his oppressors, a vengeance that would have been just, but his prayer was in vain.[43]

Even after the Indian wars in the South were over, and the Creeks removed to Arkansas and Oklahoma, the legal debate over whether the Indians should be repaid for the myriad frauds perpetrated against them had not been settled. In 1933, the U.S. Court of Claims ruled on a case that had been filed in 1924. The report of the deliberations contains a restatement of the conditions that had brought on the final fighting and the removal a hundred years earlier. Game was disappearing, and the Creeks, despite Benjamin Hawkins's efforts, never became successful farmers; the extension of Alabama civil and criminal jurisdiction over the Indians made the chiefs powerless; and the Indians were surrounded by white settlers. The treaties drawn under these circumstances—compounded by the Indians' lack of basic understanding of the terms—resulted in the "most dastardly frauds by impersonation," the court conceded. Nevertheless, U.S. agents had visited each village and worked out a fair system of assigning "reservations," the allotments provided under the treaty, to the Indians. Those who did not have an attachment to a specific parcel or who had not improved a spot of land they might claim were called "floaters," and their properties had been assigned by lot. The court found that though "gross frauds" had been perpetrated against the Indians, agents had investigated the complaints from knowing chiefs and fraudulently procured sales contracts were canceled; new ones had been drawn, certified by the president and approved by him. The court also rested its decision against the Indians on an 1856 treaty in which the Creeks relinquished all claims, with minor exceptions, to lands east *or* west of the Mississippi.[44]

The names of Indians of the Creek Nation are still found in title searches conducted when ownership of land is changing hands or being contested. In March 1943, when examining a chain of title, a Tuskegee lawyer inquired about a parcel of land, questioning whether a patent was necessary from the government. He received a reply from the commissioner of the General Land Office of the U.S. Department of the Interior that stated in part: "Our records show that the above-described lands were reserved for a Creek Indian by the name of Ich-che-yo-ho-lo. However, our records do not show that a patent has ever been issued thereon." The commissioner cited an act of June 4, 1912, whereby the United States gave up all of its lands which had previously been set aside for the Creek Nation, to "those persons, estates, firms or corporations who would be the true and lawful owners of said lands under the laws of Alabama." A patent from the U.S. government was not required—and the rights of the states, argued for by Troup and Gayle, were finally confirmed in a federal statute.[45]

The departure of the Creeks removed the need for a single artery through the section from the Chattahoochee to Line Creek. Settlers were free to fan out across the Creek Nation and were no longer compelled to travel over the one road that provided the safety of numbers, forts, taverns, and an occasional military escort. This change alone would not have been a sufficient cause for the disappearance of the Federal Road, had not other factors also obtained. Why would a road, already established, slip back into the landscape, even though it remained a principal link between the Georgia capital and a succession of Alabama capitals, from the territorial center at St.

Stephens to Cahaba, Tuscaloosa, and finally Montgomery? Why would it not be built to the highest standards of nineteenth-century road construction and justify its name as a "federal" road? Why was only a minimal amount of money ever allocated to building and maintaining the road, despite its service to the Post Office Department, the War Department, and the general population? Obviously a grand plan set forth in 1808 by Albert Gallatin, Jefferson's secretary of the treasury, calling for a national system of roads and canals—and specifying in particular a road from Athens to Natchez—was never executed. Jealous competition for sparse funds and the conflict between states and federal rights worked together to prevent its enactment.[46]

A well-researched and closely reasoned opinion on the Federal Road in its physical and political setting is buried in a report of the Board of Internal Improvement to the secretary of war made on April 11, 1826, for transmittal to the Congress. The engineers charged with reconnaissance for a national road defined three possible routes from Washington to New Orleans: the *eastern* route, through Richmond, Raleigh, Columbia, Milledgeville, and across Alabama; the *middle* route, with two options—an upper section through Charlottesville, Lynchburg, Danville, Spartanburg, Athens, and Monticello, Georgia, and a lower section through Alexandria, Fredericksburg, Cumberland Court House, Greensboro, Salisbury, Charlotte, Lawrenceville, and Monticello; and the *western* route, through Fairfax Court House, Rockfish Gap, Lexington, Salem, Abingdon, Knoxville, Centreville, and Demopolis.[47] The eastern and middle routes could join near Montgomery. The delineations indicate that, through western Georgia and Alabama, the eastern route would run near or on the Federal Road, and the upper section of the middle route would intersect the horse path of 1806 at Athens. Although the eastern route had the advantage of linking capitals of five states, the engineers described difficulties that earlier road builders, soldiers, travelers, and settlers had learned by heart. The eastern route was shorter than the western, but it required almost a mile more of bridges than the middle; also, the middle route was shortest, and in its vicinity more materials for construction were available—particularly the stone to crush for macadam.[48]

The committee's report cataloged the requisites not easily met by the eastern route: a military road was needed—and the western route would be best because Tennessee and Kentucky, as inland states, could better reinforce the maritime states; a postal road was needed—and the middle route would be better than the eastern because of the availability of forage for horses; a trading road was needed—and the middle or western routes would contribute more than the eastern "to the development of internal commerce and industry." Although the report weighs the political advantages of the eastern route, the accumulated arguments tip the balance to the western and middle routes. Population growth along the eastern route was not as great in 1824 as it was along the middle and western; moreover, the report took note of the 1:1 ratio of whites to blacks along the eastern route, as opposed to a 3:2 ratio on the middle and a 2:1 ratio on the western. Obviously more votes were distributed along the middle and western routes. Conspicuously absent is direct mention of any threat posed by the Indians; the engineers did note in italics, however, that the *probable distance* from Milledgeville to New Orleans was 479 miles because "the country being thickly settled in the Territory occupied by the Indians, the board found it difficult to keep within the line."[49]

This Internal Improvement Report, filed in 1826, looked toward the time when Indians would not be a factor in deciding where to put a national road; but the other obstacles along the lower eastern route—the many watercourses and the soil too weak to bear heavy traffic—would remain persistent foes. The country had learned a lesson from the twenty years of struggles over, and on, the Federal Road—namely, that the costs for building and maintaining a passable thoroughfare would be high where the materials for roadbed construction were scarce and the demands for bridges and causeways great. Without great political pressures to create a better road through the lower South, the status quo prevailed; even as the issue was being considered, it appeared that those who were complaining about the ordeal of overland travel by horse- or footpower via the Federal Road would be delivered from their suffering by new means of transportation.

On paper the Chattahoochee and the Alabama rivers might have seemed from the outset more satisfactory options than the hazardous horse path, later the wider but no less difficult Federal Road. The downriver journeys to Apalachicola or Mobile by canoe, dugout, or flatboat were farther, slower, and equally dangerous, however, and the poling or paddling upriver against the current was more taxing than fording streams or slogging through swamps. The movement of humans and freight, even south, was easier over the Federal Road, until the steamboats appeared.

The Federal Road had been in use for a decade when the first regular steamboat to reach Montgomery, the *Harriet*, arrived on October 23, 1821, in seven days from Mobile. The *Cotton Plant* arrived the next year, followed in 1824 by the *Osage, Elizabeth, Henderson, Arkansas,* and *Columbus.*[50] Although steamboat travel offered its own menu of disasters—explosions, fires, groundings, snaggings, and collisions—it was preferred by most travelers, as the various narratives indicate. The head of navigation on the Alabama was at Wetumpka, but Montgomery, only a few miles downstream, was near the Federal Road, which became a feeder line, increasing traffic and the growth of the city.[51] The road was also a factor in the development of Columbus, since it crossed the Chattahoochee at the falls, the head of navigation. The first steamboat to reach Columbus was the *Steubenville,* which arrived on February 22, 1828, followed in 1830 by the *Baltimore* and the *Georgian,* and in 1831 by *Herald, Plaquemine, Marion,* and *Jenkins.*[52]

For those who could afford it, steamboats also provided the additional option of no overland travel. In the 1830s, ocean passage might be taken between Charleston and Mobile; with the advent of railroads, a combination of transportation could take a traveler across the lower South entirely by steam power. In 1840, the Brunswick and Florida line advertised travel from Charleston to Brunswick, Georgia, by steamboat; by railroad to St. Marks, Florida; and from there by steamboat through the inner passage to Mobile, a circumnavigation of the Federal Road.[53] By the 1850s, as the economy improved and the traffic increased, the competition in transportation was between steamboats and railroads.[54]

The presence of steamboats gave new energy to long-standing arguments in favor of canals as the best means of internal communications and travel. In many parts of the United States, canals were an attractive option. Even in the South, federal money assisted in the construction of the Dismal Swamp Canal and the Carondelet Canal at

New Orleans—and a canal between the Tennessee River and the Tombigbee-Mobile system, not to be realized until late in the twentieth century, was also discussed. Although canals were not a precise alternative to roads and could not replace such an artery as the Federal Road, they competed well for the national dollar. Their major rival was not the Alabama-Georgia road but such major national highways as the Cumberland Road, which ran from the head of navigation on the Potomac, across Maryland, present-day West Virginia, and Pennsylvania to the Ohio River.[55]

The coming of the railroads ensured the demise of the Federal Road. With the opening of lands in the Creek Nation, the eyes of the railway men in Montgomery turned eastward. On January 20, 1832, four months before the treaty of final cession was signed in Washington, the Montgomery Railroad Company was chartered; it was rechartered two years later, and in 1841–43, it was reorganized.[56] The assets were purchased by Charles T. Pollard and eight other men, and on February 13, 1843, it was incorporated as the Montgomery and West Point Railroad Company, with Pollard as president.[57] The direction of the rail laying was west-to-east, unusual in America, and the progress was slow. By 1840, the first twelve miles east of Montgomery had been completed, and by 1847, the road had been opened for forty-nine miles to Notasulga. Rail traffic reached West Point, Georgia, by April 1851.[58] In that year a joint timetable issued by the Montgomery and West Point Railroad and the Lagrange Railroad offered a schedule by rail from Montgomery to West Point, by four-horse stagecoach from West Point to Palmetto, and thence by rail to Atlanta for connection with Georgia Railroad, the Macon & Western Railroad, and the Western & Atlantic Railroad.[59] This route went north of the Federal Road and took travelers to a part of the state that was growing and to a city that in 1868 would become the state capital. The imperfections of journeying "on the cars" inspired briefer, less eloquent complaints than the jeremiads of Federal Road travelers. For example, Daniel R. Hundley complained about a red-hot stove, and Sir Charles Lyell, accustomed to superior British trains, could not understand why Americans were satisfied with speeds of only fourteen to sixteen miles per hour.[60] George Featherstonhaugh, the British writer who had nothing good to say about travel over the Federal Road by "private conveyance," complained about the foul language used by the passengers and said that white, yellow, and black passengers were "indiscriminately packed together."[61] These criticisms were merely carpings, however; no matter how inconvenient rail travel might have been, it was preferable.

National economic issues related to trade and travel reduced travel on the Federal Road. On July 10, 1832, President Jackson vetoed the bill to recharter the Bank of United States, which was to expire in 1836. Federal money was deposited in state banks, called "pet banks" by Jackson's critics.[62] By 1835–36, speculation in land was rampant, with land sales on credit and real estate values both escalating rapidly. Bank notes were discounted, and on July 11, 1836, Jackson prohibited payment for public lands in anything but hard currency, which was in short supply.[63] In this Panic of 1837, many who had purchased land on credit lost it or settled for a reduced acreage. The demand for Alabama land was considerably reduced, and the flow of settlers down the Federal Road decreased. Emigration from eastern and tidewater lands declined for another reason as well. Due to the efforts of Edmund Ruffin, writing in the *Farmer's Register*, and others who promoted scientific farming, soils considered worn out in Virginia and the Carolinas were being improved. The renewed fertility in the years between 1820 and 1850 made the land values in tidewater Virginia alone increase by millions of dollars.[64]

Finally, the telegraph key tapped out the epitaph for the Federal Road. In 1845, one year after Samuel F. B. Morse had sent a message from Washington to Baltimore over a wire, the *Columbus Times* reported: "Space is annihilated as to the transmission of mind, almost as to matter, by the Telegraph and Steam."[65] In 1847, the Georgia city granted to the telegraph company the right to erect poles and extend its line through the city, to cross streets and commons, and to attach wires to the river bridges.[66] The "Wire Road" through Columbus was located on the Upper Federal Road, which had opened in 1833. West of Columbus it followed the Upper Federal Road to its junction with the Lower Federal Road beyond Tuskegee and from there on to Montgomery.[67] On July 18, 1848, the Montgomery-to-Macon connection to the New Orleans Telegraph line was completed.[68] It extended from Girard (formerly Sodom, now Phenix City) through Montgomery to Cahaba along the Wire Road and thence to Mobile, approximately along the railroad route. By the early 1850s, telegraph lines under private company ownership for public patronage had been extended to principal towns of the Black Belt.[69] The development of the telegraph system relieved much of the pressure for fast military and governmental communications and reduced the role of the Federal Road as a postal route through the lower South to New Orleans.

These economic factors, together with the development of faster, safer, and more reliable alternatives, and eventually the construction of a network of county, state, and U.S. highways, contributed to the demise of the Federal Road. Though it did not disappear overnight, most of the road was gone before the twentieth century demanded highways suitable for automobiles. When those roads were built, better and straighter routes and new methods of construction were possible.

Today the Federal Road is a shadowy presence, a wraith that runs beside farm-to-market roads, old U.S. highways, and its latest descendant, the interstate highway system. Several segments overlap current roads. One four-mile, unpaved stretch, still declared a public road on Macon County maps, on the ridge between Warriorstand and Fort Hull, has the appearance of the earlier Federal Road; it turns east off U.S. 29, just north of Davisville between Tuskegee and Union Springs. The banks of that section are recessed, as Lyell described them in his 1846 visit, and the road retains the look described by travelers of the 1820s and 1830s. An existing unpaved county road from Russell County 51 west to Boromville and Creek Stand nearly coincides with the Federal Road, and the old roadway itself may still be observed. The fort sites, for the most part, remain unrecognized. Fort Mitchell has been given permanent notice with the location of a national cemetery adjacent to the site in 1987, and Fort Deposit has kept its status as a post office and a town. Archaeologists will have to determine the precise location of Sand Fort in Russell County, where innkeeper Royston was besieged by Indians in 1836 and forced to make his bread from whiskey.[70]

Except for occasional notations on county maps, most of the stands are gone, too. An explorer with Macon and Russell county maps may find Creek Stand and Warriorstand and might determine the approximate location of Fort Bainbridge. Lucas Tavern, where Lafayette stayed on April 2, 1825, has been moved from its location just west of Line Creek and is handsomely restored as part of Old Alabama Town, the Landmarks Foundation project in Montgomery. The streams that imperiled the pioneers are now passed in a twinkling by travelers of Interstate 85 and 65. Line Creek, between Montgomery and Macon counties, is marked on Interstate 85, but Milly's Creek, that small stream beyond which travelers could take their turn for Fort Stoddert or St. Stephens, is crossed on a bridge too short to notice. Farther south the Federal Road forms the boundary between Conecuh and Monroe counties. The ferry from Fort Mims to Fort Stoddert has been replaced by twin, dual-lane bridges more than seven miles long, which alone cost the government more than $120 million— more than 20,000 times the original 1806 appropriation of $6,400 for opening the horse path all the way from Athens, Georgia, to the Pearl River, and about 2,500 times the $48,295 appropriated for the road during its entire history.[71] Over most of its route, the Federal Road has been reclaimed by nature, by subsequent growths of trees— though the majestic chestnuts are gone—and by a tenacious twentieth-century settler, kudzu, which in summer spreads a green blanket over the erosion of sandy soils started by the iron rims of the wagon wheels.

It will remain for archaeologists and historians, amateur and professional, to discover more about the road that is considered by many the most important in the history of Alabama. That it opened the section with a postal horse path, that it allowed military transport to protect New Orleans and the new Sabine River border, that it caused the Creek War of 1813–14 and helped win the War of 1812–15 against the British, and that it permitted tens of thousands of people from the Atlantic seaboard to come into the Old Southwest and settle in undeveloped territory must all be taken into account by way of eulogy. It would be an understatement to say that the region the horse path entered in 1806 differed from the section in which the Federal Road began to disappear in 1836. The Mississippi Territory had become two states; nationalism in the South was fading, and sectionalism had become an issue; the controversy over slavery was warming and would result in war twenty-five years later; and the state of Alabama was poised to become part of a solidifying South.

Absent from this section as a physical threat, much less a political force, were the Creeks, almost all of whom had died, fled to the Seminoles, or joined the surviving remnant in the West. From its inception, the Federal Road had spelled out their fate, and they, ironically, by their hostilities kept it defined and required that it be reinforced. When the power of the Creek Nation was broken in 1836, it was logical and inevitable that alternative routes would develop and that, in the Old Southwest, the Creek Indians and the Federal Road would become ghosts together, yoked in history, leaving the land to new stewards, moving over other roads.

NOTES

INTRODUCTION: *"But for the Federal Road..."*

1. Peter A. Brannon, "The Federal Road—Alabama's First Improved Highway," *Alabama Highways* 1 (April 1927): 7.

2. Peter Joseph Hamilton, "Early Roads of Alabama," *Transactions of the Alabama Historical Society* 2 (1897–98): 50.

3. Thomas Jefferson, *The Works of Thomas Jefferson*, ed. Paul Leicester Ford, Federal Edition, 12 vols. (New York: G. P. Putnam's Sons, 1905), 10:37.

1: THE NATIONAL PERSPECTIVE

1. Jefferson, *Works*, 8:226.

2. Ibid., 12:470–75.

3. Maurice Matloff, ed., *American Military History* (Washington, D.C.: Government Printing Office, 1969), p. 117.

4. Dumas Malone, *Jefferson and His Time: Jefferson the President, First Term, 1801–1805*, 6 vols. (Boston: Little, Brown, 1970), 4:331.

5. *Louisiana Purchase: An Exhibition* (New Orleans: The Cabildo, 1953), p. 42.

6. Cited in ibid., p. 43.

7. Malone, *Jefferson, First Term*, 4:133.

8. Quoted in William Elijius Martin, *Internal Improvements in Alabama* (Baltimore: Lord Baltimore Press, 1902), pp. 15–16.

9. Malone, *Jefferson, First Term*, 4:94.

10. *Annals of Congress*, 8th Cong., 1st sess., House of Representatives, November 2, 1803, p. 555. "Mitchill" was sometimes spelled "Mitchell."

11. *Secretary of War Letter Book H*, p. 395, cited in Merritt Bloodworth Pound, *Benjamin Hawkins: Indian Agent* (Athens: University of Georgia Press, 1951), p. 207.

12. Ibid.

13. Albert James Pickett, *History of Alabama, and Incidentally of Georgia and Mississippi from the Earliest Period* (1851; reprint, Birmingham: Webb Book, 1900), pp. 26–47; R. Reid Badger and Lawrence A. Clayton, eds., *Alabama and the Borderlands: From Prehistory to Statehood* (University: University of Alabama Press, 1985), pp. 96–127.

14. Mark E. Fretwell, *This So Remote Frontier: The Chattahoochee Country of Alabama and Georgia* (Eufaula, Ala.: Historic Chattahoochee Commission, 1980), pp. 119, 122, 143, 147; Pickett, *History of Alabama*, p. 426; James Leitch Wright, Jr., *Anglo-Spanish Rivalry in North America* (Athens: University of Georgia Press, 1971), pp. 70, 79; John McKay Sheftall, "Ogeechee Old Town: A Georgia Plantation, 1540–1860," *Richmond County History* (Georgia) 14 (Summer 1982): 27–28.

15. "Captain Fitch's Journey to the Creeks, 1725," in *Travels in the American Colonies*, ed. Newton D. Mereness, National Society of Colonial Dames in America (New York: Antiquarian Press, 1961), pp. 173–212.

16. Pickett, *History of Alabama*, p. 262.

17. "A Ranger's Report of Travels with General Oglethorpe in Georgia and Florida, 1739–1742," in *Travels in the American Colonies*, pp. 213–36.

18. "Journal of David Taitt's Travels from Pensacola, West Florida, to and through the Country of the Upper and Lower Creek, 1772," in *Travels in the American Colonies*, p. 493.

19. Ibid., pp. 491–565; John Richard Alden, *John Stuart and the Southern Colonial Frontier* (New York: Gordian Press, 1966), p. 297.

20. William Bartram, *Travels through North and South Carolina, Georgia, East and West Florida, the Cherokee Country, the Extensive Territories of the Muscogulges or Creek Confederacy, and the Country of the Chactaws* (Philadelphia: James & Johnson, 1791), pp. 379–401; Francis Harper, *The Travels of William Bartram*, naturalist's ed. (New Haven: Yale University Press, 1958), pp. 240–55, 396–405; "Extracts from the Travels of William Bartram," *Alabama Historical Quarterly* 17 (Fall 1955): 110–24.

21. Pickett, *History of Alabama*, pp. 352–55; Peter A. Brannon, "The Coosa River Crossing of British Refugees, 1781," *Alabama Historical Quarterly* 19 (Spring 1957): 149–55.

22. U.S. Congress, Senate, *Biographical Dictionary of the American Congress, 1774–1971*, 92d Cong., 1st sess., Senate Doc. 92-8 (Washington, D.C.: Government Printing Office, 1971), p. 1090 (hereinafter cited as *Biographical Dictionary*); Pound, *Benjamin Hawkins*, pp. 4, 65, 99, 249; Absalom H. Chappell, *Miscellanies of Georgia: Historical, Biographical, Descriptive* (1874; reprint, Columbus, Ga.: Gilbert Printing, 1928), pp. 59–73; Benjamin Hawkins, *A Combination of a Sketch of the Creek Country in the Years 1798 and 1799 (1848) and Letters of Benjamin Hawkins 1796–1806 (1916)* (Spartanburg, S.C.: Reprint Company, 1974), pp. 22–27, 34–90.

23. Clarence Edwin Carter, ed., *The Territorial Papers of the United States*, 26 vols. (Washington, D.C.: Government Printing Office, 1934–52), 5:306–7.

24. U.S. Congress, *American State Papers, Post Office Department* (Washington, D.C.: Gales & Seaton, 1834), pp. 35–36 (hereinafter cited as *ASP, PO*).

25. Ibid., p. 36.

26. Carter, *Territorial Papers*, 5:518–19.

27. *ASP, PO*, p. 36. Oche Haujo was a half-breed known to the colonists as Alexander Cornells and frequently used as an interpreter. See Benjamin Hawkins, "A Sketch of the Creek Country in the Years 1798 and 1799," in *Collections of the Georgia Historical Society*, vol. 3, pt. 1 (New York: William Van Woodson, 1948), p. 29.

28. *ASP, PO*, p. 36.

29. Ibid., pp. 35–38.

30. U.S. Congress, *American State Papers, Claims* (Washington, D.C.: Gales & Seaton, 1834), 10th Cong., 1st sess., March 18, 1808, no. 192, p. 362; U.S. Congress, Senate, *Report of the Committee of Claims*, 15th Cong., 1st sess., Senate Report no. 78, Senate, April 14, 1818, p. 367, and House, April 13, 1818, p. 1739. Briggs's trip, survey, and compensation also are mentioned in Randle Bond Truett, *Trade and Travel around the Southern Appalachians before 1830* (Chapel Hill: University of North Carolina Press, 1935), pp. 52–61.

31. U.S. Congress, *The Public Statutes at Large*, 8 vols. (Boston: Little, Brown, 1856), 2:337–38 (hereinafter cited as *Statutes at Large*); *Raleigh Register and North Carolina State Gazette*, April 22, 1805, p. 1.

32. U.S. Congress, House, *Inaugural Addresses of the Presidents of the United States, from George Washington, 1789, to Richard Milhous Nixon, 1969*, 91 Cong., 1st sess., House Doc. 91-142, vol. 3-3 (Washington, D.C.: Government Printing Office, 1969), p. 18.

33. William Charles Cole Claiborne, *Official Letter Book of W. C. C. Claiborne, 1801–1816*, ed. Dunbar Rowland, 6 vols. (Jackson, Miss.: State Department of Archives and History, 1917), 3:38, 83, 97.

34. Ibid., pp. 114–15, 125–26.

35. Ibid., pp. 203, 217.

36. Julian P. Bretz, "Early Land Communication with the Lower Mississippi Valley," *Mississippi Valley Historical Review* 13 (June 1926): 12.

37. Carter, *Territorial Papers*, 5:396.

38. *Annals of Congress*, 9th Cong., 1st sess., Public Acts of Congress, Appendix, pp. 1295–96.

39. *ASP, PO*, pp. 225–26, 338. Congressman Pearce represented Rhode Island from 1825 to 1837 (*Biographical Dictionary*, p. 1521).

40. Carter, *Territorial Papers*, 5:396; Leonard V. Huber and Clarence A. Wagner, *The Great Mail: A Postal History of New Orleans* (State College, Pa.: American Philatelic Society, 1949), pp. 11, 27.

41. *Statutes at Large*, 7:96–98.

42. William S. Coker and Thomas D. Watson, *Indian Traders of The Southeastern Spanish Borderlands: Panton, Leslie & Company and John Forbes & Company, 1783–1847* (Gainesville: University Presses of Florida; Pensacola: University of West Florida Press, 1986), pp. 255–66. In 1812–14, Forbes & Company was paid $21,916 for debts to the Upper Creeks; in 1805–9, the company was paid $41,787 to settle the Choctaws' debt.

43. *ASP, PO*, pp. 39–40.

44. *Statutes at Large*, 2:396–97. At that time, the western frontier of Georgia was the Ocmulgee River. This act was passed less than a month after the passage of the Act for the Cumberland Road, March 29, 1806 (ibid., p. 357).

45. *ASP, PO*, pp. 39–40.

2: Stayed Couriers

1. *Letter Book*, Postmaster General Granger to David Thomas, November 30, 1803; cited in Bretz, "Land Communication," p. 9.

2. Carter, *Territorial Papers*, 5:459.

3. Ibid., pp. 470–71.

4. *Secretary of War Letter Book H*, page 395; cited in Pound, *Benjamin Hawkins*, p. 207.

5. Carter, *Territorial Papers*, 5:470–71.

6. Ibid., pp. 474, 475.

7. "Bloomfields's Description of Road, Coweta to Tombeckby," Wheaton Papers, MS-1124, University of Georgia Libraries, Athens, Georgia (hereinafter cited as Wheaton Papers).

8. Carter, *Territorial Papers*, 5:497; *ASP, PO*, p. 20.

9. Wheaton Papers.

10. Carter, *Territorial Papers*, 5:476.

11. Ibid., p. 478.

12. Report of Gideon Granger, postmaster general, dated March 20, 1806, to the House of Representatives, 9th Cong., 1st sess., in *ASP, PO*, pp. 39–40; General Post Office Account with Joseph Wheaton, contractor, for opening the road between Appalatchy, Ga., Athens, Ga., and Fort Stoddert, no. 4, Wheaton Papers.

13. Joseph Wheaton to Gideon Granger, postmaster general, November 28, 1806, no. 2, Wheaton Papers.

14. Ibid. The remainder of the account of Wheaton's difficulties is from this source.

15. Carter, *Territorial Papers*, 9:690.

16. Granger to Wheaton, January 20, 1807, Wheaton Papers.

17. Edmund P. Gaines, Fort Stoddert, to Granger, February 12, 1807, no. 8, Wheaton Papers.

18. H. R. Graham, Ocmulgee Old Fields [now East Macon], Georgia, to Granger, March 20, 1807, no. 9, Wheaton Papers.

19. John Francis Hamtramck Claiborne, *Mississippi as a Province, Territory, and State* (Jackson, Miss.: Power & Barksdale, 1880; reprint, Baton Rouge: Louisiana State University Press, 1964), pp. 264–71; *Mississippi Provincial Archives*, vol. 3, *French Dominion, 1704–1743*, ed. Dunbar Rowland and Albert Godfrey Sanders (Jackson: Press of the Mississippi Department of Archives and History, 1932), p. 515. Accounts of the establishment of the garrison vary from 1714 to 1716.

20. W. C. C. Claiborne, *Official Letter Book*, 4:17–20; J. F. H. Claiborne, *Mississippi*, pp. 266–71. An earlier attempt on Spanish territory resulting in a failure was the Blount Conspiracy, led by William Blount, senator from Tennessee. See Pound, *Benjamin Hawkins*, pp. 126–29; Wright, *Anglo-Spanish Rivalry*, pp. 156–58; and *Biographical Dictionary*, p. 605.

21. Pickett, *History of Alabama*, pp. 488–90; Lucille Griffith, *Alabama: A Documentary History to 1900*, rev. ed. (University: University of Alabama Press, 1972), pp. 62–63; and J. F. H. Claiborne, *Mississippi*, pp. 271–89.

22. Pickett, *History of Alabama*, pp. 490–500.

23. *Letter Book*, Postmaster General Granger to J. B. Varnum, February 5, 1807, cited in Bretz, "Land Communication," p. 15.

24. Ibid.; Granger to Josiah Meigs, February 11, 1807. Meigs (1757–1822), son of Return Meigs, was president of the University of Georgia from 1801 to 1810. In 1814, he became commissioner of the General Land Office of the United States at Washington, D.C., serving in that capacity until 1818. He was brother of Col. Return Jonathan Meigs (1740–1823), U.S. Army officer, not to be confused with the latter's son, Return Jonathan Meigs, Jr. (1764–1824), senator and, from 1814 to 1823, U.S. postmaster general. See Kenneth Coleman and Charles Stephen Gurr, eds., *Dictionary of Georgia Biography*, 2 vols. (Athens: University of Georgia Press, 1983), 2:702–4; *Who Was Who in America, Historical Volume, 1607–1896* (Chicago: Marquis–Who's Who, 1963), p. 353.

25. Carter, *Territorial Papers*, 5:511–17, 518–20.

26. Joseph Wheaton, contractor, in account with the General Post Office, no. 4, Wheaton Papers.

27. Granger to Swan and Van Ness, July 9, 1808, no. 1, Wheaton Papers.

28. Alden Lewis, Athens, Georgia, to Granger, January 17, 1807, no. 16, Wheaton Papers.

29. S. P. Bloomfield to Abraham Bradley, jun., assistant postmaster general, Washington City, May 31, 1807, no. 22, Wheaton Papers.

30. Bretz, "Land Communication," p. 15.

3: THE WAR ROAD

1. Matloff, *American Military History*, p. 121; Dumas Malone, ed., *Dictionary of American Biography*, 22 vols. (New York: Charles Scribner's Sons, 1928–58), 20:222–26.

2. James Madison, *The Writings of James Madison*, ed. Gaillard Hunt, 9 vols. (New York: G. P. Putnam's Sons, 1900–1910), 8:49.

3. Carter, *Territorial Papers*, 6:76–77; John K. Mahon, *The War of 1812* (Gainesville: University of Florida Press, 1972), pp. 192–95; and David B. Warden, *Statistical, Political, and Historical Account of the United States of North America; from the Period of Their First Colonization to the Present Day*, 3 vols. (Edinburgh: Archibald Constable, 1819), 3:40–41.

4. John R. Swanton, *Early History of the Creek Indians and Their Neighbors*, Smithsonian Institute, Bureau of American Ethnology, Bulletin 73 (Washington, D.C.: Government Printing Office, 1922), plate 7.

5. Office of Chief of Engineers, Field Survey Records, 1793–1916, no. 37-4-7, Record Group 77, National Archives, Washington, D.C.; MFS-791, Samford University Library, Birmingham.

6. Ibid., p. 102.

7. Warden, 3:41–42.

8. Office of the Secretary of War, Record Group 107, no. 37-4-7.

9. Records of U.S. Army Commands, 1784–1821, Second U.S. Infantry, Register of Discharges, Deaths, and Desertions, List of Officers, and Descriptive Rolls of Companies, 1811–14, vol. 103/52, pp. 1, 4, 6, Record Group 98, National Archives, Washington, D.C.: MFS-791, Samford University Library, Birmingham.

10. Pickett, *History of Alabama*, p. 510; Timothy Horton Ball, *A Glance into the Great South-East; or, Clarke County, Alabama, from 1540 to 1877* (Chicago: Knight & Leonard, 1882; reprint, Tuscaloosa, Ala.: Willo Publishing, 1962), p. 134; Brannon, "Federal Road," p. 8; Anne Kendrick Walker, *Russell County in Retrospect: An Epic of the Far Southeast* (Richmond, Va.: Dietz Press, 1950), p. 139; Margaret Laney Whitehead and Barbara Bogart, *City of Progress: A History of Columbus, Georgia, 1828–1978* (Columbus: Georgia Office Supply, 1979), p. 85; Annie Crook Waters, *History of Escambia County, Alabama* (Huntsville, Ala.: Strode Publishers, 1983), p. 25.

11. Carter, *Territorial Papers*, 6:213–14.

12. Ibid., 5:461–63.

13. Ibid., 6:213–14.

14. Pound, *Benjamin Hawkins*, p. 210; H. Niles, ed., *Weekly Register*, October 19, 1811, p. 120; and January 18, 1812, p. 376.

15. Peter Joseph Hamilton, *Colonial Mobile: An Historical Study Largely from Original Sources of the Alabama-Tombigbee Basin, from the Discovery*

of Mobile Bay in 1519 until the Demolition of Fort Charlotte in 1821 (New York: Houghton Mifflin, 1897), pp. 354–55.

16. Arbuckle became a brevet brigadier general and built military roads near Fort Smith, Arkansas, where he died June 11, 1851; Ware became a captain and was honorably discharged June 15, 1815; Bogardus became a captain, assistant deputy quartermaster general at Mobile, and died December 23, 1814; Gaines became a brevet major general, was active in the Second Seminole War, and died in New Orleans June 6, 1849; Lawrence became a colonel, was cited for gallantry in the defense of Fort Bowyer, and died January 7, 1841; and Covington became a brigadier general and died November 14, 1813, from wounds received in the Battle of Chrystlers Field. See Francis B. Heitman, *Historical Register and Dictionary of the United States Army*, 2 vols. (Washington, D.C.: Government Printing Office, 1903), 1:168, 227, 442, 619, 646, 1002. No connection between Capt. John Roger Nelson Luckett, Second U.S. Infantry, and the Luckett family of Maryland has been found. See Harry Wright Newman, *The Lucketts of Portobacco* (Washington, D.C.: By the author, 1938), p. 22.

17. Carter, *Territorial Papers*, 5:187.

18. *Statutes of the Mississippi Territory* (Natchez, Miss.: Peter Isler, 1816), pp. 292–94; *Acts of Alabama, Passed at the First Session of the First General Assembly of the Alabama Territory; in the Forty-Second Year of American Independence*, approved February 4, 1818 (St. Stephens, Alabama Territory: Thomas Eastin, 1818; reprint, Washington, D.C.: T. L. Cole, 1912), pp. 4–6; W. E. Martin, *Internal Improvements*, p. 29.

19. This view of the Federal Road as a cause of the war is also advanced by Reginald Horsman in *Expansion and American Indian Policy, 1812–1813* (East Lansing: Michigan State University Press, 1967), pp. 163–64, as discussed in Frank Lawrence Owsley, Jr., *Struggle for the Gulf Borderlands: The Creek War and the Battle of New Orleans, 1812–1815* (Gainesville: University Presses of Florida, 1981), p. 11; by Charles H. Fairbanks and John H. Goff, *Cherokee and Creek Indians* (New York: Garland Publishing, 1974), pp. 168–69; and by Ball, *Clarke County*, p. 134.

20. Owsley, *Struggle for the Borderlands*, p. 12.

21. Pound, *Benjamin Hawkins*, p. 210.

22. Coker and Watson, *Indian Traders*, p. 250.

23. Huber and Wagner, *Great Mail*, p. 32; Carter, *Territorial Papers*, 6:390–91, citing letters from Judge Toulmin to F. L. Claiborne, July 2, 9, 31, and August 12, 1813, in Claiborne Papers, Mississippi Department of Archives and History.

24. Summaries of the major actions of the Creek War of 1813–14 are drawn from H. S. Halbert and T. H. Ball, *The Creek War of 1813 and 1814* (1895; reprint, ed. Frank L. Owsley, Jr., Southern Historical Publications no. 15, University: University of Alabama Press, 1969), p. 38; James Nelson Bloodworth, "Alexander McGillivray—Emperor of the Creeks," *Alabama Lawyer* 37 (July

1976): 314; James W. Holland, "Andrew Jackson and the Creek War: Victory at the Horseshoe," *Alabama Review* 21 (October 1968): 243–75; Frank L. Owsley, Jr., "The Fort Mims Massacre," *Alabama Review* 24 (July 1971): 192–204; Owsley, *Struggle for the Borderlands*, pp. 30–94; and Alexander Beaufort Meek, *Romantic Passages in Southwest History: Including Orations, Sketches, and Essays*, 2d ed. (Mobile: S. H. Goetzel, 1857), pp. 235–58.

25. John W. Cottier and Gregory A. Waselkov, "The First Creek War: Twilight of Annihilation," in *Clearings in the Thicket: An Alabama Humanities Reader*, ed. Jerry Elijah Brown (Macon, Ga.: Mercer University Press, 1985), p. 29.

26. The historical consensus is that the leap is fact, not legend. For accounts of the battle and reports of the leap, see Benjamin W. Griffith, Jr., *McIntosh and Weatherford, Creek Indian Leaders* (Tuscaloosa: University of Alabama Press, 1988), pp. 129–31.

27. Letter from Big Warrior, William McIntosh, Little Prince, and Alexander Cornells, Coweta, November 18, 1813, to General Floyd, Floyd Papers, Georgia Department of Archives and History, Atlanta.

28. "Historic Sites in Alabama," *Alabama Historical Quarterly* 15 (Spring 1953): 44; Pickett, *History of Alabama*, p. 586; Andrew Jackson, *Correspondence of Andrew Jackson*, ed. John Spencer Bassett, 7 vols. (Washington, D.C.: W. F. Roberts, 1926–35), 1:399, 457–59, 467, 470–71, 502–3; 2:23; Peter A. Brannon, "Macon County, Present Day Place Names Suggesting Aboriginal Influence," *Arrow Points* 5 (July 1922): 7; Brannon, "Fort Hull of 1814: A Record of a Pioneer Post Established in the Present Macon County," *Arrow Points* 14 (March 1929): 6–11; Fort Hull, File 207, Military Section, Alabama Department of Archives and History, Montgomery.

29. Peter A. Brannon, "Fort Bainbridge," *Arrow Points* 5 (August 1922): 26; Adam Hodgson, *Letters from North America*, 2 vols. (London: Hurst, Robinson; and Edinburgh: A. Constable, 1824), 1:128; Pound, *Benjamin Hawkins*, pp. 90–118, 228; Jackson, *Correspondence*, 1:501.

30. Floyd to Jackson, Fort Mitchell, December 18, 1813, Jackson, *Correspondence*, 1:399; David W. Chase, *Fort Mitchell: An Archaeological Exploration in Russell County, Alabama*, Special Publications of the Alabama Archaeological Society no. 1 (Moundville, Ala., 1974), pp. 3–4; Floyd Papers, Georgia Department of Archives and History, Atlanta; Benson John Lossing, *The Pictorial Field Book of the War of 1812* (New York: Harper & Brothers, 1869), pp. 768–69, 776–77; Joel Crawford III Papers, Georgia Department of Archives and History, Atlanta.

31. James A. Tait, "Journal of James A. Tait for the Year 1813," annotated by Peter A. Brannon, *Georgia Historical Quarterly* 8 (September 1924), 237–38.

32. Owsley, *Struggle for the Borderlands*, p. 81.

33. Ibid., pp. 87–88; John K. Mahon, *History of the Second Seminole War, 1835–1842* (Gainesville: University of Florida Press, 1967), p. 7; Matloff, *Amer-*

ican Military History, p. 146; Wilburt S. Brown, *The Amphibious Campaign for West Florida and Louisiana, 1814–1815: A Critical Review of Strategy and Tactics at New Orleans* (University: University of Alabama Press, 1969), pp. 161, 166, 168.

4: "Almost Impassable"

1. John H. Goff, "Excursion along an Old Way to the West," *Georgia Review* 6 (Summer 1952): 193–95.

2. U.S. Department of Agriculture, Bureau of Soils, *Soil Map: Alabama, Russell County Sheet* (New York: Snyder & Black, 1913), 32″ × 28″, scale 1 inch = 1 mile.

3. Charles Lyell, *A Second Visit to the United States of North America*, 2 vols. (New York: Harper & Brothers, 1849), 2:36–38.

4. U.S. Congress, *American State Papers, Miscellaneous*, 2 vols. (Washington, D.C.: Gales & Seaton, 1834), 2:273 (hereinafter cited as *ASP, Misc*).

5. Secretary of War to Jackson, September 24, 1816, Secretary of War, Letters Sent, Roll 9, p. 148, cited in Tommy R. Young, "The United States Army in the South, 1789–1835" (Ph.D. diss., Louisiana State University, 1973), p. 251.

6. U.S. Congress, *American State Papers, Military Affairs*, 7 vols. (Washington, D.C.: Gales & Seaton, 1834), 4:627.

7. Young, "United States Army," p. 251.

8. *ASP, Misc.*, 2:466–67. See chapter 6 for a longer discussion of Crawford's role in regional politics.

9. Carter, *Territorial Papers*, 18:43–45. Mitchell retired as agent for the Creek Nation in 1821.

10. Ibid., pp. 374–415.

11. Ibid.

12. Ibid., pp. 186, 287, 316–17.

13. Ibid., pp. 397–406.

14. Ibid., pp. 424–25.

15. Judge Harry Toulmin, Fort Stoddert, May 25, 1818, to John C. Calhoun, secretary of war, copy, Historic Chattahoochee Commission, Eufaula, Alabama.

16. Carter, *Territorial Papers*, 18:470, 485. See also pp. 106, 178–79, 316–17, 397, 406, 415–16, 424–25, and 442.

17. *Statutes of the Mississippi Territory*, pp. 294–95.

18. *Acts of Alabama*, pp. 4–5. Such laws remained in effect into the twentieth century, until state highway departments were formed and much of the manual labor was done by convicts.

19. *ASP, PO*, pp. 119–20.

20. W. E. Martin, *Internal Improvements*, p. 21. Clement Eaton, *The Growth of Southern Civilization, 1790–1860* (New York: Harper & Row, 1861), p. 32, confused the Upper Federal Road, opened about 1833, with the Federal Road, built in 1811.

21. Pickett, *History of Alabama*, pp. 619–22.

22. *Niles' Weekly Register*, Baltimore, March 26, 1818, p. 270.

23. Ibid., p. 271.

24. Margaret Ervin Austill, "Life of Margaret Ervin Austill," *Alabama Historical Quarterly* 6 (Spring 1944): 92–93.

25. Carter, *Territorial Papers*, 18:504, 543–45, *Biographical Dictionary*, p. 1050.

26. Kay Nuzum, *A History of Baldwin County* (Bay Minette, Ala.: Baldwin Times, 1971), pp. 78–79; Brannon, "Federal Road," p. 65; Elsie Lathrop, *Early American Inns and Taverns* (New York: Tudor Publishing, 1926), p. 233; Peter A. Brannon, *Little Journeys to Interesting Points in Alabama* (Montgomery: Paragon Press, 1930), p. 27.

27. Anne Royall, *Mrs. Royall's Southern Tour; or, Second Series of the Black Book*, 3 vols. (Washington, D.C.: n.p., 1831), 2:126, 137, 146; W. E. Martin, *Internal Improvements*, p. 27.

28. Brannon, "Federal Road," p. 65; Nuzum, *History of Baldwin County*, p. 79; Etta Blanchard Worsley, *Columbus on the Chattahoochee* (Columbus, Ga.: Columbus Office Supply, 1951), p. 47; Peter A. Brannon, *Engineers of Yesteryear* (Montgomery: Paragon Press, 1928), p. 52.

29. Nuzum, *History of Baldwin County*, pp. 77–78.

30. Alice Morse Earle, *Stage-Coach and Tavern Days* (New York: Macmillan, 1900), pp. 263–69; Margaret Parker Davis, "Stage-Coaches in Alabama before 1830," term paper, Historical Essays, Winners of Highest Awards, 1956–57, National Society of Colonial Dames in the State of Alabama, Howard College, Birmingham, 1958, 1:2–42.

31. W. E. Martin, *Internal Improvements*, pp. 27–28. Martin's source is James Silk Buckingham, *Slave States of America*, 2 vols. (London: Fisher Son, 1842). For several first-person accounts of stage travel, see chapter 5.

32. Nuzum, *History of Baldwin County*, pp. 77–78; Davis, "Stage-Coaches in Alabama," pp. 10, 14.

33. W. E. Martin, *Internal Improvements*, pp. 27–28.

34. John White, "Old Stage Road," *Area Magazine*, Southern Pine Co-Op Edition, August 1976, pp. 16–17.

35. W. E. Martin, *Internal Improvements*, p. 28.

36. John H. B. Latrobe, *Southern Travels: Journal of John H. B. Latrobe, 1834*, ed. Samuel Wilson, Jr. (New Orleans: Historic New Orleans Collection, 1986), p. 90.

37. Ibid., pp. 90–93.

38. Ibid., pp. 94–96.
39. Ibid., pp. 96–97.
40. Ibid., pp. 96–99.
41. James D. Davidson, "A Journey through the South in 1836: Diary of James D. Davidson," ed. Herbert A. Kellar, *Journal of Southern History* 1 (August 1935): 344, 370–72.
42. Nuzum, *History of Baldwin County*, p. 79.
43. Frederic Troutmann, "Alabama through a German's Eyes: The Travels of Clara von Gerstner, 1839," *Alabama Review* 36 (April 1983): 132.
44. Carter, *Territorial Papers*, 18:240.

5: PASSING STRANGERS

1. Captain Basil Hall, *Travels in North America in the Years 1827–1828*, 3 vols. (Edinburgh: Cadell, 1829), 3:278.
2. Auguste Levasseur, *LaFayette in America, in 1824 and 1825; or, Journal of a Voyage to the United States*, trans. John D. Godman, 2 vols. (Philadelphia: Carey & Lea, 1829), 2:70.
3. Peter A. Remsen, "Across Georgia and into Alabama, 1817–1818," ed. William B. Hesseltine and Larry Gara, *Georgia Historical Quarterly* 37 (December 1953): 334.
4. Thomas Hamilton, *Men and Manners in America*, 2 vols. (Edinburgh: William Blackwood, 1833), 2:270–71.
5. Hodgson, *Letters from North America*, 1:113–14.
6. Karl Bernhard, *Travels through North America during the Years 1825 and 1826*, 2 vols., trans. from German (Philadelphia: Carey, Lea & Carey, 1828), 2:22.
7. William Gilmore Simms, *The Letters of William Gilmore Simms*, ed. Mary C. Simms Oliphant, Alfred Taylor Odell, and T. C. Duncan Eaves, 5 vols. (Columbia: University of South Carolina Press, 1952), 1:23; W. Stanley Hoole, "Alabama and W. Gilmore Simms," *Alabama Review* (April and July 1963), reprinted in *According to Hoole: The Collected Essays and Tales of a Scholar-Librarian and a Literary Maverick* (University: University of Alabama Press, 1973), pp. 134–60.
8. Simms, *Letters*, p. 24.
9. Ibid., p. 26 and note.
10. Royall, *Southern Tour*, 2:126–27.
11. Ibid., p. 137; Goff, "Excursion along an Old Way," p. 191.
12. Goff, "Excursion along an Old Way," p. 191; Lorenzo Dow, *History of Cosmopolite; or, The Writings of Rev. Lorenzo Dow; Containing His Experiences and Travels in Europe and America*, 8th ed. (Cincinnati: Applegate,

1857), pp. 222, 652; Peggy Dow, *The Vicissitudes of Life*, printed with Lorenzo Dow, *The Dealings of God, Man, and the Devil* (Cincinnati: Applegate, 1859).

13. Hodgson, *Letters from North America*, 1:116.

14. Margaret Hunter Hall, *The Aristocratic Journey: Being the Outspoken Letters of Mrs. Basil Hall, Written during a Fourteen Months' Sojourn in America, 1827–1828*, ed. Una Pope Hennessy (New York: G. P. Putnam's Sons, 1831), pp. 237–38.

15. Bernhard, *Travels through North America*, 2:23.

16. Treaty of Washington, January 24, 1826, *Statutes at Large*, 7:286–90.

17. Lyell, *Second Visit*, 2:4–35.

18. Hodgson, *Letters from North America*, 1:117; Thomas Stocks, "Memorandum Taken on My Tour to Pensacola, Commencing the 15 April 1819," *Monthly Bulletin, Alabama Department of Archives and History* 2 (September 1925): 24; Bernhard, *Travels through North America*, 2:24–25.

19. Goff, "Excursion along an Old Way," pp. 197–98.

20. L. Dow, *History of Cosmopolite*, p. 652.

21. Levasseur, *Lafayette in America*, 2:75–76; Thomas S. Woodward, *Woodward's Reminiscences of the Creek or Muscogee Indians, Contained in Letters to Friends in Georgia and Alabama* (Montgomery: Barrett & Wimbish, 1859; reprint, Tuscaloosa, Ala.: Alabama Book Store, 1939), pp. 66–68.

22. Tennant S. McWilliams, "The Marquis and the Myth: Lafayette's Visit to Alabama, 1825," *Alabama Review* 22 (April 1969): 135–46.

23. Anson West, *A History of Methodism in Alabama* (Nashville: Methodist Episcopal Church, 1893; Reprint, Spartanburg, S.C.: Reprint Company, 1983), pp. 369–83.

24. Levasseur, *Lafayette in America*, 2:76.

25. For more on the last days of the McIntoshes in Alabama, see chapter 7. For more about the McIntosh family and their complicated and sometimes conflicting genealogy, see John Bartlett Meserve, "The McIntoshes," *Chronicles of Oklahoma* 10 (September 1932): 310–25; Horace Montgomery, ed., *Georgians in Profile* (Athens: University of Georgia Press, 1958), pp. 114–19, 350; Harriet Turner Porter Corbin, *A History and Genealogy of Chief William McIntosh, Jr., and His Known Descendants*, ed. Carl C. Burdick (Long Beach, Calif.: n.p., 1967), pp. 13–15, 83–85.

26. Levasseur, *Lafayette in America*, 2:77; Woodward, *Reminiscences*, pp. 66–68; McWilliams, "Marquis and Myth," p. 139. This Indian ball game was the origin of modern lacrosse.

27. Kendall Lewis, "McIntosh Brigade Creek Indian Warriors, Seminole War, 1817–1818," Military Service Records, National Archives, Washington, D.C.

28. Peter A. Brannon, "Russell County, Present Day Placenames Showing Aboriginal Influence," *Arrow Points* 1 (October 1920): 25; Chase, *Fort Mitchell*, pp. 3–4.

29. Hodgson, *Letters from North America*, 1:124; Peter A. Brannon, "Some Early Taverns in Alabama," *Arrow Points* 5 (September 1922): 53; W.P.A. Workers, "Principal Stops and Taverns in What Is Now Alabama, prior to 1840," *Alabama Historical Quarterly* 17 (Spring and Summer 1955): 84; Chase, *Fort Mitchell*, p. 4; W. Stuart Harris, *Dead Towns of Alabama* (University: University of Alabama Press, 1977), p. 46: cf. Peter Brannon, ed., *Alabama Historical Quarterly* 21 (1959): 1–71; Jackson, *Correspondence*, 1:298–99, 458n, 2:23n; Nella J. Chambers, "The Creek Indian Factory at Fort Mitchell," *Alabama Historical Quarterly* 21 (1959): 15; Truett, *Trade and Travel*, p. 153; [W. Warner Floyd, comp.], *Alabama's Tapestry of Historic Places, an Inventory* (Montgomery: Alabama Historical Commission, 1978), p. 157; Hamilton, *Men and Manners*, 2:264–69. John Crowell was a delegate from Alabama Territory in 1818 and representative from Alabama from 1819 to 1821; *Biographical Dictionary*, p. 806.

30. Peter A. Brannon, "Dueling in Alabama," *Alabama Historical Quarterly* 17 (Fall 1955): 100–101; Lucian Lamar Knight, *A Standard History of Georgia and Georgians*, 6 vols. (Chicago: Lewis Publishing, 1917), 1:518–20; William B. Collins, "The Crawford-Burnside Duel," *Gulf States Historical Magazine* 2 (July 1903): 54–57. William Harris Crawford and George Walker Crawford were first cousins, once removed.

31. Brannon, "Dueling in Alabama," pp. 100–102; John H. Martin, *Columbus, Geo., from Its Selection as a "Trading Town" in 1827 to Its Partial Destruction by Wilson's Raid in 1865*, 2 pts. (Columbus, Ga.: Thos. Gilbert, 1874; reprint, Easley, S.C.: Georgia Genealogical Reprints, 1972), pt. 1, pp. 32–33.

32. Stocks, "Memorandum on Tour," p. 30; *Map of Reconnaissances Exhibiting Country between Washington and New Orleans*, 19th Cong., 1st sess., to accompany House Document no. 156 (Washington, D.C.: n.p., 1826).

33. Hodgson, *Letters from North America*, 1:123.

34. M. H. Hall, *Aristocratic Journey*, pp. 238–39; Capt. Hall, *Travels in North America*, 3:283.

35. Royall, *Southern Tour*, 2:134–80.

36. Sol Smith, *Theatrical Management in the West and South for Thirty Years*, ed. Arthur Thomas Tees (1868; reprint, New York: Benjamin Blom, 1968), pp. 77–79; J. H. Martin, *Columbus, Geo.*, pt. 1, p. 37; Henry W. Adams, *The Montgomery Theater, 1822–1835* (University: University of Alabama Press, 1955), pp. 5–6, 25–37.

37. *Columbus* [Georgia] *Enquirer*, May 19, 1832, [p. 3].

38. "Theatrical," *Columbus Enquirer*, May 26, 1832, [p. 3].

39. Smith, *Theatrical Management*, pp. 78–79.

40. Simms, *Letters*, pp. 28–31.

41. From Simms's *Southern Passages and Pictures*, cited in Hoole, *According to Hoole*, p. 151.

42. Hoole, *According to Hoole*, p. 153.

43. J. H. Martin, *Columbus, Geo.*, pt. 1, pp. 32, 43; Walter Brownlow Posey, ed., "Alabama in the 1830's as Recorded by British Travellers," *Birmingham-Southern College Bulletin* 31 (December 1938): 17, 30.

44. Quotations, in this paragraph and the next, are from Harriet Martineau, *Society in America*, 3 vols., 2d ed. (London: Saunders & Otley, 1837), 1:286–91.

45. Lyell, *Second Visit*, 2:34–38.

46. Hodgson, *Letters from North America*, 1:123–26.

47. Peter A. Brannon, "Early Travel and Some Stage Stops in Alabama," in *The Pageant Book*, ed. Brannon (Montgomery: n.p., 1926), p. 29; W.P.A., "Principal Stage Stops," p. 84; Truett, *Trade and Travel*, p. 151; Lathrop, *Early Inns*, p. 230.

48. W.P.A., "Principal Stage Stops," p. 86; Harris, *Dead Towns*, p. 49; Truett, *Trade and Travel*, p. 153; AHC, *Alabama's Tapestry*, p. 159; Lathrop, *Early Inns*, p. 230; Brannon, *Pageant Book*, p. 30; Brannon, "Russell County Placenames," p. 26.

49. AHC, *Alabama Tapestry*, p. 147; Harris, *Dead Towns*, p. 36; H. M. King, "Historical Sketches of Macon County," *Alabama Historical Quarterly* 18 (Summer 1956): 187–217; Jackson, *Correspondence*, 2:23n; Brannon, "Russell County Placenames," p. 25; "Fort Bainbridge," *Arrow Points* 5 (August 1922): 21–28.

50. Brannon, "Early Taverns," p. 54; Brannon, "Fort Bainbridge," p. 28; Peter A. Brannon, "Lewis Tavern at Fort Bainbridge," *Alabama Historical Quarterly* 17 (Spring and Summer 1955): 78–79; W.P.A., "Principal Stage Stops," p. 80; Jackson, *Correspondence*, 2:122; "Tuckabachi Sons-in-Law: White Men Noted in Early Records Who Had Indian Wives," *Arrow Points* 14 (May 1929): 43; Woodward, *Reminiscences*, p. 62; File 5803, Seminole War, 1817–1818, McIntosh's Brigade (Creek Indians, p. 5), National Archives, Military Records Service, Washington, D.C.: Truett, *Trade and Travel*, pp. 106, 151; Lathrop, *Early Inns*, pp. 230–31.

51. Hodgson, *Letters from North America*, 1:127–33.

52. Bernhard, *Travels through North America*, 2:27–28.

53. M. H. Hall, *Aristocratic Journey*, pp. 240–41.

54 Royall, *Southern Tour*, 2:178–79.

55. George W. Featherstonhaugh, *Excursion through the Slave States* (New York: Harper & Brothers, 1844), pp. 152–53.

56. AHC, *Alabama Tapestry*, p. 108.

57. J. H. Martin, *Columbus, Geo.*, pt. 1, pp. 32, 43; pt. 2, p. 29; *Columbus Enquirer*, July 14, 1832, p. 3; and July 28, 1832, p. 3; Brannon, "Macon Place Names," p. 6; Brannon, *Historic Highways in Alabama* (Montgomery: Paragon Press, 1929), pp. 42–43; Louise Calhoun Barfield, *History of Harris County,*

Georgia, 1827–1961 (Columbus, Ga.: n.p., n.d.), p. 434; Truett, *Trade and Travel*, p. 153. Line Creek is also known as Ocfuskee, Ofuskee, Okfuskee, or Oakfuskee Creek.

58. Peter A. Brannon, "Pole Cat Springs Agency," *Arrow Points* 10 (February 1925): 24; Brannon, "Macon Place Names," p. 8; Brannon, "Fort Bainbridge," p. 28.

59. Smith, *Theatrical Management*, p. 78.

60. Ibid., p. 102.

61. Remsen, "Across Georgia and into Alabama," p. 334.

62. Featherstonhaugh, *Excursion through the Slave States*, p. 152. "McGirt" probably was James McGirth, whose grave was pointed out to General Lafayette by General Woodward (see the latter's *Reminiscences*, p. 71). No relationship between the McGirth, McQueen, and McIntosh families in the Creek Nation and Daniel McGirtt, John McQueen, and John Houstoun McIntosh, all of whom lived on Ortega Island, Jacksonville, Florida, from 1780 to about 1812, has been determined. See Dena Snodgrass, *The Island of Ortega: A History* (Jacksonville, Fla.: Ortega School, 1981), pp. 17–23.

63. Remsen, "Across Georgia and into Alabama," p. 334.

64. Featherstonhaugh, *Excursion through the Slave States*, p. 152.

65. Posey, "Alabama in the 1830's," pp. 17–21; Tyrone Power, *Impressions of America*, 2 vols., 2d American ed. (Philadelphia: Carey, Lea & Blanchard, 1836), 2:81–85, 88–90.

66. Joseph M. Field, *The Drama in Pokerville: The Bench and Bar of Jurytown, and Other Stories* (Philadelphia: A. Hurt, 1850), pp. 190–93.

67. M. H. Hall, *Aristocratic Journey*, pp. 241–44; Capt. B. Hall, *Travels in North America*, 3:289–307. Although both accounts mention Captain Triplett, Captain Hall states that it was "the house of another of the United States agent." The agency was at Pole Cat Springs; it was very near, or it may have been, Capt. William Walker's Tavern (AHC, *Alabama's Tapestry*, p. 108).

68. From 1813 to 1815, Captain Walker was with the 39th Infantry and later served in the Second Seminole War. He was in command of Fort Decatur when Gen. John Sevier died unexpectedly on September 24, 1815, attended by only a few soldiers and Indians. The general was buried with military honors by the troops and his body removed to Tennessee in 1888. Capt. William Walker was subagent at Pole Cat Springs as late as 1825 under Col. John Crowell. Captain Walker died about October 20, 1836, while commanding a regiment of Creek Warriors at Apalachicola, Florida. See Francis B. Heitman, *Historical Register and Dictionary of the United States Army from Its Organization, September 29, 1789, to March 2, 1903*, 2 vols. (Washington, D.C.: Government Printing Office, 1903), 1:997; Bounty Warrant File no. 2829, Military Service Records, National Archives, Washington, D.C.; W.P.A., "Principal Stage Stops," p. 86; AHC, *Alabama's Tapestry*, p. 108; Brannon, "Fort Hull," pp. 7, 11;

Brannon, *Pageant Book*, p. 30; Paul Sanguinetti, "My Recollections of the Trip to Milstead in 1888 at the Time of the Removal of the Remains of John Sevier," *Arrow Points* 2 (April 1921): 62; Brannon, "Pole Cat Springs," p. 25; "Historic Sites of Alabama," p. 45; Brannon, "Early Taverns," p. 54; Lathrop, *Early Inns*, p. 231; Goff, "Excursion along an Old Way," p. 200. Cf. "Tuckabachi Sons-in-Law," p. 43, as to the second wife of Captain Walker. The first post office in Macon County was at Pole Cat Springs, according to *Alabama's Tapestry*, p. 108, but it is not listed in Carter, *Territorial Papers*, 18:507–9.

69. Remsen, "Across Georgia and into Alabama," pp. 334–35.

70. Hodgson, *Letters from North America*, 1:138. For land vehicles used in this period, see Peter Bray and Barbara Brown, *Transport through the Ages* (New York: Taplinger Publishing, 1971), pp. 58–60.

71. M. H. Hall, *Aristocratic Journey*, p. 244.

72. Bernhard, *Travels through North America*, 2:30.

73. Hamilton, *Men and Manners*, 2:254.

74. Stocks, "Memorandum on Tour," pp. 30–31, 35.

75. Bernhard, *Travels through North America*, 2:30.

76. Royall, *Southern Tour*, 2:179–81.

77. Brannon, *Pageant Book*, p. 30; Lathrop, *Early Inns*, p. 231; W. G. Robertson, *Recollections of the Early Settlers of Montgomery County and Their Families* (Montgomery: Excelsior Printing, 1892; reprint, Montgomery: Society of Pioneers of Montgomery, 1961), pp. 40–41; Brannon, "Early Taverns," p. 54.

78. Woodward, *Reminiscences*, p. 71; Levasseur, *Lafayette in America*, 2:80–83. Between 1978 and 1980, Lucas Tavern was removed from its original location on Line Creek and reconstructed at Old Alabama Town, on the northeast corner of Jefferson and Hull streets in Montgomery.

79. W.P.A., "Principal Stage Stops," pp. 81, 84; Stocks, "Memorandum on Tour," pp. 30–32, 35. Evans, Montgomery, and Snowdoun made a triangle of the roads.

80. Martineau, *Society in America*, 1:293.

81. Featherstonhaugh, *Excursion through the Slave States*, p. 145.

82. Phineas Taylor Barnum, *Struggles and Triumphs; or, Forty Years of Recollections of P. T. Barnum, Written by Himself*, The Modern Reader Series (New York: Macmillan, 1930), p. 39.

83. Hodgson, *Letters from North America*, 1:140.

84. James Stuart, *Three Years in North America*, 2 vols. (New York: J. & J. Harper, 1833), 2:111, 113–14.

85. Ibid., p. 115.

86. P. Dow, *Vicissitudes*, p. 222.

87. Hodgson, *Letters from North America*, 1:141.

88. Ibid., pp. 141–42; J. F. H. Claiborne, *Life and Times of Gen. Sam Dale, the Mississippi Partisan* (New York: Harper & Brothers, 1860), pp. 169–71.

89. Stuart, *Three Years*, 2:117.

90. The name of the creek is drawn from the 1789 murder of a Colonel Kirkland of South Carolina, his son, and two other persons by a party of thieves led by John Catt, a white man who was probably from Tennessee. Catt was captured, and the Creek leader William McGillivray was informed by the Spanish governor that the Indians had jurisdiction. Catt confessed and was hanged in the suit he had taken from one of his victims. See John Forbes, *John Forbes' Description of the Spanish Floridas, 1804*, ed. William S. Coker (Pensacola: Perdido Bay Press, 1979), p. 3. Cf. Pickett, *History of Alabama*, pp. 383–84.

91. Hodgson, *Letters from North America*, 1:142–43.

92. Stuart, *Three Years*, 2:118.

93. Hodgson, *Letters from North America*, 1:143–44.

94. Stuart, *Three Years*, 2:118–20.

95. Ibid., p. 121.

96. Hodgson, *Letters from North America*, 1:146–49.

97. Stuart, *Three Years*, 2:121–22.

98. Ibid., p. 122.

99. Hodgson, *Letters from North America*, 1:149–50.

100. Stuart, *Three Years*, 2:122–23.

101. For a description of violence in Montgomery from travel narratives, see Walter Bertram Hitchcock, Jr., "Telling Observations: Early Travelers in East-Central Alabama," in *Clearings in the Thicket: An Alabama Humanities Reader*, ed. Jerry Elijah Brown (Macon, Ga.: Mercer University Press, 1985), pp. 39–62.

102. Stocks, "Memorandum on Tour," p. 30; Harris, *Dead Towns*, pp. 47, 51–52, 66, 103.

103. Joseph Thompson Hare, *The Life of the Celebrated Mail Robber and Daring Highwayman, Joseph Thompson Hare* (Philadelphia: J. P. Perry, 1844), pp. 18–23; Jonathan Daniels, *The Devil's Backbone: The Story of the Natchez Trace* (New York: McGraw-Hill, 1962), pp. 104–110; Willis Brewer, *Alabama: Her History, Resources, War Record, and Public Men, from 1540 to 1872* (Montgomery: Barrett & Brown, 1872), p. 194.

104. Edward J. Coale, *Trials of the Mail Robbers, Hare, Alexander, and Hare* (Baltimore: Edward J. Coale, 1818), pp. 14, 55, 64–71, 104, 195; Robert M. Coates, *The Outlaw Years: The History of the Land Pirates of the Natchez Trace* (New York: Literary Guild of America, 1930), pp. 103–5; Daniels, *Devil's Backbone*, p. 110.

6: Sojourners and Statehood

1. John L. Androit, ed., *Population Abstract of the United States* (McLean, Va.: Androit Associates, 1980), p. 4.

2. Pound, *Benjamin Hawkins*, p. 210.

3. Thomas Ruffin, *The Papers of Thomas Ruffin*, ed. J. G. de Roulhac Hamilton, 4 vols. (Raleigh: North Carolina Historical Commission, 1918–20), 1:198. James Graham (1793–1851) of Lincoln County, North Carolina, son of Gen. Joseph Graham and brother of Gov. William A. Graham, was in the House of Representatives 1822–24, 1828–29, 1833–43, and 1845–47 (*Biographical Dictionary*, p. 1022).

4.. U.S. Congress, *Register of Debates*, 20th Cong., 1st sess., March 26, 1828, p. 519. McKinley later served as an associate justice of the United States Supreme Court, 1837–52.

5. Frank A. Daniels, *History of Wayne County* [North Carolina], address delivered November 30, 1914 (n.p.).

6. William Faulkner, *The Hamlet* (New York: Random House, 1941; reprint, Vintage Books, 1964), p. 4.

7. P. Dow, *Vicissitudes*, pp. 222–23.

8. Gideon Lincecum, "Autobiography of Gideon Lincecum," in *Publications of the Mississippi Historical Society*, 14 vols. in 13 (Oxford: Mississippi Historical Society, 1904), 8:464–65.

9. Eaton, *Growth of Southern Civilization*, p. 33.

10. Lincecum, "Autobiography," p. 465.

11. Benjamin F. Porter, *Reminiscences of Men and Things in Alabama*, ed. Sara Walls (Tuscaloosa, Ala.: Portals Press, 1983), pp. 29–30.

12. Ibid., pp. 30–31.

13. Ibid., p. 31.

14. Joseph G. Baldwin, *The Flush Times of Alabama and Mississippi* (Americus, Ga.: Americus Book, 1853), pp. 236–39.

15. For Spain's claims to land, 1783–75, see Coker and Watson, *Indian Traders*, pp. 2–5.

16. Frances C. Roberts, "Thomas Freeman, Surveyor of the Old Southwest," *Alabama Review* 40 (July 1987): 224.

17. Alan V. Briceland, "The Mississippi Territorial Land Board East of the Pearl River, 1804," *Alabama Review* 32 (January 1979): 39–41.

18. Ibid., p. 45; James F. Doster, "Land Titles and Public Land Sales in Early Alabama," *Alabama Review* 16 (April 1963): 108–10. Land speculation was intense in Alabama. See Roy M. Robbins, *Our Landed Heritage* (Lincoln: University of Nebraska Press, 1962), p. 30.

19. Doster, "Land Titles," pp. 113–14.

20. Ibid.; Malcolm Rohrbough, *The Land Office Business: The Settlement and Administration of American Public Lands, 1789–1837* (New York: Oxford University Press, 1968), pp. 30–31, 37, 91–92, 109–27, 164.

21. Roberts, "Thomas Freeman," p. 229; Gordon T. Chappell, "John Coffee: Surveyor and Land Agent," *Alabama Review* 14 (July, October 1961): 185, 193, 247; Carter, *Territorial Papers*, 5:637; Thomas Perkins Abernethy, *The Forma-*

tive Period in Alabama, 1815–1828 (University: University of Alabama Press, 1965), p. 66.

22. Albert Burton Moore, *History of Alabama* (Nashville: Benson Printing, 1934; reprint, Tuscaloosa, Ala.: Alabama Book Store, 1951), pp. 92–93; Carter, *Territorial Papers*, 5:290; 6:26–30, 36–39, 332–39, 347–51, 358–59; William H. Brantley, *Three Capitals. A Book about the First Three Capitals of Alabama: St. Stephens, Huntsville, and Cahawba* (1947; reprint, University: University of Alabama Press, 1976), pp. 12–18.

23. Moore, *History of Alabama*, pp. 93–98; Brantley, *Three Capitals*, pp. 18–23; Carter, *Territorial Papers*, 6:601–2, 655–56, 708, 715–17, 730–31, 744–48, 763–66; 3:413, 472–73.

24. Frances C. Roberts, "Politics and Public Land Disposal in Alabama's Formative Period," *Alabama Review* 22 (July 1969): 170–71.

25. William J. Northern, ed., *Men of Mark in Georgia*, ed. John Temple Graves, 7 vols. (Atlanta: A. B. Caldwell, 1910), 2:2–3.

26. Abernethy, *Formative Period*, p. 337.

27. *Biographical Dictionary*, pp. 589, 800, 1050, 1786–87, 1831–32. Crawford and Tait had known each other in Augusta, Elberton, and Milledgeville, Georgia. See Phillip Jackson Green, *The Life of William Harris Crawford* (n.p., n.d.), p. 2; Chase Curren Mooney, *William H. Crawford, 1772–1834* (Lexington: University of Kentucky Press, 1974), pp. 7, 10.

28. Pickett, *History of Alabama*, pp. 615, 660, 680; Abernethy, *Formative Period*, pp. 49–50; Charles H. Moffat, "Charles Tait: Planter, Politician, and Scientist of the Old South," *Journal of Southern History* 14 (May 1948): 222–24.

29. Moore, *History of Alabama*, p. 114; Joel Crawford to Bolling Hall, July 30, 1819, and September 28, 1821; and Hines Holt to Bolling Hall, July 3 and September 20, 1820, Bolling Hall Papers, Alabama Department of Archives and History, Montgomery.

30. Moore, *History of Alabama*, pp. 114–16; *Biographical Dictionary*, p. 1542.

31. Robbie Lee Gillis Ross, *Your Inheritance* (Matthews, N.C.: Delmar Printing, 1972), p. 131; Ball, *Clarke County*, p. 575.

32. National Archives, "Record of First Returns Received from Postmasters, October 1789–July 1818" (Washington, D.C.: National Archives and Records Service, Micro Copy No. M 1131, 1980), Roll No. 1. Cf. Carter, *Territorial Papers*, 18:507–9; J. H. Scruggs, Jr., *Alabama Postal History* (By the author, n.d.), pp. 4–5; Bruce C. Oakley, Jr., *A Postal History of Mississippi: Stampless Period, 1799–1860* (Baldwyn, Miss.: Magnolia Publishers, 1969), pp. 13–14; Carroll Chase and Richard McP. Cabeen, *The First Hundred Years of United States Territorial Postmarks, 1787–1887* (State College, Pa.: American Philatelic Society, 1950), p. 67.

33. U.S. Congress, Senate, Committee on Public Lands and Surveys, *Natchez Trace Parkway Survey*, National Parks Service, Department of the Interior. Report prepared by Arno B. Cammerer. 76th Cong., 3d sess., Senate Doc. No. 148 (Washington, D.C.: Government Printing Office, 1941), pp. 96–100, 107; Huber and Wagner, *Great Mail*, p. 24.

34. Mable Ponder Wilson, *Some Early Alabama Churches* (Birmingham: Alabama Society, Daughters of the American Revolution, 1973), p. 12.

35. West, *History of Methodism*, pp. 181, 198, 128, 446.

36. Androit, *Population Abstract*, pp. 4, 438, 328. The population figures include slaves.

37. Moore, *History of Alabama*, p. 45.

38. Pickett, *History of Alabama*, pp. 229, 342–46; Joel Campbell Dubose, *Alabama History* (Richmond, Va.: Johnson Publishing, 1908), pp. 31–32, 39–40; Woodward, *Reminiscences*, pp. 59–61, 88–89; Louis LeClerc Milfort, *Memoirs; or, A Quick Glance at My Various Travels and My Sojourn in the Creek Nation*, trans. and ed. Ben C. McCary (Savannah, Ga.: Beehive Press, 1972), p. 135; John Walton Caughey, *McGillivray of the Creeks* (Norman: University of Oklahoma Press, 1938), pp. 9–13; L. J. Newcomb Comings and Martha M. Albers, *A Brief History of Baldwin County* (Fairhope, Ala.: Baldwin County Historical Society, 1928), p. 28; Halbert and Ball, *Creek War*, pp. 164–66.

39. James Denny Dreisbach to Lyman C. Draper, July 1874, Draper Manuscript Collection, State Historical Society of Wisconsin, Madison, Series V, p. 1008; for information on James Denny Dreisbach, see "White Men Associated with Indian Life," *Alabama Historical Quarterly* 13 (1951): 142–43; Halbert and Ball, *Creek War*, pp. 173–76.

40. Meserve, "The McIntoshes," pp. 311–13. Cf. Corbin, *Chief William McIntosh*, pp. 83–84; James C. Bonner, "William McIntosh," in *Georgians in Profile: Historical Essays in Honor of Ellis Merton Coulter*, ed. Horace Montgomery (Athens: University of Georgia Press, 1958), pp. 115–18; and *Biographical Dictionary*, pp. 1397, 1831–32. Meserve and Bonner state that Governor Troup's mother was Catherine, while Corbin has her as Margaret. Meserve states that Catherine married a British naval officer named Troup, while Corbin states that Margaret married a British army officer. Both Corbin and Meserve have Governor Troup's middle name as McIntosh, while the *Biographical Dictionary* lists it as Michael. Bonner further states (p. 350, n. 6) that both Woodward and Pickett are "in error concerning the genealogy of the McIntosh family" but does not attempt to correct any error or cite any sources as being correct.

41. Meserve, "The McIntoshes," pp. 313–15, and Corbin, *Chief William McIntosh*, pp. 84–85, are not in agreement. Details of McIntosh's death are in chapter 7.

42. Levasseur, *Lafayette in America*, 2:70.

43. Peter A. Brannon, "More about Mordacai," *Alabama Historical Quarterly* 20 (Spring 1958): 27–33; Clanton Ware Williams, *The Early History of Montgomery, and Incidentally of the State of Alabama* (University, Ala.: Confederate Publishing, 1979), pp. 13, 22.

44. Hawkins, *Sketch and Letters*, pp. 29–66.

45. See Mary G. Bryan, *Passports Issued by Governors of Georgia, 1785 to 1820* (Washington, D.C.: National Genealogical Society, 1962).

46. Enclosure no. 2, Maj. T. P. Andrews to James Barbour, July 4, 1825, House Report no. 98, 19th Cong., 2d sess. (Washington, D.C.: Gales & Seaton, 1927), pp. 257–58, contained in *New American State Papers, Indian Affairs*, 13 vols. (Wilmington, Del.: Scholarly Resources, 1972), vol. 7, *Southeast*, pp. 279–80.

47. Peter A. Brannon, "Removal of Indians from Alabama," *Alabama Historical Quarterly* 12 (1950): 96.

48. Inferred from figures in Androit, *Population Abstract*, p. 4.

49. James Silk Buckingham, *Slave States of America*, 2 vols. (London: Fisher Son, 1842), 1:497–98. See also Hitchcock, "Early Travelers," pp. 39–62.

7: TWO GHOSTS

1. Pat Jackson Jemian, *Chattahoochee Coverlets* (Auburn, Ala.: Auburn University Center for the Arts and Humanities, 1987), p. 17.

2. *Statutes at Large*, see vol. 7; U.S. Congress, *American State Papers, Indian Affairs*, 2 vols. (Washington, D.C.: Gales & Seaton, 1832–61); Commissioner of Indian Affairs, *Treaties between the United States of America and the Several Indian Tribes, from 1778 to 1837* (Washington, D.C.: Langtree & O'Sullivan, 1837), pp. xxiv–xxix (hereinafter cited as *U.S.-Indian Treaties*).

3. *American Mirror*, Tuscaloosa, March 30, p. 3; April 6, p. 4; and April 27, 1824, p. 4; John H. Goff, "The Path to Oakfuskee: Upper Trading Route in Georgia to the Creek Indians," *Georgia Historical Quarterly* 39 (March, June 1955): 24–25, 160–62.

4. *U.S.-Indian Treaties*, pp. 323–26.

5. Cited in U.S. Department of Interior, *Federal Indian Law* (Washington, D.C.: Government Printing Office, 1958; reprint, Dobbs Ferry, N.Y.: Oceana Publications, 1966), p. 193.

6. *Federal Indian Law*, p. 193.

7. *Niles' Weekly Register*, March 19, 1825.

8. Meserve, "The McIntoshes," pp. 315–17, 320–21; Grant Foreman, *Indians & Pioneers: The Story of the American Southwest before 1830*, rev. ed. (Norman: University of Oklahoma Press, 1936), pp. 250–57.

9. Levasseur, *Lafayette in America*, 1:76.

10. *Federal Indian Law*, p. 193n.

11. Dexter Perkins and Glyndon G. Van Densen, *The United States of America: A History*, 2 vols. (New York: Macmillan, 1962), 1:344–45; *U.S.-Indian Treaties*, pp. 323–27, 391–95; *Federal Indian Law*, pp. 191–95.

12. *Statutes at Large*, 7:286–90.

13. J. H. Martin, *Columbus, Geo.*, pt. 1, p. 10.

14. *Indian Office Letter Books, Series II*, no. 7, p. 422, cited in *Federal Indian Law*, p. 194.

15. *Federal Indian Law*, p. 194.

16. Grant Foreman, *Indian Removal: The Emigration of the Five Civilized Tribes of Indians* (Norman: University of Oklahoma Press, 1932), pp. 107–90; Angie Debo, *The Road to Disappearance* (Norman: University of Oklahoma Press, 1941), pp. 72–107.

17. Brannon, "Removal of Indians," p. 96.

18. Frank L. Owsley, Jr., "Francis Scott Key's Mission to Alabama in 1833," *Alabama Review* 23 (July 1970): 182–84.

19. Ibid., pp. 184–85.

20. Ibid., pp. 185–86.

21. Ibid., pp. 187–88.

22. Journal of Sarah Haynesworth Gayle, December 1833, Gorgas Family Papers, Amelia Gayle Gorgas Library, University of Alabama; cited in Owsley, "Francis Scott Key," p. 191.

23. Ibid., p. 192.

24. Foreman, *Indian Removal*, p. 114.

25. J. H. Martin, *Columbus, Geo.*, pt. 1, pp. 51–79.

26. Jacob Rhett Motte, *Journey into Wilderness: An Army Surgeon's Account of Life in Camp and Field during the Creek and Seminole Wars, 1836–1838*, ed. James F. Lundsman (Gainesville: University of Florida Press, 1953), pp. 18–19.

27. Ibid., p. 20.

28. Ibid., p. 21; George White, *Historical Collections of Georgia*, 3d ed. (New York: Pudney & Russell, 1855; reprint, Baltimore: Genealogical Publishing, 1969), pp. 638–39.

29. Davidson, "Journey through the South," pp. 344, 370–72.

30. Motte, *Journey into Wilderness*, p. 21.

31. Ibid., p. 22.

32. Ibid., pp. 35–37.

33. Brannon, "Removal of Indians," p. 91.

34. Angie Debo, *And Still the Waters Run: The Betrayal of the Five Civilized Tribes* (Princeton: Princeton University Press, 1940), p. iii.

35. J. Leitch Wright, Jr., *Creeks and Seminoles: The Destruction and Regen-*

eration of the Muscogulge People (Lincoln: University of Nebraska Press, 1986), pp. 284–85.

36. Brannon, "Removal of Indians," p. 99.

37. Mahon, *Second Seminole War*, p. 185. David Moniac's biography is sketched above in chapter 6.

38. Ibid., p. 183. For details of Walker's activities on the Federal Road, see chapter 5 above.

39. Ibid., p. 144–51. Gaines is mentioned above in chapters 1–4.

40. Ibid., pp. 82–83, 252.

41. *Statutes at Large*, 7:366–68, 411–12.

42. Mary Elizabeth Young, *Redskins, Ruffleshirts, and Rednecks: Indian Allotments in Alabama and Mississippi, 1830–1860* (Norman: University of Oklahoma Press, 1961), pp. 73–74.

43. Levasseur, *Lafayette in America*, p. 82.

44. *The Creek Nation v. The United States*, 77 Court of Claims 226 (1933), at pp. 252, 260. See also *Federal Indian Law*, pp. 194–95.

45. Commissioner of the General Land Office, U.S. Department of the Interior, to William M. Russell, Esquire, March 23, 1943. Private papers of William M. Russell, Jr., attorney-at-law, Tuskegee, Alabama.

46. John Lauritz Larson, " 'Bind the Republic Together': The National Union and the Struggle for a System of Internal Improvements," *Journal of American History* 74 (September 1987): 371–74.

47. U.S. Congress, House, *Report of the Board of Internal Improvement upon the Subject of a National Road from the City of Washington to New Orleans*, 19th Cong., 1st sess., 1826, pp. 9–10.

48. Ibid., pp. 9–10, 20.

49. Ibid., pp. 14, 21–28.

50. Peter A. Brannon, *Romance of Beginnings of Some Alabama Industries: An American Pilgrimage Address* (Birmingham: Birmingham Publishing, 1939), p. 193. Cf. Charles Grayson Summersell, *Alabama History for Schools*, 3d ed. (Montgomery: Viewpoint Publications, 1965), p. 188.

51. Moore, *History of Alabama*, p. 305; J. H. Scruggs, Jr., *Alabama Steamboats, 1819–1869* (By the author, n.d.), pp. 4–16; Mell A. Frazer, *Early History of Steamboats in Alabama*, Alabama Polytechnic Institute Historical Series, Third Series (Auburn, Ala., 1907), p. 24; Bert Neville, *Directory of River Packets in the Mobile-Alabama-Warrior-Tombigbee Trades (1818–1832)* (Selma, Ala.: Coffee Printing, 1962), pp. 12–29; Bert Neville, *Directory of Steamboats, with Illustrations and Lists of Landings on Chattahoochee-Apalachicola-Flint-Chipola Rivers* (Selma, Ala.: n.p., 1961).

52. Martin, *Columbus, Geo.*, pt. 1, pp. 14, 22, 24–25; Dorothy Sue Parsons, "Boats on the Alabama River," term paper, Colonial Dames Historical Essays, Howard College, Birmingham, 1960, 3:131–38.

53. Brannon, *Engineers of Yesteryear*, p. 8.

54. Moore, *History of Alabama*, p. 305.

55. Joseph Hobson Harrison, Jr., "The Internal Improvement Issue in the Politics of the Union, 1783–1825" (Ph.D. diss., University of Virginia, 1954).

56. Among the thirteen commissioners were Abner McGehee, Andrew Dexter, Charles T. Pollard, and S. W. Goode. Andrew Dexter was its engineer in 1835, and A. McGehee, its president. See Marshall L. Bowie, *A Time of Adversity—and Courage: A Story of Montgomery and West Point Rail Road, a Predecessor Company of the Western Railway of Alabama, and Its Activities during the War Between the States, 1861–1865* (N.p., 1961), pp. 1–2; N. P. Renfro, Jr., *The Beginnings of Railroads in Alabama*, Alabama Polytechnic Institute Historical Studies, Fourth Series (Auburn, Ala., 1910), p. 7.

57. J. Arch Avery and Marshall L. Bowie, *The West Point Route: A Story of the Atlanta and West Point Rail Road, the Western Railway of Alabama* (Atlanta: n.p., 1954), p. 3.

58. Renfro, *Beginnings of Railroads*, pp. 14–17; Ulrich Bonnell Phillips, *A History of Transportation in the Eastern Cotton Belt to 1860* (New York: Columbia University Press, 1908; reprint, New York: Octagon Books, 1968), p. 365.

59. Bowie, *Montgomery and West Point Rail Road*, p. 4.

60. Eugene Alvarez, *Travel on Southern Antebellum Railroads* (University: University of Alabama Press, 1974), p. 112.

61. George William Featherstonhaugh, *A Canoe Voyage up the Minnay Soto; with an Account of the Land and Copper Deposits in Wisconsin; of the Gold Region in the Cherokee Country; and Sketches of Popular Manners* (London, 1847), 2:187–88; cited in Alvarez, *Southern Antebellum Railroads*, p. 128.

62. Robert V. Remini, *Andrew Jackson and the Bank War: A Study in the Growth of Presidential Power* (New York: W. W. Norton, 1967), p. 82.

63. Ibid., p. 173; Charles S. Sydnor, *The Development of Southern Sectionalism, 1819–1848*, vol. 5 of *A History of the South* (Baton Rouge: Louisiana State University Press, 1948), pp. 261–64.

64. Avery Craven, *Edmund Ruffin, Southerner: A Study in Secession* (Hamden, Conn.: Archon Books, 1964), pp. 61–64.

65. J. H. Martin, *Columbus, Geo.*, pt. 1, p. 159.

66. Ibid., pt. 2, pp. 21, 29.

67. W. E. Martin, *Internal Improvements*, p. 21.

68. Peter A. Brannon, *Historic Highways in Alabama: Stories of Incidents with the Early Roadways in the State* (Montgomery: Paragon Press, 1929), pp. 42–43.

69. Phillips, *History of Transportation*, p. 385.

70. W. E. Martin, *Internal Improvements*, pp. 20–21.

71. Brannon, "Federal Road," p. 10.

BIBLIOGRAPHY

PRIMARY SOURCES

Manuscript Materials

Crawford, Joel, III. Papers. Manuscript Section, Alabama Department of Archives and History, Montgomery.

————. Papers. Georgia Department of Archives and History, Atlanta.

Creek War Letters. Files 205 and 207, Military Section, Alabama Department of Archives and History, Montgomery.

Dreisbach, James Denny, to Lyman C. Draper, July 1874. Series V, Draper Manuscript Collection, State Historical Society of Wisconsin, Madison.

Floyd, John. Forts. Files 205 and 207, Military Section, Alabama Department of Archives and History, Montgomery.

————. Papers. Georgia Department of Archives and History, Atlanta.

Hall, Bolling. Papers. Manuscript Section, Alabama Department of Archives and History, Montgomery.

Military Service Records. National Archives, Washington, D.C.

Office of the Chief of Engineers. Field Survey Records, 1793–1916. Record Group 77, National Archives, Washington, D.C. MFS-791, Samford University Library, Birmingham.

Office of the Secretary of War. Letters Received, #L 189(5) 1811. Record Group 107, National Archives, Washington, D.C. MFS-791, Samford University Library, Birmingham.

Pickens, Israel. Papers. Manuscript Section, Alabama Department of Archives and History, Montgomery.

Records of U.S. Commands. Vol. 103/52. Record Group 98, National Archives, Washington, D.C. MFS-791, Samford University Library, Birmingham.

Stiggins, Joseph N., to Lyman C. Draper, February 5, 1874. Draper Manuscript Collection, State Historical Society of Wisconsin, Madison.

Toulmin, Harry. Copy of letter to John C. Calhoun, May 25, 1818. Historic Chattahoochee Commission, Eufaula, Alabama.

U.S. Register of Enlistments, Year 1804. Records of Men Enlisted in the U.S. Army prior to the Peace Establishment, May 17, 1815. National Archives, Washington, D.C.

Wheaton, Joseph. Papers. University of Georgia Libraries, Athens.

Public Documents

Acts of Alabama, Passed at the First Session of the First General Assembly of the Alabama Territory; in the Forty-Second Year of American Independence. St. Stephens, Alabama Territory: Thomas Eastin, 1818. Reprint. Washington, D.C.: T. L. Cole, 1912.

Alabama, *Code of Alabama.* Prepared by John J. Ormond, Arthur P. Bagby, and George Goldthwaite. With headnotes and index by Henry C. Semple. Published by Act of the General Assembly. Approved February 5, 1852. Montgomery: Brittain & DeWolf, 1852.

Bryan, Mary G. *Passports Issued by Governors of Georgia, 1785 to 1820.* Washington, D.C.: National Genealogical Society, 1962.

Commager, Henry Steele, ed. *Documents of American History.* 8th ed. 2 vols. New York: Meredith Corporation, 1968.

Commissioner of Indian Affairs, comp. *Treaties between the United States of America and the Several Indian Tribes, from 1778 to 1837.* Washington, D.C.: Langtree & O'Sullivan, 1837.

The Creek Nation v. The United States. 77 Court of Claims 226 (1933).

[Floyd, W. Warner, comp.]. *Alabama's Tapestry of Historic Places, an Inventory.* Montgomery: Alabama Historical Commission, 1978.

Georgia. *Road Laws of the State of Georgia.* Columbus, Ga.: Louis F. Gerrard, 1878.

Heitman, Francis B. *Historical Register and Dictionary of the United States Army from Its Organization, September 29, 1789, to March 2, 1903.* 2 vols. Washington, D.C.: Government Printing Office, 1903.

Horn, David Bayne, and Mary Ransome, eds. *English Historical Documents.* 12 vols. New York: Oxford University Press, 1955–77.

Mississippi Provincial Archives. Vol. 3, *French Dominion, 1704–1743.* Edited by Dunbar Rowland and Albert Godfrey Sanders. Jackson: Press of the Mississippi Department of Archives and History, 1932.

National Archives. "Record of First Returns Received from Postmasters, October 1789–July 1818." Washington, D.C.: National Archives and Records Services, Micro Copy No. M 1131, 1980.

Statutes of the Mississippi Territory. Natchez, Miss.: Peter Isler, 1816.

Thorpe, Francis Newton, comp. *The Federal and State Constitutions: Colonial Charters, and Other Organic Laws of the States, Territories, and Colonies, Now or Thereafter Forming the United States of America.* 7 vols. 59th Cong., 2d sess. House Document 357. Washington, D.C.: Government Printing Office, 1909.

"United States Land Grants, Milledgeville, Ga., Aug. 4, 1817–Nov. 1818, and Cahawba, Ala., Dec. 1818." Typewritten MS. Peter Forney Chapter, D.A.R., Montgomery, 1937.

U.S. Congress. *American State Papers: Documents, Legislative and Executive of the Congress of the United States . . . Selected and Edited under the Authority of Congress.* 38 vols. Washington, D.C.: Gales & Seaton, 1832–61.

———. *Annals of Congress: Debates and Proceedings in the Congress of the United States, 1789–1824.* 42 vols. Washington, D.C.: Gales & Seaton, 1834–56.

———. *The New American State Papers: Indian Affairs.* 13 vols. Wilmington, Del.: Scholarly Resources, 1972.

———. *The Public Statutes at Large.* 8 vols. Boston: Little, Brown, 1856.

———. *Register of Debates in Congress, 1825–1837.* 29 vols. Washington, D.C.: Gales & Seaton, 1825–37.

U.S. Congress. House. *Inaugural Addresses of the Presidents of the United States, from George Washington, 1789, to Richard Milhous Nixon, 1969.* 91st Cong., 1st sess. House Doc. 91-142, vol. 3-3. Washington, D.C.: Government Printing Office, 1969.

———. *Report of the Board of Internal Improvement upon the Subject of a National Road from the City of Washington to New Orleans.* 19th Cong., 1st sess. House Doc. 156. 1826.

———. *Statistical Atlas to the United States, Based upon Results of the Eleventh Census.* 52d Cong., 1st sess. Misc. Doc. no. 40, pt. 29, Serial 3811. 1898.

U.S. Congress. Senate. *Biographical Dictionary of the American Congress, 1774–1971.* 92d Cong., 1st sess. Senate Doc. 92-8. Washington, D.C.: Government Printing Office, 1971.

———. Committee on Public Lands and Surveys. *Natchez Trace Pathway Survey.* Report prepared by Arno B. Cammerer. 76th Cong., 3d sess. Doc. No. 148. Washington, D.C.: Government Printing Office, 1941.

———. *Report of the Committee of Claims.* 15th Cong., 1st sess. Senate Report No. 78. January 23, 1818.

U.S. Department of Interior. *Biographical and Historical Index of American Indians and Persons Involved in Indian Affairs.* 8 vols. Boston: G. K. Hall, 1966.

———. *A Compendium of the Ninth Census (June 1, 1870).* Francis A. Walker, Superintendent of Census, Washington, D.C.: Government Printing Office, 1872.

———. *Federal Indian Law.* Washington, D.C.: Government Printing Office, 1958. Reprint. Dobbs Ferry, N.Y.: Oceana Publications, 1966.

Whitaker, Arthur Preston, trans. and ed. *Documents Relating to the Commercial Policy of Spain in the Floridas, with Incidental References to Louisiana.* Deland: Florida State Historical Society, 1931.

Published Personal Accounts

Austill, Margaret Ervin. "Life of Margaret Ervin Austill." *Alabama Historical Quarterly* 6 (Spring 1944): 92–93.

Baldwin, Joseph Glover. *The Flush Times of Alabama and Mississippi*. Americus, Ga.: Americus Book, 1853.

Ball, T. H. *A Glance into the Great South-East; or, Clarke County, Alabama, and Its Surroundings from 1540 to 1877*. Chicago: Knight and Leonard, 1882. Reprint. Tuscaloosa, Ala.: Willo Publishing, 1962.

Barnum, Phineas Taylor. *Struggles and Triumphs; or, Forty Years' Recollections of P. T. Barnum, Written by Himself*. The Modern Reader Series. New York: Macmillan, 1930.

Bartram, William. *Travels through North and South Carolina, Georgia, East and West Florida, the Cherokee Country, the Extensive Territories of the Muscogulges or Creek Confederacy, and the Country of the Chactaws*. Philadelphia: James & Johnson, 1791.

Bernhard, Karl, Duke of Saxe-Weimar Eisenach. *Travels through North America during the Years 1825 and 1826*. 2 vols. Translated from German. Philadelphia: Carey, Lea & Carey, 1828.

Buckingham, James Silk. *Slave States of America*. 2 vols. London: Fisher Son, 1842.

Carter, Clarence Edwin, ed. *The Territorial Papers of the United States*. 26 vols. Washington, D.C.: Government Printing Office, 1934–52.

Cauthen, Charles E., ed. *Family Letters of the Thomas Ward Hamptons*. Columbia: University of South Carolina Press, 1953.

Claiborne, John Francis Hamtramck. *Life and Times of Gen. Samuel Dale, the Mississippi Partisan*. New York: Harper & Brothers, 1860.

————. *Mississippi as a Province, Territory, and State, with Biographical Notices of Eminent Citizens*. Jackson, Miss.: Power & Barksdale, 1880. Reprint. Baton Rouge: Louisiana State University Press, 1964.

Claiborne, William Charles Cole. *Official Letter Book of W. C. C. Claiborne, 1801–1816*. Edited by Dunbar Rowland. 6 vols. Jackson, Miss.: State Department of Archives and History, 1917.

Coale, Edward J., reporter. *Trials of the Mail Robbers, Hare, Alexander, and Hare*. Baltimore: Edward J. Coale, 1818.

Cummins, Ebenezer H. *Summary Geography of Alabama, One of the United States*. Philadelphia: William Brown, 1819.

Darby, William. *The Emigrant's Guide to the Western and Southwestern States and Territories*. New York: Kirk & Mercein, 1817.

Davidson, James D. "A Journey through the South in 1836: Diary of James D. Davidson." Edited by Herbert A. Kellar. *Journal of Southern History* 1 (August 1935): 344, 370–72.

Dow, Lorenzo. *History of Cosmopolite; or, The Writings of Rev. Lorenzo Dow, Containing His Experiences and Travels in Europe and America, up to Near His Fiftieth Year*. 8th ed. Cincinnati: Applegate, 1857.

Dow, Peggy. *The Vicissitudes of Life*. Printed with *The Dealings of God, Man, and the Devil*, by Lorenzo Dow. Cincinnati: Applegate, 1859.

Ellicott, Andrew. *The Journal of Andrew Ellicott*. Philadelphia, 1803. Reprint, Americana Classics no. 7. Chicago: Quadrangle Books, 1962.

Featherstonhaugh, George W. *Excursion through the Slave States*. New York. Harper & Brothers, 1844.

Field, Joseph M. *The Drama in Pokerville: The Bench and Bar of Jurytown, and Other Stories*. Philadelphia: A. Hurt, 1850.

Fitch, Tobias. "Journal of Captain Tobias Fitch's Mission from Charleston to the Creeks, 1726." In *Travels in the North American Colonies*, ed. Newton D. Mereness. National Society of Colonial Dames of America. New York: Macmillan, 1916.

Forbes, John. *John Forbes' Description of the Spanish Floridas, 1804*. Edited by William S. Coker. Pensacola: Perdido Bay Press, 1979.

Hall, Captain Basil. *Travels in North America in the Years 1827–1828*. 3 vols. Edinburgh: Cadell, 1829.

Hall, Margaret Hunter (Mrs. Basil). *The Aristocratic Journey: Being the Outspoken Letters of Mrs. Basil Hall, Written during a Fourteen Months' Sojourn in America, 1827–1828*. Edited by Una Pope Hennessy. G. P. Putnam's Sons, 1831.

Hamilton, Thomas. *Men and Manners in America*. 2 vols. Edinburgh: William Blackwood, 1833.

Hare, Joseph Thompson. *The Life of the Celebrated Mail Robber and Daring Highwayman, Joseph Thompson Hare*. Philadelphia: J. B. Perry, 1844.

Hawkins, Benjamin. *A Combination of a Sketch of the Creek Country in the Years 1798 and 1799 (1848) and Letters of Benjamin Hawkins, 1796–1806 (1916)*. Spartanburg, S.C.: Reprint Company, 1974.

———. "Letters of Benjamin Hawkins, 1796–1806." In *Collections of the Georgia Historical Society*, vol. 9. Savannah, Ga.: Morning News, 1916.

Hodgson, Adam. *Letters from North America, Written during a Tour of the United States and Canada*. 2 vols. London: Hurst, Robinson; and Edinburgh: A. Constable, 1824.

Jackson, Andrew. *Correspondence of Andrew Jackson*. Edited by John Spencer Bassett. Carnegie Institute of Washington, Publication no. 371. 7 vols. Papers of the Division of Historical Research. Washington, D.C.: W. F. Roberts, 1926–35.

Jefferson, Thomas. *The Works of Thomas Jefferson*. Edited by Paul Leicester Ford. Federal Edition. 12 vols. New York: G. P. Putnam's Sons, 1904–5.

Jones, Kathleen Paul, and Pauline Jones Gandrud, comps. *Alabama Records*.

245 vols. Easley, S.C.: Southern Historical Press, 1981.

"Journals of the Passage of Sergeant Wright to the Upper Creek Nation, 1771." In *Colonial Captivities, Marches, and Journeys*, by Isabel M. Calder, pp. 236–43. New York: Macmillan, 1935.

Latrobe, John H. B. *Southern Travels: Journal of John H. B. Latrobe, 1834.* Edited by Samuel Wilson, Jr. New Orleans: Historic New Orleans Collection, 1986.

Levasseur, Auguste. *La Fayette in America in 1824 and 1825; or, Journal of a Voyage to the United States.* Translated by John D. Godman. 2 vols. Philadelphia: Carey & Lea, 1829.

Lincecum, Gideon. "Autobiography of Gideon Lincecum." In *Publications of the Mississippi Historical Society*, 14 vols. in 13, 8:443–519. Oxford: Mississippi Historical Society, 1904.

Lossing, Benson John. *The Pictorial Field Book of the War of 1812.* New York: Harper & Brothers, 1869.

Lyell, Charles. *A Second Visit to the United States of North America.* 2 vols. New York: Harper & Brothers, 1849.

Madison, James. *The Papers of James Madison.* Edited by M. C. Rachal and R. A. Rutland. 8 vols. Chicago: University of Chicago Press, 1962.

―――. *The Writings of James Madison.* Edited by Gaillard Hunt. 9 vols. New York: G. P. Putnam's Sons, 1900–1910.

Martin, Francois-Xavier. *The History of Louisiana from the Earliest Period.* New Orleans: James A. Gresham, 1882.

Martineau, Harriet. *Society in America.* 3 vols. 2d ed. London: Saunders & Otley, 1837.

Meek, Alexander Beaufort. *Romantic Passages in Southwest History: Including Orations, Sketches, and Essays.* 2d ed. Mobile: S. H. Goetzel, 1857.

Mereness, Newton D., ed. *Travels in the American Colonies.* National Society of Colonial Dames in America. New York: Antiquarian Press, 1961.

Milfort, Louis LeClerc. *Memoirs; or, A Quick Glance at My Various Travels and My Sojourn in the Creek Nation.* Translated and edited by Ben C. McCary. Savannah, Ga.: Beehive Press, 1972.

Motte, Jacob Rhett. *Journey into Wilderness: An Army Surgeon's Account of Life in Camp and Field during the Creek and Seminole Wars, 1836–1838.* Edited by James F. Lundsman. Gainesville: University of Florida Press, 1953.

Porter, Benjamin F. *Reminiscences of Men and Things in Alabama.* Edited by Sara Walls. Tuscaloosa, Ala.: Portals Press, 1983.

Posey, Walter Brownlow, ed. "Alabama in the 1830's as Recorded by British Travellers." *Birmingham-Southern College Bulletin* 31 (December 1938): 1–47.

Power, Tyrone. *Impressions of America.* 2 vols. 2d American ed. Philadelphia:

Carey, Lea & Blanchard, 1836.

"A Ranger's Report of Travels with General Oglethorpe in Georgia and Florida, 1739–1742." In *Travels in the American Colonies*, ed. Newton D. Mereness. National Society of Colonial Dames of America. New York: Macmillan, 1916.

Remsen, Peter A. "Across Georgia and into Alabama, 1817–1818." Edited by William B. Hesseltine and Larry Gara. *Georgia Historical Quarterly* 37 (December 1953): 329–40.

Robertson, W. G. *Recollections of the Early Settlers of Montgomery County and Their Families*. Montgomery: Excelsior Printing, 1892. Reprint. Montgomery: Society of Pioneers of Montgomery, 1961.

Royall, Anne. *Mrs. Royall's Southern Tour; or, Second Series of the Black Book*. 3 vols. Washington, D.C.: n.p., 1831.

Ruffin, Thomas. *The Papers of Thomas Ruffin*. 4 vols. Edited by J. G. de Roulhac Hamilton. Raleigh: North Carolina Historical Commission, 1918–20.

Sanguinetti, Paul. "My Recollections of the Trip to Milstead in 1888 at the Time of the Removal of the Remains of John Sevier." *Arrow Points* 2 (April 1921): 62–64.

Simms, William Gilmore. *The Letters of William Gilmore Simms*. Vol. 1, *1830–1844*. Collected and edited by Mary C. Simms Oliphant, Alfred Taylor Odell, and T. C. Duncan Eaves. Columbia: University of South Carolina Press, 1952.

Smith, Sol. *Theatrical Management in the West and South for Thirty Years*. Edited by Arthur Thomas Fees. 1868. Reprint. New York: Benjamin Blom, 1968.

Stocks, Thomas. "Memorandum Taken on My Tour to Pensacola, Commencing the 15 April 1819." *Monthly Bulletin, Alabama Department of Archives and History* 2 (September 1925): 24–36.

Stuart, James. *Three Years in North America*. 2 vols. New York: J. & J. Harper, 1833.

Tait, James A. "Journal of James A. Tait for the Year 1813." Annotated by Peter A. Brannon. *Georgia Historical Quarterly* 8 (September 1924): 229–39.

Taitt, David. "David Taitt's Journal of a Journey through the Creek Country, 1772." In *Travels in the American Colonies*, ed. Newton D. Mereness. National Society of Colonial Dames of America. New York: Macmillan, 1916.

Trumbull, Henry. *History of the Discovery of America*. Boston: Stephen Sewell, 1819.

Warden, David B. *Statistical, Political, and Historical Account of the United States of North America; from the Period of Their First Colonization to the Present Day*. 3 vols. Edinburgh: Archibald Constable, 1819.

Washington, George. *The Writings of George Washington*. 12 vols. Edited by Jared Sparks. Boston: Ferdinant Andrews, 1839.

Wilkinson, James. *Memoirs of My Own Times*. 3 vols. Philadelphia: Abraham Small, 1816.

Woodward, Thomas Simpson. *Woodward's Reminiscences of the Creek or Muscogee Indians, Contained in Letters to Friends in Georgia and Alabama*. Montgomery: Barrett & Wimbish, 1859. Reprint. Tuscaloosa, Ala.: Alabama Book Store, 1939.

Maps (listed chronologically)

U.S. Bureau of American Ethnology. *Territory between the Chattahoochee and the Mississippi Rivers*. Compiled by Baron de Crenay, Commandant of Mobile, March, 1733. Washington, D.C.: Government Printing Office, 1922.

U.S. Department of Interior, General Land Office. [Map of conjunction of Tombigbee and Alabama rivers from St. Stephens to Fort Stoddert.] MS map in National Archives, Washington, D.C., ca. 1805.

Cary, John, engraver. *A New Map of the United States of North America, Containing the Carolinas and Georgia. Also the Florida and Part of the Bahama Islands, etc.* . . . London: J. Cary, February 1, 1806.

Melish, John. *Map of the Seat of War among the Creek Indians, from the Original Drawing in the War Department*. J. Melish, delineavit, H. S. Tanner, sculpsit. Philadelphia: John Melish, 1814.

Darby, William. *State of Mississippi and Alabama Territory*. New York: Olmstead, 1817.

Thomson, John. *Southern Provinces of the U.S.* Edinburgh: J. Thomson, 1817.

Melish, John. *Map of Alabama Constructed from Surveys in the General Land Office and Other Documents*. Philadelphia: John Melish, 1818.

U.S. Bureau of American Ethnology. *Towns of the Creek Confederacy as Shown in the Early Maps of Georgia, 1818*. Washington, D.C.: Government Printing Office, 1922.

Cary, John. *A New Map of Part of the United States of North America, Containing the Carolinas and Georgia. Also the Floridas and Part of the Bahama Islands, etc.* . . . London: J. Cary, January, 1819.

Buchon, Jean Alexandre C. *Carte Geographique, Statistique, et Historique d'Alabama*. [Paris]: J. Carey, [1823].

Tanner, Henry Schenck. *Georgia and Alabama*. Philadelphia: H. S. Tanner, 1823.

Finley, Anthony. *Map of Louisiana, Mississippi, and Alabama, Constructed from the Latest Authorities*. J. H. Young, sculpsit, and D. H. Vance, delineavit. Philadelphia: [A. Finley], 1826.

Map of Reconnaissance Exhibiting the Country between Washington and

New Orleans, with the Routes Examined in Reference to a Contemplated National Road between These Two Cities. 19th Cong. 1st sess. To accompany House Doc. no. 156. Washington, D.C.: n.p., 1826.

Finley, Anthony. *Alabama.* Young and Delleker, sculpsits. Philadelphia: A. Finley, [1829–32].

Tanner, Henry Schenck. *The Traveller's Pocket Map of Alabama with Its Roads and Distances from Place to Place, along the Stage and Steamboat Routes.* Philadelphia: W. Brose, c. 1830.

Fenner, Sears, and Company. *Map of the States of Alabama and Georgia.* London: I. T. Hinton, Simkin & Marshall, 1831.

Williams, Calvin S. *Mississippi, Alabama, and Louisiana.* New Haven: C. S. Williams, 1832.

Society for the Diffusion of Useful Knowledge. *Georgia, with Parts of North Carolina, Tennessee, Alabama, and Florida.* J. & C. Walker, sculpsit. London: Baldwin & Craddock, 1833.

La Tourrette, John. *An Accurate Map of the State of Alabama and West Florida Carefully Compiled from the Original Surveys of the General Government; Designed to Exhibit at One View Each Section and Fractional Section, So That Each Person Can Point to the Tract on Which He Lives.* New York: S. Stiles; Colton, 1838.

U.S. Department of Agriculture. Bureau of Soils. *Soil Map: Alabama, Russell County Sheet.* New York: Synder & Black, 1913.

Hale, Fletcher. "The Old Federal Road." Montgomery: Alabama Department of Archives and History, 1947.

Letford, William. "The Old Federal Road as Traced." Montgomery: Alabama Department of Archives and History, 1971.

Newspapers

American Mirror, Tuscaloosa, Alabama. March 30, April 6, 27, 1824.

Columbus [Georgia] *Enquirer.* May 19, 26, July 14, 1832.

Farmer's Register, Petersburg, Va., Edmund Ruffin, ed., 1836.

Mobile Commercial Register. June 1, 1827.

Montgomery Advertiser. December 18, 1932.

Natchez [Mississippi] *Herald.* October 7, 1806.

Niles, H., ed. *Weekly Register*, Baltimore. October 19, 1811; January 18, 1812.

Niles' Weekly Register, Baltimore. March 26, 1818; February 26, 1820; March 19, 1825.

Raleigh Register and North Carolina Gazette. April 22, 1805.

SECONDARY SOURCES

Articles, Dissertations, and Theses

Bloodworth, James Nelson. "Alexander McGillivray—Emperor of the Creeks." *Alabama Lawyer* 37 (July 1976): 305–15.

Bonner, James C. "William McIntosh." In *Georgians in Profile: Historical Essays in Honor of Ellis Merton Coulter*, ed. Horace Montgomery, pp. 114–43. Athens: University of Georgia Press, 1958.

Brannon, Peter A. "Alabama's First State Highway." *Alabama Highways* 2 (March 1929): 3, 5–6.

———. "The Coosa River Crossing of British Refugees, 1781." *Alabama Historical Quarterly* 19 (Spring 1957): 149–55.

———. "Creek Indian War, 1836–1837." *Alabama Historical Quarterly* 13 (1951): 156.

———. "Dueling in Alabama." *Alabama Historical Quarterly* 17 (Fall 1955): 97–109.

———. "The Federal Road—Alabama's First Improved Highway." *Alabama Highways* 1 (April 1927): 7–10, 19.

———. "Fighting at Fort Mitchell." *Montgomery Advertiser*, December 18, 1932.

———. "Fort Bainbridge." *Arrow Points* 5 (August 1922): 21–28.

———. "Fort Hull of 1814: A Record of a Pioneer Post Established in the Present Macon County." *Arrow Points* 14 (March 1929): 6–11.

———. "Lewis Tavern at Fort Bainbridge." *Alabama Historical Quarterly* 17 (Spring and Summer 1955): 78–79.

———. "Macon County, Present Day Place Names Suggesting Aboriginal Influence." *Arrow Points* 5 (July 1922): 5–8.

———. "More about Mordecai." *Alabama Historical Quarterly* 20 (Spring 1958): 27–33.

———. "Pole Cat Springs Agency." *Arrow Points* 10 (February 1925): 24–26.

———. "Removal of Indians from Alabama." *Alabama Historical Quarterly* 12 (1950): 91–117.

———. "Russell County, Present Day Placenames Showing Aboriginal Influence." *Arrow Points* 1 (October 1920): 24–26.

———. "Some Early Taverns in Alabama." *Arrow Points* 5 (September 1922): 52–58.

———, ed. [Special Issue.] *Alabama Historical Quarterly* 21 (1959): 1–71.

Bretz, Julian P. "Early Land Communication with the Lower Mississippi Valley." *Mississippi Valley Historical Review* 13 (June 1926): 3–29.

Briceland, Alan V. "The Mississippi Territorial Land Board East of the Pearl River, 1804." *Alabama Review* 32 (January 1979): 38–68.

Chambers, Nella J. "The Creek Indian Factory at Fort Mitchell." *Alabama Historical Quarterly* 21 (1959): 15–53.

Chappell, Gordon T. "John Coffee: Surveyor and Land Agent." *Alabama Review* 14 (July, October 1961): 180–95, 243–50.

Chase, Mary Ida. "The Old Federal Road in Alabama." Master's thesis, Birmingham-Southern College, 1936.

Cherry, F. L. "The History of Opelika and Her Agricultural Tributary Territory." *Alabama Historical Quarterly* 15 (1953): 175–537.

Cleveland, Gordon Baylor. "Social Conditions in Alabama As Seen by Travelers, 1840–1850." *Alabama Review* 2 (January, April 1949): 3–23, 122–38.

Collins, William B. "The Crawford-Burnside Duel." *Gulf States Historical Magazine* 2 (July 1903): 54–57.

Crenshaw, Mrs. Myra W. (Richard). "Butler County Beginnings." *Publications of the Butler County Historical Society* 1 (March 1965): 1–10.

Davis, Margaret Parker. "Stage Coaches in Alabama before 1830." Term paper, Colonial Dames Historical Essays, Howard College, Birmingham, 1958, 1:2–42.

Doster, James F. "Land Titles and Public Land Sales in Early Alabama." *Alabama Review* 16 (April 1963): 108–24.

Duffee, Mary Gordon. "Sketches of Alabama: Jones Valley." 2 vols. Works Progress Administration, typed transcript at Birmingham Public Library, Birmingham, 1937. Originally published as *The Weekly Iron Age*, Birmingham, 1886.

"Extracts from the Travels of William Bartram." *Alabama Historical Quarterly* 17 (Fall 1955): 110–24.

Fairbanks, Charles Herron. "Ethnographic Report on the Royce Area 79; Chickasaw, Cherokee, Creek." In *Cherokee and Creek Indians*, by Charles H. Fairbanks and John H. Goff, pp. 31–285. New York: Garland Publishing, 1974.

Fretwell, Mark E. "Two Early Letters from Alabama." *Alabama Review* 9 (January 1956): 54–65.

"Ft. Mitchell, Alabama." *Alabama Historical Quarterly* 21 (1959): 1–17.

Goff, John Hedges. "Excursion along an Old Way to the West." *Georgia Review* 6 (Summer 1952): 188–202.

———. "The Path to Oakfuskee: Upper Trading Route in Georgia to the Creek Indians." *Georgia Historical Quarterly* 39 (March, June 1955): 1–36, 152–71.

———. "The Steamboat Period in Georgia." *Georgia Historical Quarterly* 12 (September 1928): 236–54.

Hamilton, Peter Joseph. "Early Roads of Alabama." *Transactions of the Ala-*

bama *Historical Society* 2 (1897–98): 39–56.

Harrison, Joseph Hobson, Jr. "The Internal Improvement Issue in the Politics of the Union, 1783–1825." Ph.D. diss., University of Virginia, 1954.

Hesseltine, William, and Larry Gary, eds. "Across Georgia and into Alabama, 1817–1818." *Georgia Historical Quarterly* 37 (December 1953): 329–40.

"Historic Sites in Alabama." *Alabama Historical Quarterly* 15 (Spring, Summer 1953): 25–55, 340–75.

Holland, James W. "Andrew Jackson and the Creek War: Victory at the Horseshoe." *Alabama Review* 21 (October 1968): 243–75.

Johnston, James Ambler. "The War Did Not End at Yorktown." *Virginia Magazine of History and Biography* 60 (July 1952): 444–57.

King, H. M. "Historical Sketches of Macon County." *Alabama Historical Quarterly* 18 (Summer 1956): 187–217.

Larson, John Lauritz. " 'Bind the Republic Together': The National Union and the Struggle for a System of Internal Improvements." *Journal of American History*, 74 (September 1987): 363–87.

McWilliams, Tennant S. "The Marquis and the Myth: Lafayette's Visit to Alabama, 1825." *Alabama Review* 22 (April 1969): 135–46.

Meserve, John Bartlett. "The McIntoshes." *Chronicles of Oklahoma* 10 (September 1932): 310–25.

Moffett, Charles H. "Charles Tait: Planter, Politician, and Scientist of the Old South." *Journal of Southern History* 14 (May 1948): 206–33.

Neeley, Mary Ann Oglesby. "Lachlan McGillivray: A Scot on the Alabama Frontier." *Alabama Historical Quarterly* 36 (Spring 1974): 5–14.

Nelson, Harold L. "Military Roads for War and Peace—1791–1836." *Military Affairs* 19 (Spring 1955): 1–14.

"The Old Federal Road." *Escambia County Historical Society Quarterly* 2 (December 1974): 4.

Owsley, Frank L., Jr. "The Fort Mims Massacre." *Alabama Review* 24 (July 1971): 192–204.

———. "Francis Scott Key's Mission to Alabama in 1833." *Alabama Review* 23 (July 1970): 181–92.

Parsons, Dorothy Sue. "Boats on Alabama Rivers." Term paper, Colonial Dames Historical Essays, Howard College, Birmingham, 1960, 3:121–44.

Pound, Merritt Bloodworth. "Benjamin Hawkins—North Carolinian—Benefactor of the Southern Indians." *North Carolina Historical Review* 19 (January, April 1942): 1–21, 168–86.

"Revolutionary War Soldiers Buried in Alabama." *Alabama Historical Quarterly* 6 (Winter 1944): 523–678.

Roberts, Frances C. "Politics in Public Land Disposal in Alabama's Formative Period." *Alabama Review* 22 (July 1969): 163–74.

———. "Thomas Freeman, Surveyor of the Old Southwest." *Alabama Re-*

view 40 (July 1987): 216–30.

Scribner, Robert Leslie. "A Short History of Brewton, Alabama." *Alabama Historical Quarterly* 11 (1949): 1–131.

Sheftall, John McKay. "Ogeechee Old Town: A Georgia Plantation, 1540–1860." *Richmond County History* (Georgia) 14 (Summer 1982): 27–42.

Shingleton, Royce Gordon. "Stages, Steamers, and Stations in the Ante-Bellum South: A British View." *Georgia Historical Quarterly* 56 (Summer 1972): 243–58.

Southerland, Henry deLeon, Jr. "Crossing the Creeks: The Old Federal Road, 1806–1836." Master's thesis, Samford University, 1983.

———. "The Federal Road, Gateway to Alabama, 1806–1836." *Alabama Review* 39 (April 1986): 96–109.

Tarvin, Marion Elisha. "The Muscogees or Creek Indians, 1519–1893." *Alabama Historical Quarterly* 17 (Fall 1955): 125–45.

Troutmann, Frederic. "Alabama through a German's Eyes: The Travels of Clara von Gerstner, 1839." *Alabama Review* 36 (April 1983): 129–42.

"Tuckabachi Sons-in-Law: White Men Noted in Early Records Who Had Indian Wives." *Arrow Points* 14 (May 1929): 43.

Waters, Annie C. "A Documentary History of Fort Crawford." *Escambia County Historical Quarterly* 3 (September 1975): 1–24.

White, John. "Old Stage Road." *Area Magazine*, Southern Pine Co-op Edition, August 1976, pp. 16–17.

"White Men Associated with Indian Life." *Alabama Historical Quarterly* 13 (1951): 140–54.

Williams, Clanton Ware. "Early Ante-Bellum Montgomery: A Black Belt Constituency." *Journal of Southern History* 7 (November 1941): 495–525.

W.P.A. Workers. "Principal Stage Stops and Taverns in What Is Now Alabama, Prior to 1840." *Alabama Historical Quarterly* 17 (Spring and Summer 1955): 80–87.

Yamaguchi, Elizabeth Hughes. "Macon County, Alabama: Its Lands and Its People from Prehistory to 1870." Master's thesis, Auburn University, 1981.

Young, Tommy R. "The United States Army in the South, 1789–1835." Ph.D. diss., Louisiana State University, 1973.

Books

Abernethy, Thomas Perkins. *The Formative Period in Alabama, 1815–1828.* University: University of Alabama Press, 1965.

Adams, Henry W. *The Montgomery Theater, 1822–1835.* University: University of Alabama Press, 1955.

Adler, James B., ed. *CIS, U.S. Serial Set Index.* Congressional Information Service. 12 pts. 36 vols. Pt. 1, *American State Papers* and the 18th–34th Congresses, 1789–1857. Washington, D.C.: Congressional Information Services, 1977.

Alden, John Richard. *John Stuart and the Southern Colonial Frontier.* New York: Gordian Press. 1966.

Alvarez, Eugene. *Travel on Southern Antebellum Railroads.* University: University of Alabama Press, 1974.

Androit, John L., ed. *Population Abstract of the United States.* McLean, Va.: Androit Associates, 1980.

Avery, J. Arch, and Marshall L. Bowie. *The West Point Route: A Story of the Atlanta and West Point Rail Road, the Western Railway of Alabama.* Atlanta: n.p., 1954.

Badger, R. Reid, and Lawrence A. Clayton, eds. *Alabama and the Borderlands: From Prehistory to Statehood.* University: University of Alabama Press, 1985.

Barfield, Louise Calhoun. *History of Harris County, Georgia, 1827–1961.* Columbus, Ga.: n.p., n.d.

Bears, Ed, and Arrell M. Gibson. *Fort Smith, Little Gibraltar on the Arkansas.* 2d ed. Norman: University of Oklahoma Press, 1979.

Black, Robert C. *Railroads of the Confederacy.* Chapel Hill: University of North Carolina Press, 1952.

Blue, Matthew Powers. *City Directory and History of Montgomery, Alabama.* Montgomery: T. C. Bingham, 1878.

Bowie, Marshall L. *A Time of Adversity—and Courage: A Story of Montgomery and West Point Rail Road, a Predecessor Company of the Western Railway of Alabama, and Its Activities during the War Between the States, 1861–1865.* N.p., 1961.

Brannon, Peter A. *Engineers of Yesteryear.* Montgomery: Paragon Press, 1928.
———. *Historic Highways in Alabama: Stories of Incidents with the Early Roadways in the State.* Montgomery: Paragon Press, 1929.
———. *Little Journeys to Interesting Points in Alabama.* Montgomery: Paragon Press, 1930.
———. *Romance of Beginnings of Some Alabama Industries: An American Pilgrimage Address.* Birmingham: Birmingham Publishing, 1939.
———. *A Travel Log: One of a Series of Historic Stories of Trips through Alabama, Prepared for Alabama Highways.* Montgomery: Paragon Press, 1928.
———. *Turning the Pages in Alabama.* Montgomery: Paragon Press, 1932.
———, ed. *The Pageant Book.* Montgomery: n.p., 1926.

Brant, Irving, ed. *James Madison: The President, 1809–1812.* Indianapolis: Bobbs-Merrill, 1956.

Brantley, Mary E. *Early Settlers along the Old Federal Road in Monroe and Conecuh Counties, Alabama*. Baltimore: Gateway Press, 1976.

Brantley, William H. *Three Capitals. A Book about the First Three Capitals of Alabama: St. Stephens, Huntsville, and Cahawba.* 1947. Reprint. University: University of Alabama Press, 1976.

Bray, Peter, and Barbara Brown. *Transport through the Ages*. New York: Taplinger Publishing, 1971.

Brewer, Willis. *Alabama: Her History, Resources, War Record, and Public Men, from 1540 to 1872*. Montgomery: Barrett & Brown, 1872.

Brown, Jerry Elijah, ed. *Clearings in the Thicket: An Alabama Humanities Reader*. Macon, Ga.: Mercer University Press, 1985.

Brown, Wilburt S. *The Amphibious Campaign for West Florida and Louisiana, 1814–1815: A Critical Review of Strategy and Tactics at New Orleans*. University: University of Alabama Press, 1969.

Buker, George Edward. *Swamp Sailors: Riverine Warfare in the Everglades, 1835–1842*. Gainesville: University Presses of Florida, 1975.

Cammeror, Arno B. *Natchez Trace Parkway Survey*. National Park Service, Department of Interior. Senate Document No. 148, 76th Cong., 3d sess. Washington, D.C.: Government Printing Office, 1941.

Carstensen, Vernon Rusco, ed. *The Public Lands: Studies in the History of the Public Domain*. Madison: University of Wisconsin Press, 1963.

Caughey, John Walton. *McGillivray of the Creeks*. Norman: University of Oklahoma Press, 1938.

Chappell, Absalom H. *Miscellanies of Georgia: Historical, Biographical, Descriptive*. 1874. Reprint. Columbus, Ga.: Gilbert Printing, 1928.

Chase, Carroll, and Richard McP. Cabeen. *The First Hundred Years of United States Territorial Postmarks, 1787–1887*. State College, Pa.: American Philatelic Society, 1950.

Chase, David W. *Fort Mitchell: An Archaeological Exploration in Russell County, Alabama*. Special Publications of the Alabama Archaeological Society no. 1. Moundville, Ala., 1974.

Clark, Thomas D., ed. *Travels in the Old South: A Bibliography*. 2 vols. Norman: University of Oklahoma Press, 1956.

Coates, Robert M. *The Outlaw Years: The History of the Land Pirates of the Natchez Trace*. New York: Literary Guild of America, 1930.

Coker, William S., and Thomas D. Watson. *Indian Traders of the Southeastern Spanish Borderlands: Panton, Leslie & Company and John Forbes & Company, 1783–1847*. Gainesville: University Presses of Florida; Pensacola: University of West Florida Press, 1986.

Coleman, Kenneth, ed. *A History of Georgia*. Athens: University of Georgia Press, 1977.

Coleman, Kenneth, and Charles Stephen Gurr, eds. *Dictionary of Georgia*

Biography. 2 vols. Athens: University of Georgia Press, 1983.

Coles, Harry L. *The War of 1812*. The Chicago History of Civilization Series. Chicago: University of Chicago Press, 1956.

Comings, L. J. Newcomb, and Martha M. Albers. *A Brief History of Baldwin County*. Fairhope, Ala.: Baldwin County Historical Society, 1928.

Corbin, Harriet Turner (Porter). *A History and Genealogy of Chief William McIntosh, Jr., and His Known Descendants*. Edited by Carl C. Burdick. Long Beach, Calif.: n.p., 1967.

Corkran, David H. *The Creek Frontier, 1540–1783*. Norman: University of Oklahoma Press, 1967.

Cotterill, Robert Spencer. *The Southern Indians: The Story of the Civilized Tribes before Removal*. Norman: University of Oklahoma Press, 1954.

Coulter, Harold S. *A People Courageous: A History of Phenix City, Alabama*. Columbus, Ga.: Howard Printing, 1976.

Cox, Isaac Joslin. *The West Florida Controversy, 1798–1813*. Baltimore: Johns Hopkins Press, 1918. Reprint. Gloucester, Mass.: Peter Smith, 1967.

Craven, Avery. *Edmund Ruffin, Southerner: A Study in Secession*. Hamden, Conn.: Archon Books, 1964.

Cullum, George W. *Biographical Register of the Officers and Graduates of the U.S. Military Academy at West Point, N.Y., from Its Establishment, March 16, 1802, to the Army Reorganization of 1866–67*. 2 vols. New York: D. Van Nostrand, 1868.

Daniels, Frank A. *History of Wayne County* [North Carolina]. Address delivered November 30, 1914. N.p.

Daniels, Jonathan. *The Devil's Backbone: The Story of the Natchez Trace*. The American Trails Series. New York: McGraw-Hill, 1962.

Davis, Charles S. *The Cotton Kingdom in Alabama*. Montgomery: State Department of Archives and History, 1939.

Debo, Angie. *And Still the Waters Run: The Betrayal of Five Civilized Tribes*. Princeton: Princeton University Press, 1940.

————. *The Road to Disappearance*. Norman: University of Oklahoma Press, 1941.

Dictionary of National Biography. London: Oxford University Press, 1921.

Donaldson, Thomas Convin. *The Public Domain: Its History, with Statistics*. Introduction by Paul W. Gales. Washington, D.C.: Government Printing Office, 1884. Reprint. New York: Johnson Reprint, 1970.

Dubose, Joel Campbell. *Alabama History*. Richmond, Va.: Johnson Publishing, 1908.

Earle, Alice Morse. *Stage-Coach and Tavern Days*. New York: Macmillan, 1900.

Eaton, Clement. *The Growth of Southern Civilization, 1790–1860*. New York: Harper & Row, 1961.

Fairbanks, Charles H., and John H. Goff. *Cherokee and Creek Indians*. New York: Garland Publishing, 1974.

Faulkner, William. *The Hamlet*. New York: Random House, 1941. Reprint. Vintage Books, 1964.

Foreman, Grant. *The Five Civilized Tribes*. Norman: University of Oklahoma Press, 1934.

———. *Indian Removal: The Emigration of the Five Civilized Tribes of Indians*. Norman: University of Oklahoma Press, 1932.

———. *Indians and Pioneers: The Story of the American Southwest before 1830*. Rev. ed. Norman: University of Oklahoma Press, 1936.

Frazer, Mell A. *Early History of Steamboats in Alabama*. Alabama Polytechnic Institute Historical Series. Third Series. Auburn, Ala., 1907.

Fretwell, Mark E. *This So Remote Frontier: The Chattahoochee Country of Alabama and Georgia*. Eufaula, Ala.: Historic Chattahoochee Commission, 1980.

Goff, John Hedges. *Place Names of Georgia: Essays of John H. Goff*. Edited by Frances Lee Utley and Marion R. Hemperley. Athens: University of Georgia Press, 1975.

Graham, John Simpson. *History of Clarke County*. Birmingham: Birmingham Printing, 1923.

Green, Philip Jackson. *The Life of William Harris Crawford*. N.p., n.d.

Griffith, Benjamin W., Jr. *McIntosh and Weatherford, Creek Indian Leaders*. Tuscaloosa: University of Alabama Press, 1988.

Griffith, Lucille. *Alabama: A Documentary History to 1900*. Rev. ed. University: University of Alabama Press, 1972.

Hahn, Marilyn Davis. *Butler County in the Nineteenth Century*. Birmingham: By the author, 1978.

———. *Old Cahaba Land Office Records: Military Land Warrants, 1817–1853*. Mobile: Old Southland Publishing, 1981.

———. *Old St. Stephen's Land Office Records and American State Papers: Public Lands*. Vol. 1, *1768–1888*. Easley, S.C.: Southern Historical Press, 1983.

Halbert, H. S., and T. H. Ball. *The Creek War of 1813 and 1814*. Montgomery: White, Woodruff, & Fowler, 1895. Reprint, edited by Frank L. Owsley, Jr., Southern Historical Publications no. 15. University: University of Alabama Press, 1969.

Hamilton, Peter Joseph. *Colonial Mobile: An Historical Study Largely from Original Sources of the Alabama-Tombigbee Basin, from the Discovery of Mobile Bay in 1519 until the Demolition of Fort Charlotte in 1821*. New York: Houghton Mifflin, 1897.

Harper, Francis. *The Travels of William Bartram*. Naturalist's ed. New Haven: Yale University Press, 1958.

Harris, W. Stuart. *Dead Towns of Alabama*. University: University of Alabama Press, 1977.

Harris, Walter A. *Here the Creeks Sat Down*. Macon, Ga.: J. W. Burke, 1958.

Hay, Thomas Robson, and M. R. Werner. *The Admirable Trumpeter: A Biography of General James Wilkinson*. Garden City, N.Y.: Doubleday, Doran, 1941.

Hoole, W. Stanley. *According to Hoole: The Collected Essays of a Scholar-Librarian and Literary Maverick*. University: University of Alabama Press, 1973.

Huber, Leonard V., and Clarence A. Wagner. *The Great Mail: A Postal History of New Orleans*. State College, Pa.: American Philatelic Society, 1949.

Jacobs, James Ripley. *Tarnished Warrior*. New York: Macmillan, 1938.

Jemian, Pat Jackson. *Chattahoochee Coverlets*. Auburn, Ala.: Auburn University Center for the Arts and Humanities, 1987.

Julich, Louise Milan, chairman. *Roster of Revolutionary War Soldiers and Patriots in Alabama*. Alabama Society, Daughters of the American Revolution. Montgomery: Parchment Press, 1979.

Knight, Lucian Lamar. *Georgia's Landmarks, Memorials, and Legends*. 2 vols. Atlanta: Byrd Printing, 1914.

————. *A Standard History of Georgia and Georgians*. 6 vols. Chicago: Lewis Publishing, 1917.

Lathrop, Elsie. *Early American Inns and Taverns*. New York: Tudor Publishing, 1926.

Lewis, Marcus W. *The Development of Early Emigrant Trails in the United States East of the Mississippi River*. Washington, D.C.: National Genealogical Society, 1933.

Little, John Buckner. *The History of Butler County, Alabama, from 1815 to 1885*. Cincinnati: Elm St. Printing, 1885. Reprint. Greenville, Ala.: John Goodwin Little, Jr., 1972.

Louisiana Purchase: An Exhibition. New Orleans: The Cabildo, 1953.

MacGill, Caroline E. *History of Transportation in the United States before 1860*. Washington, D.C.: Carnegie Institution, 1917. Reprint. [New York]: Peter Smith, 1948.

McLemore, Richard Aubrey. *A History of Mississippi*. Hattiesburg: University and College Press of Mississippi, 1973.

McLendon, S. Guyton. *History of the Public Domain of Georgia*. Atlanta: Foote & Davies, 1924.

McMillan, Malcolm C. *The Land Called Alabama*. Austin, Tex.: Steck-Vaughn, 1975.

McMullin, Phillip W., ed. *Grassroots of America: A Computerized Index to the American State Papers, Land Grants, and Claims (1789–1839), with Other Aids to Research*. Salt Lake City, Utah: Gendex Corporation, 1972.

McReynolds, Edwin C. *The Seminoles*. Norman: University of Oklahoma Press, 1957.

Mahon, John K. *History of the Second Seminole War, 1835–1842*. Gainesville: University of Florida Press, 1967.

———. *The War of 1812*. Gainesville: University of Florida Press, 1972.

Malone, Dumas. *Jefferson and His Time*. Vol. 4, *Jefferson the President: First Term, 1801–1805*. Boston: Little, Brown, 1970.

———, ed. *Dictionary of American Biography*. 22 vols. New York: Charles Scribner's Sons, 1928–58.

Martin, John H. *Columbus, Geo., from Its Selection as a "Trading Town" in 1827 to Its Partial Destruction by Wilson's Raid in 1865*. Columbus, Ga.: Thos. Gilbert, 1874. Reprint. Easley, S.C.: Georgia Genealogical Reprints, 1972.

Martin, William Elijius. *Internal Improvements in Alabama*. Baltimore: Lord Baltimore Press, 1902.

Matloff, Maurice, ed. *American Military History*. Army Historical Series. Washington, D.C.: Government Printing Office, 1969.

Montgomery, Horace, ed. *Georgians in Profile: Historical Essays in Honor of Ellis Merton Coulter*. Athens: University of Georgia Press, 1958.

Mooney, Chase Curren. *William H. Crawford, 1772–1834*. Lexington: University of Kentucky Press, 1974.

Moore, Albert Burton. *History of Alabama*. Nashville: Benson Printing, 1934. Reprint. Tuscaloosa, Ala.: Alabama Book Store, 1951.

Myer, William Edward. *Indian Trails of the Southeast*. Nashville: Blue & Gray Press, 1971.

Neville, Bert. *Directory of River Packets in the Mobile-Alabama-Warrior-Tombigbee Trades, 1818–1832*. Selma, Ala.: Coffee Printing, 1962.

———. *Directory of Steamboats, with Illustrations and List of Landings on Chattahoochee-Apalachicola-Flint-Chipola Rivers*. Selma, Ala.: n.p., 1961.

Newman, Harry Wright. *The Lucketts of Portobacco*. Washington, D.C.: By the author, 1938.

Northern, William J., ed. *Men of Mark in Georgia*. Edited by John Temple Graves. 7 vols. Atlanta: A. B. Caldwell, 1907–12.

Nuzum, Kay. *A History of Baldwin County*. Bay Minette, Ala.: Baldwin Times, 1971.

Oakley, Bruce C., Jr. *A Postal History of Mississippi: Stampless Period, 1799–1860*. Baldwyn, Miss.: Magnolia Publishers, 1969.

Owen, Marie Bankhead. *The Story of Alabama: A History of the State*. 5 vols. New York: Lewis Publishing, 1949.

Owsley, Frank L., Jr. *Struggle for the Gulf Borderlands: The Creek War and the Battle of New Orleans, 1812–1815*. Gainesville: University of Florida Presses, 1981.

Parton, J. *The Life and Times of Aaron Burr: Lieutenant Colonel in the Army of the Revolution, United States Senator, Vice President of the United States, etc.* New York: Mason Brothers, 1860.

Perkins, Dexter, and Glyndon G. Van Densen. *The United States of America: A History.* 2 vols. New York: Macmillan, 1962.

Phillips, Ulrich Bonnell. *A History of Transportation in the Eastern Cotton Belt to 1860.* New York: Columbia University Press, 1908. Reprint. New York: Octagon Books, 1968.

————. *Life and Labor in the Old South.* Boston: Little, Brown, 1929.

Pickett, Albert James. *History of Alabama, and Incidentally of Georgia and Mississippi from the Earliest Period.* 1851. Reprint. Birmingham: Webb Book, 1900.

Pound, Merritt Bloodworth. *Benjamin Hawkins: Indian Agent.* Athens: University of Georgia Press, 1951.

Prouty, William Frederick. *Roads and Road Materials of Alabama.* State Highway Bulletin no. 2; Geological Survey Bulletin no. 11; Geological Survey of Alabama. Montgomery: Brown Printing, 1911.

Remini, Robert. *Andrew Jackson.* New York: Harper & Row, 1966–69.

————. *Andrew Jackson and the Bank War: A Study in the Growth of Presidential Power.* New York: W. W. Norton, 1967.

Renfro, N. P., Jr. *The Beginnings of Railroads in Alabama.* Alabama Polytechnic Institute Historical Studies. Fourth Series. Auburn, Ala., 1910.

Richardson, Jesse M. *Alabama Encyclopedia.* Vol. 1, *Book of Facts.* Northport, Ala.: American Southern Publishing, 1965.

Riley, Benjamin Franklin. *History of Conecuh County, Alabama.* Columbus, Ga.: Thomas Gilbert, 1881. Reprint. Blue Hill, Maine: Weekly Packet, 1964.

Robbins, Roy M. *Our Landed Heritage.* Lincoln: University of Nebraska Press, 1962.

Rohrbough, Malcolm. *The Land Office Business: The Settlement and Administration of American Public Lands, 1789–1837.* New York: Oxford University Press, 1968.

Ross, Robbie Lee Gillis. *Your Inheritance.* Matthews, N.C.: Delmar Printing, 1972.

Rouse, Parke. *The Great Wagon Road: From Philadelphia to the South.* New York: McGraw-Hill, 1973.

Royce, Charles C. *Cessions of Land by Indian Tribes to the U.S.* 1st Annual Report, Bureau of Ethnology. Washington, D.C.: Government Printing Office, 1891.

Scruggs, J. H., Jr. *Alabama Postal History.* Birmingham: By the author, n.d.

————. *Alabama Postal Roads with Maps, 1818–1845. Also Early Forts—First Line of Communication, 1736-1744-1812.* Birmingham: By the author, n.d.

————. *Alabama Steamboats, 1819–1869*. Birmingham: By the author, 1953.

Silver, James W. *Edmund Pendleton Gaines: Frontier General*. Baton Rouge: Louisiana State University Press, 1949.

Smith, George Gillman. *The Story of Georgia and the Georgia People, 1732–1860*. Macon, Ga.: By the author, 1900.

Snodgrass, Dena. *The Island of Ortega: A History*. Jacksonville, Fla.: Ortega School, 1981.

Spalding, Phinizy. *Oglethorpe in America*. Chicago: University of Chicago Press, 1977. Reprint. Athens: University of Georgia Press, 1984.

Stephens, Lucinda Frances. *Crawford Genealogy*. Macon, Ga.: J. W. Burke, 1936.

Stewart, Frank Ross. *United States Land Office Record, Huntsville, Mississippi Territory, 1809–1811*. Troy, Ala.: Alabama Genealogical Society, 1964.

Stockbridge, Frank Parker, and John Holliday Perry. *Florida in the Making*. New York: de Bower Publishing, 1926.

Student Writers Club of Selma. *Some Old Churches of the Black Belt*. Birmingham: Banner Press, 1962.

Summersell, Charles Grayson. *Alabama History for Schools*. 3d ed. Montgomery: Viewpoint Publications, 1965.

Swanton, John Reed. *Early History of the Creek Indians and Their Neighbors*. Smithsonian Institute, Bureau of American Ethnology, Bulletin 73. Washington, D.C.: Government Printing Office, 1922.

Sydnor, Charles S. *A History of the South*. Vol. 5, *The Development of Southern Sectionalism, 1819–1848*. Baton Rouge: Louisiana State University Press, 1948.

Telfair, Nancy. *A History of Columbus, Georgia, 1828–1928*. Columbus, Ga.: Historical Publishing, 1929.

Truett, Randle Bond. *Trade and Travel around the Southern Appalachians before 1830*. Chapel Hill: University of North Carolina Press, 1935.

U.S. Congress. Senate. Committee on Public Lands and Surveys. *Natchez Trace Parkway Survey*. 76th Cong., 3d sess. Document No. 148. Washington, D.C.: Government Printing Office, 1941.

Vanderbilt, Frank Armstrong Crawford. *Laurus Crawfurdiana*. New York: By the author, 1883.

Walker, Anne Kendrick. *Russell County in Retrospect: An Epic of the Far Southeast*. Richmond, Va.: Dietz Press, 1950.

Wandell, Samuel H., and Meade Minigerode. *Aaron Burr: A Biography Compiled from Rare and, in Many Cases, Unpublished Sources*. 2 vols. New York: G. P. Putnam's Sons, 1925.

Waters, Annie C. *A Documentary History of Fort Crawford*. Brewton, Ala.: East Brewton Bicentennial Commission, 1975.

————. *History of Escambia County, Alabama*. Huntsville, Ala.: Strode Publishers, 1983.

Werner, M. R. *Barnum*. Garden City, N.Y.: Garden City Publishing, 1926.

West, Anson. *A History of Methodism in Alabama*. Nashville: Methodist Episcopal Church, 1893. Reprint. Spartanburg, S.C.: Reprint Company, 1983.

Wheeler, John H. *Reminiscences and Memoirs of North Carolina and Eminent North Carolinians*. Washington, D.C.: n.p., 1878. Reprint. Baltimore: Genealogical Publishing, 1966.

Whitaker, Arthur Preston. *The Spanish-American Frontier, 1783–1795*. Introduction by Samuel Eliot Morison. Boston and New York: Houghton Mifflin, 1927. Reprint. Gloucester, Mass.: Peter Smith, 1962.

White, George. *Historical Collections of Georgia, Containing the Most Interesting Facts, Traditions, Biographical Sketches, Anecdotes, etc. Relating to Its History and Antiquities from Its First Settlement to the Present Time*. New York: Pudney & Russell, 1855. Reprint. Baltimore: Genealogical Publishing, 1969.

————. *Statistics of the State of Georgia*. Savannah, Ga.: Thorne Williams, 1849.

Whitehead, Margaret Laney, and Barbara Bogart. *City of Progress: A History of Columbus, Georgia, 1828–1978*. Columbus: Georgia Office Supply, 1979.

Who Was Who in America, Historical Volume, 1607–1896. Chicago: Marquis–Who's Who, 1963.

Williams, Clanton Ware. *The Early History of Montgomery, and Incidentally of the State of Alabama*. University, Ala.: Confederate Publishing, 1979.

Wilson, Mable Ponder, chairman. *Some Early Alabama Churches*. Birmingham: Alabama Society, Daughters of the American Revolution, 1973.

Worsley, Etta Blanchard. *Columbus on the Chattahoochee*. Columbus, Ga.: Columbus Office Supply, 1951.

Wright, James Leitch, Jr. *Anglo-Spanish Rivalry in North America*. Athens: University of Georgia Press, 1971.

————. *Creeks and Seminoles: The Destruction and Regeneration of the Muscogulge People*. Lincoln: University of Nebraska Press, 1986.

Yellow Hammer Club. *A History of Russell County*. Phenix City, Ala.: Central High School, 1948.

Young, Mary Elizabeth. *Redskins, Ruffleshirts, and Rednecks: Indian Allotments in Alabama and Mississippi, 1830–1860*. Norman: University of Oklahoma Press, 1961.

INDEX

190

71, 72, 77, 113, 136, 137
Mills's Tavern, 97
Milly's Creek, 91, 92, 142
Milly's Tavern (Old Milly's), 92, 119. *See also* Evans's
Milton, Homer V., 47
Mims Ferry, 40, 68
Mississippi River, 112, 125
Mississippi Territory, 33, 108, 110, 111, 115, 119, 142
Mitchell, David B., 43, 53, 54–55, 59
Mitchill, Samuel Latham, 12
Mobile, Ala., 12, 13, 68, 69, 119, 138, 140
Mobile River, 29, 35, 55, 139
Moniac, David, 118, 123, 131, 133
Monroe, James, 9, 53, 113
Monroe County, Ala., 41, 55, 106, 142
Montgomery, Ala., 23, 29, 57, 60, 63, 66, 68, 77, 78, 79, 87, 89, 92, 133, 136, 138, 140
Montgomery County, Ala., 60, 117, 142
Montgomery Railroad Company, 139
Montgomery & West Point Railroad, 139
Monticello, Ga., 77, 136
Mordecai, Abraham, 119
Morse, Samuel F. B., 140
Motte, Jacob, 130
Mount Vernon, Ala., 2, 98
Mount Meigs, Ala., 92
Mrs. Harris's Hotel, 84
Mrs. Mills's Tavern, 97
Murder Creek, 96
Muscogees. *See* Creeks

Nashville, Tenn., 32, 38, 53, 56
Natchez, Miss., 38, 56, 111, 112, 116, 136
Natchez Trace, 10, 21, 32, 56, 101, 116
Natchitoches, 34
National road routes, 136–37
Natural Bridge, 82
New Inverness, Ga., 118
New Orleans, La., 9, 19, 21, 29, 32, 35, 56, 83, 116, 119, 132, 136, 137, 139, 141, 142; 1802 exports, 9; Jefferson's attitude toward, 9; mileage from Washington, 17

New Philadelphia, 92
Norcoce Chappo Creek, 92
Notasulga, Ala., 139

Oche Haujo, 15, 20. *See also* Cornells, Alexander
Ocmulgee River, 26, 29, 71, 72, 105, 124
Oconee River, 2, 23, 29, 67
Ogle-Stroud slaying, 57, 95, 96
Oglethorpe, James Edward, 13
Ohio River, 139
O'Kelley, John, 121
Okfuskee, 13, 29. *See also* Line Creek
Old Alabama Town (Old North Hull Street Historic District), 142
Old Southwest, 6, 67, 79, 102, 142, 143
Old Southwest humor, 79, 86, 107–8
Old Stage Road, 117
Olive Branch Baptist Church, 117
Opelika, Ala., 130
Orleans Territory, 108
Osceola, 118
Owens, Hardeman, incident, 129

Palmetto, Ga., 139
Panic of 1837, 140
Panton, Leslie & Company, 20, 39
Pascagoula River, 112
Pearce, Dutee Jerauld, 19
Pearl River, 35, 108
Peebles's Tavern, 97
Pensacola, 25, 32, 39, 49, 99, 119
"People's Line," 60
Perkins, Nicholas, 28
Persimmon Creek, 54
Persimmon Swamp, 87
"Pet banks," 140
Phenix City, Ala., 81, 140. *See also* Girard; Sodom
Pickens, Israel, 53, 66, 115
Pickett, Albert James, 3, 119
Pinchony Creek, 95
Pinkneyville, Miss., 35
Pintlala Creek, 35, 117
Pole Cat Springs Indian Agency, 90, 133
Poindexter, George, 112